Where to wat

Cumbria, La
& Cheshire

Jonathan Guest and Malcolm Hutcheson

OTHER *WHERE TO WATCH BIRDS* BOOKS PUBLISHED BY CHRISTOPHER HELM

Where to Watch Birds in Bedfordshire, Berkshire, Buckinghamshire, Hertfordshire and Oxfordshire
Brian Clews, Andrew Heryet and Paul Trodd

Where to Watch Birds in Devon and Cornwall
David Norman and Vic Tucker

Where to Watch Birds in Dorset, Hampshire and the Isle of Wight
George Green and Martin Cade

Where to Watch Birds in East Anglia
Peter and Margaret Clarke

Where to Watch Birds in France
Ligue Française pour la Protection des Oiseaux

Where to Watch Birds in Kent, Surrey and Sussex
Don Taylor, Jeffrey Wheatley and Tony Prater

Where to Watch Birds in Scotland
Mike Madders and Julia Welstead

Where to Watch Birds in Somerset, Avon, Gloucestershire and Wiltshire
Ken Hall and John Govett

Where to Watch Birds in the West Midlands
Graham Harrison and Jack Sankey

Where to Watch Birds in Wales
David Saunders

Where to watch birds in
Cumbria, Lancashire & Cheshire

Jonathan Guest and Malcolm Hutcheson

Illustrated by David Mead

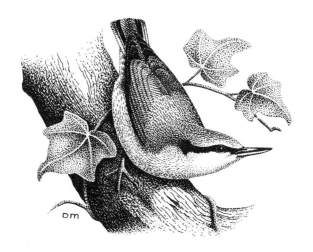

Christopher Helm
A&C Black · London

© 1992 Jonathan Guest and Malcolm Hutcheson
Line illustrations by David Mead

Christopher Helm (Publishers) Ltd,
a subsidiary of A & C Black (Publishers) Ltd,
35 Bedford Row, London WC1R 4JH

ISBN 0-7136-3519-3

A CIP catalogue for this book
is available from the British Library

10 9 8 7 6 5 4 3 2 1

Typeset by Florencetype Ltd, Kewstoke, Avon
Printed and bound by Biddles Ltd, Guildford, Surrey in Great Britain

CONTENTS

Contents

LIST OF ILLUSTRATIONS

ACKNOWLEDGEMENTS

We would like to thank the following people for their help in providing information, records or comments and corrections on the first proof of this book:–

I. Armstrong (RSPB), Miss K.M. Atkinson, S. & G. Barber, M. Bailey (English Nature), M.F. Carrier, P. Carty (National Trust), Adam Davison (Mersey Valley Warden Service), A.F. Gould, I. Kinley, Rev. H. Linn, P. Marsh, B. Martin (Woolston Eyes Conservation Group), D. Messenger, J. Miles (RSPB), D.G. Newell, D.J. Radford (RSPB), R. Rhodes (North West Water), J. & M. Turner, C. Wells (RSPB), J. Wilson (RSPB) and G. Yates.

We also obtained useful information from various publications, as acknowledged in our Select Bibliography (p. 218).

Special thanks to Mrs Ann Hutcheson for her patience and typing skills in setting out part of the basic manuscript.

Finally, thanks to the staff of Christopher Helm (Publishers) Ltd for their encouragement and professional guidance.

INTRODUCTION

The counties of Cumbria, Lancashire and Cheshire, together with Merseyside and Greater Manchester which are, for convenience, subsumed within the title of this book, make up the north-west of England, running from the Welsh border and the Ellesmere moraine (limit of the last glaciation) in the south, to the Scottish border in the north. The region encompasses the mountainous Lake District, where the higher hills exceed 750 m (2,500 ft) above sea level, and the western flank of the Pennine hills to the east, as well as the more fertile lowlands of the Fylde and the Lancashire–Cheshire Plain. The uplands are devoted largely to sheep-rearing, with some heather management for grouse. In the south of the region, the Cheshire moors have dwindled, large areas having been converted to grazing land, while in the north particularly, though not exclusively, there has been increasing emphasis on forestry.

Hill reservoirs in the southern Pennines, constructed within the last two hundred years, have suffered from the acidifying pollution that accompanied the Industrial Revolution. Many of them are steep-sided, with sparse vegetation and a limited aquatic fauna. All of them attract birds from time to time, and might reward regular coverage as a local patch, but only a selection of the more productive are included in this book.

The waters of the Lake District vary from small, clear upland tarns to large, reed-fringed meres, the best of which are ornithological sites of high quality, with excellent scenery too. Many of the Cheshire meres, also glacial in origin, are difficult of access. The cluster around Marbury, near the Shropshire border, attracts many birds but, with the exception of Marbury itself, is best left to the attentions of local watchers who can arrange ready access with landowners. Cheshire and south Lancashire contain many subsidence 'flashes', stretches of water in hollows resulting from salt or coal extraction respectively. These, like the pools caused by extraction of sand, clay and gravel, are industrial sites of benefit to birds.

The Cheshire and Lancashire lowlands contain only small fragments of ancient woodland, with further relic oak woods dotted along the southern Pennines. A thriving coppicing industry survived into the twentieth century in the Lake District, where far more broad-leaved woods survive. The lowland mosses of the region, which formerly housed Large Heath butterflies, have now all but vanished, and the few remnants are still exploited for gardeners' peat. Very often their sites are marked by Birchwoods or – scandalously – in Cheshire, by rubbish tips.

The coastline is for the most part low-lying, with extensive sand-dunes and beaches, and estuarine mudflats.

The region's climate is heavily influenced by its west coast position. Winter temperatures along the Cumbrian coast and the Cheshire–Lancashire plain are a couple of degrees warmer than on the east coast, with fewer frosts, increasing the importance of these areas for wintering birds. Rainfall is typically 75–100 mm (30–40 in) per year on the plain, with 150 mm (60 in) or more in the central Lake District and locally elsewhere in the hills, where snow often lies in winter.

FEATURES OF THE REGION'S BIRDLIFE

Virtually the whole coastline from the Dee to the Duddon is connected at low tide by a series of sandbanks which, with the mudflats of several large estuaries, provide winter and passage quarters for hundreds of thousands of waders. Wildfowl too are well represented, both in the estuaries and on inland waters. The Lancashire mosslands hold huge winter flocks of Pink-footed Geese, thousands of Pochards frequent waters along the Mersey valley, and over a hundred Ruddy Ducks gather on certain waters. The Irish Sea has relatively narrow entrances at the north and south, causing many migrant seabirds to detour round the west of Ireland. Consequently, seawatching tends to be disappointing except in strong onshore winds, particularly in autumn. Furthermore the sandy coastline lacks rugged headlands, so breeding seabirds are scarce, although several colonies of terns exist, and a few gulleries, notably Europe's largest at South Walney.

Walney is the southernmost breeding site for Eiders on the west coast of Britain. Other northern species that occasionally enter the region are England's only breeding Black Guillemots and Golden Eagles. Moorland species such as Golden Plover, Merlin and Black Grouse are found on the Pennine moors, but are coming under increasing pressure from forestry, ramblers and the deterioration of moorland habitats, especially in the south of the region. Conversely, a number of birds with southerly distributions peter out in the north-west of the region. Reed Warblers have their northernmost outpost around Leighton Moss, but are vigorously colonising any newly suitable sites. Nuthatches and Lesser Spotted Woodpeckers, which were formerly seen only south of the Mersey, have spread northwards as nineteenth-century plantations have matured, and the twentieth-century neglect of broad-leaved woods has allowed nesting cavities to develop in trees. Turtle Doves, on the other hand, are fading fast, and Little Owls, although numerous in the south of the region, are scarce north of Hadrian's Wall.

This region's birdwatchers have to work harder than their east coast counterparts to find rarities. However, small numbers of eurasian landbird rarities do find their way through to the western coastline in the days following arrivals on the east coast. The best chance of finding a rare bird lies in persistent scanning of wildfowl and wader flocks for transatlantic strays, hence what some see as disproportionate interest by the region's watchers in wetland species. As authors, we may be accused of perpetuating this emphasis in our choice of sites. This is partly because it is difficult to identify agricultural or moorland sites that can absorb visitors without consequential harm to the birds. In general, however, the status of wetland species is far better understood than that of many landbirds. In giving details of passage movement through Macclesfield Forest, by way of example, we hope to raise interest in identifying east-west corridors for migrants through the Pennines and elsewhere.

Manifestations of the 'ecological crisis' are the spread of intensive agribusiness into lowland parts of the region, and increasing weedkilling and reseeding in hill-pastures, obliterating the former tapestry of variations in local wildlife; threats to impound several estuaries for the energy industry – estuaries are not renewable; and the decline of trans-Saharan migrants, notably Whitethroat and Whinchat, which cannot make the increasingly formidable desert crossing.

HOW TO USE THIS BOOK

The sites included in this book are grouped into regions, each with a map to give a general idea of their position. From north to south these regional maps cover Solway and the Border Country, the Vale of Eden, the Lake District, Cumbrian Coast, Morecambe Bay, North Lancashire, South Lancashire (including Greater Manchester and North Merseyside) and Cheshire with Wirral.

The format standard to the rest of this series of guides has not been adopted rigidly, nevertheless for many sites the sub-headings of 'Habitat', 'Species', 'Access', 'Timing' and 'Calendar' have been employed. The 'Species' and 'Calendar' sections in particular were often found to overlap, and in such cases the 'Calendar' heading has been dropped.

Habitat
A brief description of the habitat is given. The availability of habitat types is in itself a guide to which species of birds are likely to appear. For example any site with exposed mud is likely to attract waders from time to time even where these species are not specifically mentioned as occurring at that site. Any special protection or other details of ownership and status are also given. In some cases, reference is made to other aspects of natural history for which a site is noted.

Species
For each site, an account is given of the species likely to be seen through the varying seasons of the year. Speciality birds are given particular attention. There are, however, several sites in the region which, by their nature and because they are constantly watched at passage seasons, attract a number of rarities annually. Rare birds are just that. Their occurrence can not be predicted with confidence, and a mention of past occurrences in the text does not mean that those occurrences will be repeated, even though that possibility remains.

Access
For most sites, there is a map showing access routes. In all cases access from nearby towns or main roads is described. Where we are aware of restrictions on access, these are detailed. The region contains a number of valuable ornithological sites of industrial nature, whose accessibility depends on the consent of the owners. In many cases good relations have been built up over the years between birdwatchers and landowners or tenants. Changes in policy towards access by such landowners may change overnight. It is vital that all visitors respect the authority and property of landowners, both to maintain good relations and good will towards the birds, and to spare us, the authors, from embarrassment.

Several of the sites in this book are accessible by permit only. Permit systems are established in order to avoid excessive disturbance at conservation sites, to provide a source of funding for conservation bodies, and in a few cases to meet the legal requirements (insurance etc) of the landowners. Addresses are included from which permits can be obtained.

Timing

For coastal sites, visits may need to be timed to coincide with certain states of the tide. Country parks inland may be thronged with people and apparently birdless on sunny weekends. Wind direction and other weather conditions are critical at many sites. At some sites such factors matter little, but for those where they do, recommendations are made for the best times to visit.

Calendar

This section summarises in brief note form the possible highlights at each season. There is no guarantee that all the species listed will be present on any given date. At a few sites, where interest is seasonal, there may be entries for only a part of the year. This does not necessarily mean that the site is not worth visiting at other seasons. It may indicate a lack of available information.

THE MAPS

In addition to the regional maps which indicate the general position of sites, simple larger scale maps accompany most site descriptions. These are intended to help the visitor to locate the site with confidence. (Very often there will be birdwatchers present on site – north-western birders are generally friendly and willing to share any information they may have.) Little topographical or vegetational detail is given. A key to the maps is provided below.

Key to Maps

Motorway/ dual carriageway		Mudflat or sandflat	
A or B road		Church	
Minor road		Car Park	
Track or footpath		Hide	
Railway		Level crossing	
Boundary		Woodland or forest	
Lake and river		Urban area	
		LWM Low water mark	

ABBREVIATIONS USED IN THE TEXT

CCT	Cheshire Conservation Trust	NNR	National Nature Reserve
		NT	National Trust
CWT	Cumbria Wildlife Trust	SSSI	Site of Special Scientific
EH	English Heritage		Interest
LNR	Local Nature Reserve	WWT	Wildfowl and Wetlands
LTNC	Lancashire Trust for Nature Conservation		Trust

THE SOLWAY PLAIN AND THE BORDER COUNTRY

1   Longtown Marsh
2A   Rockliffe Marsh
2B   Burgh Marsh
2C   Bowness-on-Solway
2D   Grune Point and Moricambe Bay
3A   Silloth Docks and Shore
3B   Mawbray Banks
3C   Dubmill Point
3D   Tarns Dub

This area of Cumbria has not been closely studied by natural historians
generally. It stretches from the slopes of the northern Pennines with their
wide expanse of moorland, interspersed with large blocks of coniferous
woodland, into the kinder territory of mixed cattle and sheep farms at the
lower altitudes. Moving westwards past Carlisle, into the Solway Plain,
the lushness of the fields and hedgerows is punctuated with mixed
woodland, remnant peat mosses, and raised bogs isolated by the advance of land reclamation. The whole area is drained by many rivers and
streams. The River Esk flowing from Scotland is joined by the River Lyne
and Liddle Water which is for some of its length the border between
England and Scotland. The River Eden, having meandered through

Carlisle, empties into the Solway headwater near the mouth of the Esk. Between the two is a vast expanse of saltmarsh – Rockcliffe Marsh. Further west the Rivers Wampool and Waver empty into Moricambe Bay, another very large tidal saltmarsh. From Silloth to Maryport the Outer Solway provides a coastal habitat complete with dune slack systems and pebble strewn shores. The farmland in this area is generally flat and uninspiring although the occasional small tarn (lake) offers a pleasant break to this.

Species

The upland area to the east of the region is the home of typical Pennines species, with open moorland holding Skylark, Meadow Pipit, Wheatear, Short-eared Owl and the occasional Merlin and Hen Harrier. The forestry zones here hold Redpoll, Siskin, Goldcrest and a few Crossbills. Sparrow-hawk and Long-eared Owl also occur.

The agricultural countryside from the Pennine foothills to the Solway Coast hold species such as Curlew, Lapwing and Redshank in the summer months with Whooper Swan, Pink-footed Goose and winter thrushes roaming the fields in winter.

The mosses with alder, birch and scrub are the favoured sites for Willow Tit, Whinchat, Tree Sparrow and the odd Lesser Whitethroat. Corn Buntings, which are scarce in Cumbria, are found around Wigton and near the coast in the Allonby area.

The river systems are home for Common Sandpipers, Red-breasted Merganser and Goosander with Dipper and Grey Wagtail in the higher reaches. Kingfishers also occur but are not common. Near the lower reaches wildfowl are regular in winter: the River Esk is noted for Goldeneye and Green Sandpiper whilst in summer Little Gulls are often seen.

The saltmarshes are the most important bird habitat of this region, as they are the breeding site for waders, gulls and a few terns. In winter they provide a feeding area for wildfowl and waders, particularly in the latter part of winter when thousands of Barnacle and Pink-footed Geese gather prior to their migration northwards. Wader passage is also strong here with large numbers of Grey Plover, Knot and Dunlin, for example. Grune Point on Moricambe Bay is a good migration watch point for smaller migrants which in recent years have included rarer species such as Golden Oriole, Hoopoe and Barred and Yellow-browed Warblers. Offshore, Great Shearwater, Storm and Leach's Petrels and three species of Skua have occasionally been 'storm-bound' here in adverse conditions.

Along the Solway Coast large parties of Scaup are found in winter along with Red-throated Diver and Great Crested Grebe in lesser numbers. Glaucous and Mediterranean Gulls both occur here from time to time. Among the tidewrack in the dune areas small flocks of Goldfinch and Twite are regular, the odd Snow Bunting and – more unusually – Shore Lark have occasionally appeared here.

1 LONGTOWN AND OAKBANK GRAVELPITS

OS Map 85
NY 37

Habitat

The village of Longtown is situated eight miles (13 km) north of Carlisle on the east bank of the River Esk. Beyond the river, on the opposite side lie three flooded gravel pits, two being rather exposed, while the third, smaller one is surrounded by alder-fringed reedbed. A mile (2 km) to the north at Oakbank Farm are two larger gravel pits which are also exposed. The Carlisle and District Coarse Angling Association have the rights to the Longtown pits whereas Oakbank gravel pits are run by Oakbank Fisheries who have the fishing rights.

Species

The winter months and autumn and spring passage times are the best periods here. Although there is disturbance from the fishing activities, the wildfowl tend to move between Longtown and Oakbank, with the River Esk the final refuge if constantly disturbed. It is an important site for wildfowl in winter with Whooper and Bewick's Swans and geese frequenting local fields. It is the most regular site in Cumbria to find Smew. Great Crested Grebe and the odd diver occasionally appear. Rarer wildfowl have included grebes, Ferruginous Duck and the first Cumbrian record of Ruddy Duck in 1969. The cover of the reed bed at Longtown has held Bittern and the odd Reed Warbler which is rare this far north. Spring passage brings large numbers of hirundines and a few Black Tern. The River Esk at this time is a popular place for Little Gull and Green Sandpipers. In autumn large flocks of waders, including good numbers of Golden Plovers, gather on the surrounding fields. The gravel pits often hold the odd wader and passage tern. The reed bed in autumn has a

3

large hirundine roost and the occasional Water Rail, and sub-rarities have appeared at this time of year.

Timing

General visits are best made early in the day to avoid the anglers. In winter a gull roost is worth checking at the latter part of the day. During periods of south-westerly gales in May and October the pits are well worth checking as seabirds are occasionally storm-bound here.

Access

The Longtown pits can be viewed from the A7 Carlisle–Edinburgh and the A6071 Longtown–Gretna roads. From Longtown, on the A6071, a small parking area used by the Carlisle Angling Association can be reached by turning left at Smalstown at NY 367687 and crossing the railway bridge. The reed bed can be viewed from this point. Access along the west bank of the River Esk is by a footpath at NY 377689 to Kirkandrews. Oakbank pits can be viewed at one end from the minor road that leaves the A7 at Dickstree Cottage. It is a private site and permits to enter the area should be obtained from the Oakbank Fisheries, Longtown, CA6 5NA.

Calendar

All year: Little Grebe, Great Crested Grebe, Teal, Shoveler, Pochard, Tufted Duck, Kingfisher, Grey Wagtail, Reed Bunting.

November/March: Whooper Swan, occasional divers, 'grey' geese, Pintail, Wigeon, Goldeneye, Smew, Goosander, common waders, Gull roost, occasional Kittiwake, Red-necked Grebe, Slavonian and Black-necked Grebes, Bittern and Long-tailed Duck.

March/May: Gadwall, Shelduck, Green and Common Sandpiper, Whimbrel, Little Gull, Black Tern, Grasshopper Warbler, Lesser Whitethroat, Whinchat and Redpoll. Sub-rarities have included Night Heron, Hobby and Mediterranean Gull.

June/July: Canada Goose, Ringed Plover, Green and Wood Sandpipers, Spotted Redshank and Little Gull with Spotted Sandpiper and Whiskered Tern also having been recorded.

August/October: Moulting Mute Swans, Peregrine, Merlin, Dunlin, Ruff, Greenshank, Common and Arctic Tern, Chiff-chaff, Sedge Warbler, Stonechat and large flocks of mixed finches, Tree Sparrow and Yellowhammer. Sub-rarities have included Ferruginous Duck, Ruddy Duck, Osprey, Jack Snipe, Roseate Tern, Yellow-browed Warbler.

Habitat

The Solway is one of Britain's major estuaries and is of high international importance for both wildfowl and waders. The English shore has extensive saltmarshes from Rockcliffe to Grune Point, all scheduled as Grade I SSSIs. The shoreline from Port Carlisle to Bowness and, thereafter, the Cardurnock Flatts are expanses of sand and boulder-strewn shingle. Grune Point on the south side of Moricambe Bay is a shingle promontory with a mixed scrub cover of gorse, thorn and bramble and is a well-known Cumbrian migration watch point. At Silloth, the Solway becomes much wider and deeper and as a consequence is a site for sea-duck and other seabirds.

Species

The saltmarshes of the Inner Solway are well known for wintering geese, particularly the Barnacle and Pink-footed Geese. They normally arrive in March and build up to around 10,000 birds in the case of Barnacle and 15,000 birds in the case of the Pink-footed before departing in April to their breeding grounds. Other wildfowl for which the area is important include Cormorant, Whooper Swan, Shelduck, Scaup and Goldeneye. Waders, too, reach figures of national importance here including Oystercatcher, Golden Plover, Lapwing, Knot, Dunlin, Bar-tailed Godwit, Curlew, Redshank and Turnstone. Up to 100,000 gulls roost here in winter. Other wintering wildfowl and waders include Greylag, Wigeon, Teal, Shoveler, Red-breasted Merganser, divers and grebes, Ringed and Grey Plovers, Black-tailed Godwit and Greenshank. Short-eared and Barn Owls, Hen Harrier, Merlin and Peregrine often prey on this abundance of shore birds. Flocks of Goldfinch, Twite, Meadow Pipit and Skylark frequent the saltmarshes with the occasional group of Snow Bunting being seen.

Scaup

Bowness and Grune Point are favourite sites to visit in spring when migration is quite marked in the area. Recent years have shown May as a good month to see passage Skuas on the Inner Estuary, including Great, Arctic and Pomarine Skuas, as well as shearwaters, Fulmar, Gannet and terns. At Grune Point migrant warblers and hirundines abound, often with a sub-rarity such as Golden Oriole, Wryneck, Black Redstart or Red-backed Shrike being seen. The saltmarshes at this season are alive with the noise of breeding waders and it is also now that birds like Little Egret and Spoonbill may appear, Black Tern and Little Gull often being seen at high tide. Passage Sanderling are at their most numerous in May. It is an important breeding site for wildfowl, waders, gulls and Common Tern.

The first return migrants of autumn appear in July and often include Whimbrel, Ruff, Little Stint, and Curlew Sandpiper as passage increases. Black-tailed Godwit appear in numbers large enough to be of national importance on Cardurnock Flatts and around Bowness for a brief few weeks in August and September. October often brings stormy conditions and the chance of something rarer being 'storm-bound' in the natural funnel of the estuary. Great Shearwater, Storm and Leach's Petrels, Long-tailed Skua and Grey Phalarope have been seen in this month. Rare waders have also occurred, for example Pectoral and Buff-breasted Sandpipers and in 1987 two Long-billed Dowitchers together at Anthorn in Moricambe Bay. Autumn passage of passerines can be obvious on Grune Point with large flocks or groups of warblers, finches and winter thrushes. Amongst them have occurred birds such as Firecrest, Yellow-browed Warbler, Ring Ousel, Great Grey Shrike, Wryneck and Lapland Bunting. Gull and tern movements can be interesting at this time with stormy conditions bringing flocks of Kittiwake and Fulmar, Gannet, auks and other seabirds. Both Whiskered and White-winged Black Terns occurred out in the Inner Firth in 1987. As well as three species of skua being recorded in autumn, rarer gulls such as Mediterranean and Ring-billed have been seen.

Timing

A large estuary like this can be attractive to birdwatchers all the year round, but the best times are spring and autumn for waders and passerines and late winter for wildfowl, especially large concentrations of geese and birds of prey. An hour or so either side of full tide is the best time to see most of the shorebirds as they are pushed up on to their high tide roost sited on the saltmarsh.

Access
2A ROCKCLIFFE MARSH

OS ref: NY 334648

This is an important site for breeding waders and as such is wardened throughout the summer months by Cumbria Wildlife Trust. Access is limited and strictly by permit. In winter it is popular with wildfowlers. Take the A74(T) north from Carlisle, four miles (6.5 km) to Todhills and follow the minor road to Rockcliffe Village, turn right to Castletown House and Rockcliffe Cross two miles (3 km) from the village. Follow the lane half a mile (1 km) to the Esk Boathouse where you must leave your car. A track round the inner marsh runs along the top of the grass sea-protection embankment giving good views across the whole marsh.

Barnacle Geese

2B BURGH MARSH

OS ref: NY 328608 and NY 294594

This large saltmarsh is owned by the National Trust and there are two access points. Follow the B5307 in Carlisle to Bellevue where you take a minor road to the right to Kirkandrews and Burgh-by-sands. At the crossroads in the centre of the latter village turn right for the King Edward I monument. After approximately one mile (2 km) the road becomes a track: follow this on foot to the monument where there is a good vista of the northern part of the saltmarsh. A track to the north of this point leads to the estuary of the River Eden at Old Sandfield. The second access is at the west end of the village where the minor road to Drumburgh and Bowness follows the line of Hadrians Wall. There are good views along the tideline and the southern half of the saltmarsh two miles (3 km) west of Burgh-by-sands. Beware of high tides, which may cover the road.

2C BOWNESS-ON-SOLWAY

OS ref: NY 224628

The minor road from Burgh-by-sands through Port Carlisle and Bowness-on-Solway to Cardurnock travels along the shoreline of the Inner Solway near Bowness for three miles (2.5 km) with good view-points along its length. The best viewpoints are at the car park just east of Bowness (OS ref: NY 233628), the embankment of the old Solway viaduct at Herdhill Scar (NY 212628) and at Campfield Farm (NY 194610), now an RSPB reserve for studying Campfield Marsh.

2D GRUNE PPOINT AND MORICAMBE BAY

OS ref: 144569

Good views of this bay can be had on the eastern shore from the wireless station to the village of Anthorn. The western shore can be covered from Grune Point and Skinburness. To reach Grune Point take the B5302 from

Carlisle to Silloth where a minor road northwards takes you to Skinburness Park near the Skinburness Hotel where you can walk along the edge of Skinburness Marsh (at NY 128559) to Grune Point or along the shoreline from the private road behind the Hotel. This makes a good circular tour of the area covering all the various habitats.

Calendar

All year: Cormorant, Oystercatcher, Redshank, Lapwing, Spotted Redshank, Greenshank, Curlew, Snipe, Teal, Shoveler, Greylag, Heron, gulls, Grey Wagtail, Stonechat, Reed Bunting.

November/March: Great Crested Grebe, Red-necked Grebe, Whooper Swan, Pink-footed Goose, Barnacle Goose, Pintail, Wigeon, Goldeneye, Scaup, Red-breasted Merganser, Eider (occasionally), Sanderling, Dunlin, Knot, Golden and Grey Plovers, Bar-tailed Godwit, Jack Snipe, Turnstone, Kittiwake, Guillemot, Short-eared Owl, Barn Owl, Hen Harrier, Merlin, Peregrine, Rock Pipit, Twite, Snow Bunting.

March/May: 'Grey' geese, ten species of duck, Green and Common Sandpiper, Ruff, Black-tailed Godwit, Little Gull, terns, skuas (Arctic, Pomarine and Great), Black Tern, Wheatear, Whinchat, Black Redstart and hirundines. Sub-rarities include Little Egret, White Stork, Garganey, Storm Petrel, Mediterranean Gull, Crane and Bluethroat.

June/July: Fulmar, Manx Shearwater (during gales), Gannet, terns, skuas, Wood Sandpiper, Whimbrel, Ruff, Lesser Whitethroat, Grasshopper Warbler.

August/November: Returning geese, ducks, swans and waders, Little Ringed Plover, Little Stint, Curlew Sandpiper, Grey Plover, Black-tailed Godwit, Spoonbill, terns, skuas, gulls. Excellent passage of passerines on Grune Point at this time. Sub-rarities include Great Shearwater, Storm and Leach's Petrels, Pectoral and Buff-breasted Sandpipers, Short-billed Dowitcher, Long-tailed Skua, Wryneck, Golden Oriole, Red-backed Shrike, Yellow-browed and Barred Warblers, Firecrest and Lapland Buntings.

Habitat

This region of the Solway Firth has a low, mixed coastline of sand dunes and shingle. It offers a panoramic view across to the Scottish side, Criffel being the dominant mountain. The sand dunes at South Silloth and Mawbray Banks (NT) are the two largest areas of dune slack on the English shore of the Solway and provide habitat for Natterjack Toads and a good dune flora as well as birds. Between Silloth and Allonby, at low tide, several large 'scars' come into view: these are banks of deposited large stones and shingle with small pools where many shore birds feed. The landward side has little in the way of ornithological interest except Tarns Dub, east of the village of Holme St. Cuthbert, and Salta Moss north of Allonby.

Species

The shore here holds several groups of waders and wildfowl not usually seen in the Inner Solway. In autumn and winter Mallard, Wigeon, Scaup, Goldeneye and Red-breasted Merganser predominate whilst Ringed Plover, Bar-tailed Godwit, Sanderling and Turnstone are in the majority among the waders. Wintering Great Crested Grebe are also a feature with up to 100 birds recorded recently. Red-necked and Slavonian Grebes have appeared as well as various auks and the odd Arctic and Great Skua. Gulls feature strongly, Kittiwake, Little, Mediterranean, Iceland and Glaucous Gulls often appearing in the winter months. Rock Pipit often feed on the tideline with the odd party of Twite or Goldfinch. During periods of heavy snow this coastline is often a narrow 'green' corridor and large flocks of Redwing, Fieldfare, Meadow Pipit and Skylark move in from the neighbouring countryside. It is an important breeding area for shore birds like Oystercatcher, Ringed Plover and the occasional pair of Little Tern. Stonechat, Whitethroat, Lesser Whitethroat and Corn Bunting also breed here, the latter becoming a rare bird in Cumbria.

Timing

The best conditions for watching the wildfowl and waders of this area occur one or two hours before and after high water when the birds are closer to the shore. The Silloth outfall attracts large numbers of gulls, Scaup and Goldeneye. The highest tides of the year often push the waders off their roost sites into neighbouring fields. Many gulls will move inland to wash and roost at Tarns Dub, where the odd Iceland or Mediterranean may be found in the winter. South-westerly gales can often be rewarding in bringing to the Outer Solway numbers of divers, auks, skuas and other seabirds. Spring and autumn passage of landbirds is often noteworthy and 'hard weather' movements in winter can be heavy.

Access

Access to the shore is good as the B5300 Maryport to Silloth road runs along the coast with car parks at regular intervals.

3A SILLOTH DOCKS AND SHORE

OS ref: NY 105535

Habitat and Species

The high and low water mark in Silloth Bay are close together. The promenade leading along the shoreline north east of the town to the lighthouse and beyond to East Cote overlooks the whole of the Solway Firth. The town's public park has small groups of pines and ornamental shrubberies and is a good place to find landbird migrants amongst the high population of Collared Doves. In winter a wide selection of wildfowl, waders and gulls can be seen in the Bay, including good numbers of Great Crested Grebe, Goldeneye, Scaup and Red-breasted Merganser. Waders can best be seen at low tide as the sandbanks and scars in the Firth are exposed. Good numbers of Oystercatcher, Knot, Dunlin, Sanderling, Bar-tailed Godwit and Curlew can be seen. The outfall attracts many gulls at high tide with the odd Mediterranean Gull having been recorded. Arctic Skua sometimes 'harry' those birds. Seabirds are often recorded in the Bay with Red-throated Diver, Gannet, Shag and auks being the most regular. The docks have two large grain warehouses and a large flock of Collared Dove and 'feral' pigeons reside here. The grain also attracts Chaffinch, Greenfinch, Brambling and Yellowhammer which in turn attract the regular Sparrowhawk and the occasional Merlin and Peregrine. Stonechat and Twite have also been recorded here. A large flock of gulls is also present in the docks, sometimes including Glaucous Gull. Scaup, Common Scoter, Goldeneye, Red-breasted Merganser and Shag have been recorded in the docks, which form an excellent vantage point for observers.

Access

From the centre of Silloth, both the Docks and the promenade car park are well signposted.

3B MAWBRAY BANKS

OS ref: NY 083475

This is a mile (1.5 km) long fixed sand dune system with some gorse and scrub cover. The shore consists of pebbles and mussel beds. Waders on the shore include Oystercatcher, Ringed Plover, Redshank, Turnstone, Sanderling, Bar-tailed Godwit, Curlew and the odd Purple Sandpiper. Mallard and Wigeon are the most common wildfowl, with occasional grebes, Shelduck, Scaup, Goldeneye and Red-breasted Merganser. Passage waders include Greenshank, Common Sandpiper, Knot and Dunlin whilst in summer the commoner gulls share the site with sea terns. The dunes are habitat for Skylark, Meadow Pipit and Short-eared Owl during migration. Large flocks of Starling roam the dune slacks in autumn and are often joined by Redwing and Fieldfare in bad weather conditions. Spring migration in the dunes is the site for 'chats' – Stonechat, Whinchat and Wheatear – with Kestrel and Sparrowhawk looking for small bird prey. Barn Owl are seen in the area. Pink-footed Geese sometimes use the coastal fields, especially in cold conditions, and small finch flocks with Reed Bunting, Yellowhammer and the odd Corn Bunting are found. Stock Doves replace Wood Pigeon in this area. Mawbray Banks was the site for a wintering Hoopoe in 1988/89.

Access

The B5300 traverses the site and access to the shore is from Mawbray down a track at the road junction for The Tarns (NY 083469).

3C DUBMILL POINT

OS ref: NY 076458

The shoreline at Dubmill Point is dominated by Dubmill Scar, a large mussel bed and shingle bank where large groups of waders assemble at high tide. As well as the commoner waders this is the gathering ground for Curlew, Bar-tailed Godwit, Knot and Sanderling at peak tide time. Numbers of Bar-tailed Godwits may exceed a hundred. Grey Plover,

Greenshank, Whimbrel and Spotted Redshank can be found here at migration time. Red-throated Diver, Great Crested Grebe, Whooper Swan, Eider and Common Scoter are regular wildfowl visitors and Glaucous Gull have been recorded with the gulls. The short turf along the shoreline is, as well as a roosting point for gulls, a feeding area for a sizeable flock of Twite in winter. Wheatear use this area in migration periods, large numbers having been recorded. (The first British record of Isabelline Wheatear was found in Victorian days near Allonby). With them are Skylark, Meadow Pipit and Wagtail. On the landward side of Dubmill Point lies Salta Moss: this wetland area attracts Short-eared and Barn Owls with the odd Hen Harrier or Peregrine. Stonechat, Whinchat, Grey Wagtail, Reed Bunting, Redpoll and Siskin can also be found here. The point where Crookhurst Beck runs into the sea at Allonby is the favourite site for roosting gulls. Flocks of Ringed Plover, Turnstone, Redshank, Knot and Sanderling gather here at high tide to feed and to wash in fresh water.

Access
Access to Allonby is relatively easy as there are several coastal car parks in and near the town. Dubmill Point itself is a bit more difficult and is best approached along the road or shore from Allonby.

3D Tarns Dub

OS ref: NY 115474

This small inland lake or 'dub', some three miles (5 km) from the coast, is a regular roost site for gulls. They also use it as a site to wash, preen and rest whilst on passage. More unusual species may occur among the large flocks of Herring, Lesser Black-backed, Common and Black-headed Gulls. The lake is deep and reed-fringed with alders growing on one side, and at the west end there is a large area of bog and associated marsh plants. Apart from the gulls, the lake attracts wildfowl such as Tufted Duck, Pochard and Goldeneye, with Teal in the marshy fringes. Barn Owl, Short-eared Owl, Hen Harrier and Merlin have all been seen quartering the marsh and surrounding fields. Sedge and Grasshopper Warblers frequent the marsh in summer and Redpoll are attracted to the alders.

More unusual species recorded here include Iceland and Glaucous Gulls, Kittiwake and the occasional tern, Jack Snipe and Water Rail; a Crane has been recorded nearby at Wolsty.

Access
To view Tarns Dub take the minor road to The Tarns from Mawbray: half a mile (1 km) past Holme St Cuthbert, Tarns Dub can be viewed from the road. Views of the site can also be had from the B5301 Silloth to Aspatria road (NY 118474).

VALE OF EDEN

4   Geltsdale Tarn and Tindale Tarn
5   Talkin Tarn
6   Castle Carrock Reservoir
7A Lazonby
7B Langwathby

7C Culgaith Area
7D Kirkby Thore
7E Whinfell Forest, Cliburn
8   Sunbiggin Tarn

This sheltered, agriculturally rich valley lies on the western side of the northern Pennines. This protects the area from cold east winds in winter. It stretches for forty miles from Carlisle nearly to the source of the River Eden beyond Kirkby Stephen. The river is the area's dominant feature as it meanders its way north and is particularly interesting as it deepens from Appleby northwards. Although it is rich pastureland with a percentage of mixed arable farming it has, by and large, kept its character over the years. Many hedgerows and trees have been retained and only as the valley nears Carlisle does the trend for larger fields appear.

To the east of Carlisle lies Talkin Tarn, a Country Park run by Cumbria County Council, whilst higher up, on the lower slopes of the Pennines, is the more isolated Tindale Tarn. The moorland and forestry sweep of Geltsdale is complemented by Castle Carrock Reservoir at its foot.

The area where the River Eamont joins the Eden is the most interesting for birds, particularly wildfowl. Here, near Culgaith and Langwathby, large flocks of geese and duck gather during the winter. On the west side of the Vale, at Cliburn, south of Penrith, lies Whinfell Forest. This is the largest expanse of coniferous woodland in this part of Cumbria with interesting birds. Sunbiggin Tarn is an upland lake and area of bog which is a historically known site for ornithological study, particularly migration.

Species

Eden Valley is best known for its visiting wildfowl in the winter months. Noteable are large flocks of 'grey' Geese and Whooper Swans. Cormorant, Wigeon, Goldeneye, Red-breasted Merganser and Goosander also gather in good numbers. Waders are also prominent, particularly during migration periods, Oystercatcher, Golden Plover, Lapwing, Curlew, Snipe and Redshank forming the bulk of this movement. The river system also has Dipper, Grey Wagtail, Kingfisher and several large Sand Martin colonies. Sparrowhawk, Peregrine and Short-eared Owl are regular though Buzzard is not as common as in the other parts of the county. Ravens are regular. Of the smaller birds, the woodlands hold Redstart, a few Pied Flycatcher, Wood Warbler and Siskin, with Crossbill occurring in a few areas. In the open fields large flocks of finches gather, particularly where oilseed rape has been harvested. The large Black-headed Gull colony at Sunbiggin Tarn attracts occasional terns and Little Gull as well as predatory Short-eared Owl, Peregrine and Buzzard. Ravens also scavenge here.

4 GELTSDALE (RSPB) AND TINDALE TARN

OS Map 86
NY 55/65

Habitat and Species

This is a moorland reserve in the Northern Pennines where the wild spectacular landscape can be awe-inspiring, giving one a feeling of loneliness. The fells of the Kings Forest of Geltsdale are mainly covered with moorland grasses with smaller areas of heather cover. Many parts are boggy, with small streams, and some of the highest regions are bare and stone-covered. This makes for good breeding habitat for Red Grouse, Golden Plover, Curlew, Raven and Ring Ousel.

Passage migrants at these levels include Hen Harrier, Short-eared Owl, Peregrine, Merlin, Dunlin, Twite and Snow Bunting. On the lower pastures Lapwing, Skylark, Wheatear and Meadow Pipit breed. Sparrow-hawk, Kestrel, Common and Jack Snipes, Redshank, Whinchat, Linnet and Yellowhammer are also found here. Along the path which passes through woodland of oak and beech, by the steep-sided Rivers Gelt and Irthing are breeding Dipper, Grey Wagtail and Common Sandpiper with Redstart, Pied Flycatcher, Wood Warbler and Tree Pipit in the woods. Tindale Tarn, a typical moorland lake, is well worth a visit in winter as Whooper Swan, Pochard, Tufted Duck, Goldeneye and Goosander are regular here.

Access

There is access to three walks at all times. For Geltsdale itself, park at Jockey Shield east of Castle Carrock on the B6413 and walk across the River Gelt (NY 542562) for the bridleways. Alternatively, from the small car park at Low Gelt Bridge, just east of the A69 (NY 520592) follow the marked path through Lower Gelt Woods, or start this walk at the railway viaduct turning west off the B6413, three miles (5 km) south of Brampton – at this end it is suitable for wheelchairs and pushchairs. For Tindale Tarn, park at Tindale off the A689 (NY 542562) to walk along the old railway line.

Calendar

All year: Red Grouse, Raven, Short-eared Owl, Peregrine, Merlin, Dipper, Twite.

November/March: Whooper Swan, Wigeon, Tufted Duck, Pochard, Goldeneye, Goosander, Hen Harrier, Brambling, Snow Bunting.

March/July: Golden Plover, Curlew, Redshank, Dunlin, Ring Ousel, Redstart, Pied Flycatcher, Tree Pipit, Wood Warbler. Migrant Barnacle and Pink-footed Geese often seen moving from the Solway north-east to the east coast and northern Europe.

July/October: Return of wildfowl, large flocks of migrant thrushes, Brambling, Snow Bunting. Overflighting of seabirds such as Kittiwake and Fulmar. Unusual birds seen at this site have included Red-crested Pochard, Rough-legged Buzzard, Golden Eagle, Osprey, Dotterel and Whiskered Tern.

5 TALKIN TARN (CUMBRIA COUNTY COUNCIL)

OS Map 86
NY 545588
(see map p. 15)

Habitat and Species

This is a large lake used for recreational purposes as part of a Country Park under the auspices of Cumbria County Council. However, it is a well known site for wildfowl, passage waders and terns. In winter, wildfowl include Greylag Goose, Wigeon, Pochard, Tufted Duck, Goldeneye, Goosander and Red-breasted Merganser. Almost anything may turn up with Whooper Swan, Black-necked Grebe and Smew appearing in recent years. Breeding birds include Tufted Duck, Canada Goose, Common Sandpiper and Grey Wagtail while the surrounding woodland holds breeding Redstart, Wood Warbler and Tree Pipit. Passage waders and terns have appeared in spring and autumn and have included Avocet, Green and Wood Sandpiper, Greenshank, Black-tailed Godwit, Dunlin and Turnstone. Black Tern and Little Gull have also appeared at this time of year. The mature beech and oak around the shoreline hold a good range of woodland birds.

Access

The main car park is signposted to the left from the B6413, three miles (5 km) south of Brampton, immediately you have crossed the level crossing at NY 540592. Footpaths from the car park give good access to all of the lake and most of the woodland area. Timing is important as the Country Park is popular at the weekends for canoeists and windsurfers.

6 CASTLE CARROCK RESERVOIR (NORTH WEST WATER)

Habitat and Species

This reservoir is situated to the south of the village of Castle Carrock on the lower slopes of the Northern Pennines. It is planted on three sides with a mixture of conifer, larch and oak. The western edge has several areas of tall grasses and reed giving food and cover to some birds.

In winter it holds a wide selection of waterfowl including Greylag Goose, Whooper Swan, Wigeon, Teal, Pochard, Tufted Duck, Goldeneye, Red-breasted Merganser and Goosander. Rarer wildfowl such as Black-necked Grebe, Long-tailed Duck, Smew and Common Scoter are seen from time to time. Coot also gather in large numbers here in winter and there is a noteworthy gull roost of around 1,000 Black-headed and Common Gulls. Lapwing, Redshank, Curlew and Common Sandpiper breed here. Wader species increase during spring and autumn migration and can include Ringed Plover, Golden Plover, Dunlin, Snipe, Greenshank and Green Sandpiper; less frequent are Sanderling, Ruff, Jack Snipe and Whimbrel. Common Terns appear occasionally along with the odd Black Tern and Little Gull.

The conifer woodland holds Goldfinch, Redpoll, Siskin and parties of tits and Goldcrest. Birds of prey to be seen include Buzzard, Sparrow Hawk, Peregrine, Merlin, Kestrel and Tawny Owl. Long-eared Owl have been recorded too. Osprey have occurred but Barn Owl are now scarce here as elsewhere in the county.

Access

From Castle Carrock take the B6413 south to Croglin, turn first left on a minor road to Tottergill. Excellent views can be had of most of the reservoir at NY 543540 on a footpath to Tottergill.

Habitat

The central area, between Armathwaite and Appleby, is the most interesting part of the Eden Valley for birdwatchers. The large flat fields in the
regions east of Penrith, particularly where the River Eamont joins the
River Eden near Culgaith, are host to large numbers of geese and other
wildfowl during the winter months. It is a mixed farming locality with
arable, dairy and sheep being of roughly equal importance. Being on the
lee of the highest part of the Pennines adds interest as migrant birds
often travel the length of the valley between the Solway and the East
Coast, over Stainmore. Forestry is being developed in this area with new
stands of deciduous and coniferous woodland. Of particular interest is
the Whinfell Forest at Cliburn, which is mature conifer woodland with a
rotating forestry practice.

Species

This is a rich area for water-associated birds. Wildfowl such as Canada Goose, Red-breasted Merganser and Goosander breed here as do Heron, Common Sandpiper, Redshank, Oystercatcher and the odd pair of Ringed Plover, Dipper and Grey Wagtail. There are several large colonies of Sand Martin. During the winter months the wildfowl species increase with Cormorant, Greylag Goose, Whooper Swan, Wigeon, Teal and Goldeneye. Lapwing, Golden Plover and Curlew gather in riverside fields.

Whooper Swans

The arable fields, particularly where oilseed rape has been harvested, hold very large finch flocks of up to a thousand birds. These comprise Greenfinch, Chaffinch, Brambling and Linnet, with a few Goldfinch, Tree Sparrow, Yellowhammer and Reed Bunting. Small flocks of Stock Dove can also be found here. The finch flocks attract birds of prey down from the bleaker parts of the Pennines and Sparrow Hawk, Merlin and Peregrine can all be seen when the finches are present. The deciduous woodland is home for both Green and Great Spotted Woodpeckers, and Little and Tawny Owls. Breeding birds include Tree Pipit, Redstart, Spotted Flycatcher, Wood and Garden Warblers and Blackcap. Smaller numbers of Willow Tit, Siskin, Pied Flycatcher and Chiffchaff also occur. In the birch and willow woodland that is regularly found in areas of raised peat bog, flocks of Siskin, Goldfinch and Redpoll (including some Mealy Redpoll) are seen in winter. The conifer woods are less popular with birds but Coal Tit, Siskin, a few Crossbill and Long-eared Owl are at home here. Of the migrant species, gulls and waders are often seen flighting west or east along the river. Geese and winter thrushes also migrate along this route, as do hirundines and other small passerines in summer. Unusual birds also appear from time to time: Black-throated Diver, Little Auk, Bean Goose, Smew, Red Kite, Grey Phalarope, Glaucous Gull, Firecrest and Yellow-browed Warbler have been recorded in the winter months, while in summer Night Heron, Black and White Storks, Avocet, Wood Sandpiper, Osprey, Wryneck and Red-backed Shrike have occurred.

7A LAZONBY

OS Map 86
NY 53/54

Habitat and Access

The village of Lazonby lies eight miles (13 km) north of Penrith. Take the
A6 to Carlisle and at Plumpton take the B6413 to Lazonby. Pass through
the village to the majestic red sandstone Eden Bridge where there is a car
park by the river (NY 562404). The parkland to the east of the river and
fields to the west often hold large flocks of Greylag and Canada Geese in
winter. Whooper Swan occur along with Goldeneye, Red-breasted
Merganser and Goosander. Common Sandpiper, Dipper, Sand Martin
and Grey Wagtail are some of the summer residents.

7B LANGWATHBY

OS Map 90/91
NY 53

Species and Access

Take the A686 to Alston from Penrith and after five miles (8 km)
Langwathby is reached. The fields west of the metal girder bridge over
the River Eden (NY 565338) attract a large flock of Whooper Swan in
winter with Bewick's Swan in small numbers occasionally. These fields
sometimes flood, which attracts good numbers of Mallard, Teal and
Wigeon. Summer months bring Green Sandpiper, Heron, Goldfinch and
Redpoll.

7C CULGAITH AREA

OS Map 91
NY 53 and 63

Species and Access

Where the River Eamont joins the River Eden (NY 587310) there is an
area of arable farming with large flat fields. This is one of the most
attractive areas for birds in the whole Eden Valley. Good views of the area
can be had from the hillside by the B6412 Langwathby to Culgaith road at
NY 588312. The river at this point also attracts good numbers of wildfowl;
there is a Cormorant roost too. Merlin and Peregrine often hunt here and
the fields attract finches, pigeons and Stock Doves. Less common birds
that have been seen here include Black-throated Diver, Bean,
White-fronted and Barnacle Geese, Red Kite, Mealy Redpoll and Corn
Bunting. If the goose flocks are not present they may well be at Aigill
Sike, north of the village of Culgaith at NY 615317.

7D KIRKBY THORE

OS Map 91
NY 62

Species and Access

This is another area of large fields at a river junction. Here the Trout Beck joins the River Eden to the west of the village. The area may be viewed from two sites, one at a layby on the A66 on the site of the old railway station (NY 642240), the other north along the A66 from the village, taking the first lane left. From the railway bridge to the bend in the lane good views of the area can be obtained. Whooper Swan, 'grey' geese, Wigeon, Short-eared Owl and Peregrine are among the species seen here.

7E WHINFELL FOREST, CLIBURN

OS Map 91
NY 52

Species and Access

North of the village of Cliburn lies Whinfell Forest, a large part of which is a major forestry plantation with mature and semi-mature Sitka Spruce and Scots Pine. Surrounding the main forest area are several woods of Oak, Birch and Sycamore. The trackbed of the old Penrith to Darlington railway divides the forest from Cliburn Moss which is a mature Scots Pine woodland with raised bog heathland flora and all the wildlife associated with such a site. The forest holds plentiful birdlife: apart from the more common woodland species you may also find Sparrowhawk, Buzzard, Woodcock, Tawny and Long-eared Owl, Tree Pipit, Whinchat, Willow Tit, Siskin, Redpoll and occasional Crossbill.

Access to the area is limited, as large parts of the forest are private. However, a minor road to Cliburn leaves the A66 two miles north west of Temple Sowerby at NY 595286 and passes through the eastern side of the forest. From this minor road a footpath through the forest starts at NY 587268, leading to Sawmill Cottages and eventually to the A66. Further along the minor road at NY 585264, another track leads to South Whinfell and Cliburn Moss, the latter being situated along the Penrith to Cliburn road.

8 SUNBIGGIN TARN

Habitat

Sunbiggin Tarn lies at 1,000 feet in a basin of undulating moorland and is surrounded by large areas of exposed Westmorland limestone pavement and outcrops. The southern and western sides of the basin are low-lying, forming large phragmites reedbeds from which the tarn drains into the Rais Beck, a tributary of the River Lune. Sunbiggin Tarn covers about ten acres (4 hectares) and is connected to a smaller and shallower piece of water known as Cow Dub. Between the two is a large area of floating bog and reedbed which is the breeding site for one of the county's major Black-headed Gull colonies, holding 4–5,000 pairs. This gullery has been in existence since the late 1880s and has in recent years expanded to all sides of the tarn. To the west of the tarn the outflow stream runs into a calcareous bog known as Tarn Sike which is now a reserve of the Cumbria Wildlife Trust. Here flourishes local flora, for example Birdseye Primrose, Marsh Cinquefoil and Moonwort Fern, all Westmorland flora specialities.

Species

The winter months provide interest with a wealth of waterfowl at Sunbiggin. Whooper Swan, Cormorant, Teal, Wigeon, Gadwall, Tufted Duck, Pochard, Goldeneye, Red-breasted Merganser and Goosander are regularly present. Water Rail frequent the reedbeds, as do Snipe and the odd Jack Snipe. Short-eared Owl, Buzzard, Merlin and Peregrine haunt the area for prey and Raven often gather in small groups looking for carrion. Few small land birds are present at this time but Skylark, Meadow Pipit, the odd Stonechat and small flocks of Goldfinch, Linnet or Twite may occur. Spring and autumn passage brings mainly migrant waders, with waterfowl and terns sometimes appearing. In spring the noise and spectacle of the gathering large flocks of Black-headed Gulls at their breeding site may mask the presence of passage birds like Black-necked Grebe, Shelduck, Scaup, Pintail, Shoveler, Common Scoter and Long-tailed Duck. Hen Harrier and Osprey have appeared at this season. Flocks of Golden Plover and Curlew gathering on the neighbouring fellsides, where Red Grouse breed, have diminished in recent years but Ringed Plover, Oystercatcher, Dunlin, Ruff, Greenshank and Common Sandpiper are regular while Snipe, Redshank, some Curlew and the odd Dunlin stay to breed. Less common passage waders recorded in the last few years include Dotterel, Grey Plover, Sanderling, Little Stint, Pectoral Sandpiper, Turnstone and Red-necked Phalarope. Passage terns include Common, Arctic, Little and Black while Kittiwake and Fulmar have been observed in stormy weather conditions and Little Gull may appear in mid-summer. Hirundines gather in large numbers to roost in the reedbeds in autumn while numbers of breeding Sedge Warbler vary from year to year. Passage landbirds have included Kingfisher, Dipper, Redstart, Whinchat and Grasshopper Warbler. Among rarities recorded here are Bittern, Ring-necked Duck, Rough-legged Buzzard, Red Kite and Osprey. Breeding waterfowl include Gadwall, Teal, Wigeon, Tufted Duck and occasionally, Shoveler.

Timing
The tarn is the centre of a local shooting and fishing syndicate so observations here are best done in the close season. During passage migration early morning or late afternoon, when birds use the site to feed or roost, are the appropriate times to visit. September gales or the occasional spring storm may bring something more unusual.

Access
Good views can be had from the minor road overlooking the tarn. Take the Orton road at the junction of the M6 and the A685 north of Kendal. Leave Orton on the B6261 and after half a mile (1 km) take the minor road to Raisbeck and Sunbiggin. The tarn is four miles (6.5 km) onto the moor along the road to Little Asby from Raisbeck. Tarn Sike can be viewed from the track which leaves the road at the cattle grid at NY 666074. A high viewpoint on the moorland (NY 674077) looks over the reedbeds and the Cow Dub.

Calendar
All year: Teal, Gadwall, Wigeon, Tufted Duck, Sparrowhawk, Buzzard, Peregrine, Red Grouse, Coot, Snipe, Gulls and Raven.

November/March: Cormorant, Whooper Swan, Shoveler, Pochard, Goldeneye, Red-breasted Merganser and Goosander, possible Pintail, Scaup and Long-tailed Duck. Merlin, Short-eared Owl, winter thrushes, Stonechat and Twite.

June/August: Little Grebe, Shoveler, the odd Common Scoter, Ruff, Black-tailed Godwit, Wood Sandpiper, Little Gull, Common Tern, Kingfisher, Hirundines, Sedge Warbler and Twite.

April/May and July/October: Black-necked Grebe, Grey Heron, Shelduck, Hen Harrier, Osprey, Merlin, Ringed Plover, Dotterel, Golden Plover, Sanderling, Little Stint, Whimbrel, Spotted Redshank, Greenshank, Green and Common Sandpipers, Turnstone and Black Tern.

THE LAKE DISTRICT

9   Bassenthwaite Lake
10 Ullswater
11 Brothers Water and Dovedale
12 Haweswater and Wet Sleddale Reservoirs
13 Coniston Water
14 Grizedale Forest
15 Lake Windermere and Esthwaite Water
16 The Kent Valley

The Lake District has always been a popular venue for tourism, attracting many people to venture onto the mountains and lakes and into the forests. Records of good bird sites in the area have in the past been a little vague and only in recent years has the importance of some of the larger lakes like Coniston and Bassenthwaite as well as some smaller ones like Esthwaite and Elterwater come to light. Good mountain habitat is obviously under threat by the sheer numbers of visitors although there are still a few quiet areas where birds of prey, Raven, Ring Ousel and other species can breed in relative peace. The sheer size of Grizedale Forest has encouraged the Forestry Commission to try and attract people there in order to lessen the pressures on other parts of the region and as a consequence the knowledge of forest birdlife has increased.

The southern extremes of the Lake District around the limestone districts of Whitbarrow and Scout Scar with the flat pasture land of the Lyth Valley dividing them has proved to be very rich in birdlife in recent years. Included in this area is the Kent valley and the town of Kendal. The River Kent, which passes through the town, although the shortest and fastest flowing in the country, has a good birdlife attached to it, particularly in the quieter areas such as near its source in Kentmere and its outflow in Levens Park.

The Lake District is, with these various habitats, important for breeding birds like Peregrine, Goosander, Dotterel, Pied Flycatcher, Redstart, Wood Warbler, Crossbill, Siskin and Hawfinch. The lakes have good numbers of wildfowl in winter, Windermere holding five per cent of the European population of Goldeneye at this time of year, and the Cormorant, which is a sparse breeder in the County, is widespread throughout this area.

Warning: It is essential to wear adequate clothing and stout footwear on the fells, even in summer.

9 BASSENTHWAITE LAKE

Habitat

Bassenthwaite Lake is an SSSI, and as it is the fourth largest of the lakes any disturbance is kept to a minimum. The large catchment area at the south end of the lake, with its fluctuating water level and shallow nature has produced an area of fen known as Braithwaite Bog. This mix of mire, reedbed and alder and birch scrub is very scarce now in the Lake District. Access is minimal, and as a consequence a good range of birds can be found here, particularly breeding waterbirds. At this end of the lake there are several shingle banks and islands which are roost and breeding sites for wildfowl, waders and gulls. The western shore of the lake is dominated by steep sloping fellsides which are clothed for a large part by the mixed mature woodlands of Wythop Wood. Along this shore runs the A66 trunk road providing good views along its length. The eastern shore with its dominant Skiddaw skyline is less accessible. Here scattered shallow bays and inlets hold a good aquatic flora and are favourite areas for dabbling ducks. A footpath round the wooded headland at Bowness Bay to Scarness is the best access to this shore. The local sailing club restricts its activities to the northern end of the lake. Two hides have been erected by the CWT on either side of the south end of the lake.

Species

The reedbeds and fen at the southern end of the lake are an important breeding site for waterfowl, some waders and Sedge and Grasshopper Warblers and Yellow Wagtail, a bird that is scarce in the Lake District. During the winter months the number of wildfowl using the lake can reach 2,000. Cormorant, Whooper Swan, Wigeon, Goldeneye and Pochard join the resident grebes, Greylag Goose, Red-breasted Merganser and Goosander. Common Scoter, Scaup and Long-tailed Duck, along with a few Ruddy Duck, are irregular visitors. Over Braithwaite Bog hunt Sparrowhawk, Buzzard, Peregrine, Merlin and Short-eared Owl. Hen Harrier, Barn Owl and Great Grey Shrike visit from time to time, while in the reedbeds Water Rail are frequent and the Bittern is an occasional visitor. Unusual species and rarities appear from time to time, including Red-throated Diver, Osprey, Great Skua, Roller, Hoopoe and Water Pipit.

Buzzards

Timing

Spring and autumn migration periods and the winter months are the best times to visit. Early in the day most wildfowl are visible but they tend to move to the centre of the lake in the middle of the day and are easily disturbed by the activities of the sailing club, especially at weekends.

Access

A lakeside footpath on the western shore gives excellent views of the lake from Dubwath (NY 202309) to Blackstock Point. Over the stream and along a further 100 yards (90 m) from the latter point is one of the public hides (NY 225265) overlooking the southern end of the lake and Braithwaite Bog. The hide on the eastern shore is accessible from the A591 at Little Crosthwaite where there is a car park. The hide is down a footpath at NY 232277.

10 ULLSWATER

Habitat and Species

The second largest lake in the region is very beautiful and unspoilt. It is a little over eight miles (13 km) long and is at least 180 ft (55 m) deep off Glencoyne. It winds its way around steep sloping fells and mountains which mellow to a typical placid, reed-fringed lake at its outflow to the north at Pooley Bridge. Ullswater is accessible around two thirds of its shore and has a varied habitat from shingle shore and shallow bays to steep sided wooded slopes and the odd area of reedbed. The area at Skelly Nab is named after a white fish unique to Ullswater – the Schelly or freshwater herring. Huge quantities of this fish were caught at one time in a net laid across the lake at this point. During the winter the lake has an enormous gull roost with up to 15,000 birds, mainly Common and Black-headed Gulls with smaller groups of the larger gulls. In winter wildfowl numbers increase with the arrival of Cormorant, Greylag Goose, Whooper Swan, Wigeon, Pochard, Tufted Duck, Goldeneye and Goosander. Great-crested Grebe are scarce but Black-necked Grebe, Common Scoter, Scaup and Long-tailed Duck are sometimes seen. Breeding waterbirds include Red-breasted Merganser, Coot, Redshank, Common Sandpiper, Dipper and Grey Wagtail. The oak woods of Glencoyne, Gowbarrow and Sandwick hold Buzzard, Sparrowhawk, Tawny Owl, Woodpeckers, Nuthatch, Redstart, Pied Flycatcher, Wood Warbler, Siskin and Redpoll. Of the more unusual species, Great Northern Diver, Bewick's Swan, Barnacle Goose, Smew, Goshawk, Osprey, Hoopoe, Wryneck and Red-backed Shrike have been recorded here.

Timing

Ullswater is popular with tourists and holidaymakers, so it is advisable to avoid a visit in peak holiday season and on Bank Holidays. Visits to the shoreline are most rewarding in the morning during migration seasons and in the late afternoon during the winter for the large gull roost assembly. Spring, when most of the trees have no leaves, is best for passage migrants in the woodland areas.

Access

The A592 traverses the whole length of the western shore. There are parking areas along the length of this road with larger long-stay car parks at Glenridding, Glencoyne Wood, Aira Force and Pooley Bridge. Information centres at Glenridding and Pooley Bridge will provide local details and reports on conditions on the paths around the lake and on to the nearby mountains.

11 BROTHERS WATER AND DOVEDALE

Habitat and Species

Brothers Water lies at the foot of the Kirkstone Pass near the village of Hartsop. It is one of the smallest lakes, low-lying with bog and reedbed to the south and wet pasture to the north. Low Wood rises steeply from its western shore. Dovedale Beck feeds Brothers Water from the south west and from its source flows rapidly down through Dovedale. Resident birds of the lake include Little Grebe, Heron, Tufted Duck and Goosander. Snipe frequent the boggy shores along with Dipper and Reed Bunting. In winter Whooper Swan, Greylag Goose, Wigeon, Shoveler, Pochard, Goldeneye and Red-breasted Merganser enlarge the wildfowl population while in the reedbeds roam small parties of tits, Siskin and Redpoll. The summer migrant visitors include Oystercatcher, Redshank, Common Sandpiper, Yellow Wagtail and Sedge Warbler. Along the wooded shore-line and up on to the higher ground of Dovedale are the resident pairs of Buzzard and Raven. In the woods are Woodcock, Woodpeckers,

31

Peregrines

Treecreeper, Nuthatch and finches; these are joined in winter by Redwing and Fieldfare and by Redstart, Pied and Spotted Flycatchers, Tree Pipit and warblers in summer.

Higher up the valley into Dovedale the boulder-strewn scree slopes have scattered specimen trees of oak, rowan, ash and hawthorn with juniper and gorse scrub. Sparrowhawk and Peregrine hunt here and migrant species like Wheatear, Ring Ousel and Whinchat occur in summer. Recently recorded scarce birds include Black-necked Grebe, Osprey, Gadwall and Ferruginous Duck.

Access
Brothers Water lies three miles (5 km) north of the Kirkstone Pass on the A592. Beyond the lake at NY 402134 is a car park with access to a footpath along the western shore, leading to Dovedale and beyond to the fells and Fairfield Summit. Near the waterfalls in Dovedale is a viewpoint near a prominent tree (NY 382117). Look out here for Raven, Peregrine and Ring Ousel in the screes. Avoid visiting in peak holiday periods as the track is very popular with tourists, fellwalkers and ramblers.

12 HAWESWATER AND WET SLEDDALE RESERVOIR

OS Map 90
NY 41, NY 51

Habitat and Species

The reservoir of Haweswater is situated in a horseshoe of the fells of the High Street mountain range. It is three miles (5 km) long and half a mile (1 km) wide and is best known for England's only breeding pair of Golden Eagles. They frequent a site near the head of the valley which is wardened by the RSPB at an observation post throughout the spring and summer. The rugged surrounding fells have breeding Kestrel, Wheatear, Ring Ousel and Raven. Look out also for Peregrine. At the northern end the huge dam wall is landscaped well into the surrounding length of Naddle Forest. This is a mixture of conifer and hardwood and has breeding Buzzard, Sparrowhawk, Woodpeckers, Redstart, Pied Fly-catcher, Garden and Wood Warblers, Woodcock and the odd pair of Black Grouse. Amongst the waterside species are Greylag Goose, Teal, Red-breasted Merganser, Common Sandpiper and gulls. (Of the gulls, Herring and Lesser Black-backed Gulls have recently started to breed on a small island to the northern end of Haweswater.) The reservoir is an important roost for Common and Black-headed Gulls through the winter months. The numbers peak at around 12,000 birds. Typically, the gulls divide into rafts of about 2,000 each of the same species.

The Wet Sleddale reservoir is at the head of a small valley running south westwards from Shap Summit. The wet meadows at the inflow to the reservoir are excellent habitat for Teal, Snipe, Curlew and Redshank. It is an important site for wildfowl, particularly Greylag and Canada Geese and Goosander. Passage migrants at both of these sites have included a few rare birds and include all three Divers, Gannet, Bewick's and Whooper Swans, Wigeon, Pintail, Shoveler, Pochard, Tufted Duck, Scaup, Long-tailed Duck, Common Scoter, Goldeneye, Hen Harrier,

Golden Eagles

33

Merlin, Ringed and Golden Plovers, Sanderling, Dunlin, Ruff, Whimbrel, Spotted Redshank, Turnstone, Kittiwake, Common and Arctic Terns, Short-eared Owl, Yellow Wagtail, Waxwing, Nuthatch, Twite, Crossbill, Hawfinch and Snow Bunting. Rarer migrants include Slavonian Grebe, Red Kite, Osprey, Goshawk, Rough-legged Buzzard, Water Pipit, Firecrest, Golden Oriole and Red-backed Shrike. This area also has a rich variety of mountain flowers on the fells and red squirrels frequent the forest.

Access

From the A6 in Shap Village take the minor road to Haweswater and Bampton Grange. Turn left over the bridge past the church in Bampton Grange at NY 522180 for Burnbanks. Here the road winds round the dam at NY 510162 and along the western shore for three miles (5 km) past Mardale Hotel to the car parking area at the head of the reservoir at NY 469108. Good views of the reservoir and fellside are obtained along the length of the road.

Wet Sleddale is reached from the A6 a mile (1.3 km) south of Shap Village where a minor road at NY 567128 to Wet Sleddale leads to the car park by the dam wall (NY 555114). A footpath leads into the Shap Fells from this car park, giving good views of the reservoir and the wet meadows beyond. Access along the top of the dam gives good views of the other shore and the roost site for wildfowl, waders and gulls. Motorway access to both sites is from junction 39 on the M6 turning right along the A6 for Penrith.

Timing

Minor roads in both areas are single-track with passing places and are very narrow at some points. Avoid Bank Holidays as Haweswater is popular with holidaymakers and potential 'eagle spotters'. The best time to see Golden Eagle here is late summer and autumn when the young are on the wing and disturbance to the breeding birds is less.

13 CONISTON WATER

OS Map 96/97
SD 28/29 and 39

Habitat

This lake is popular with visitors to the Lake District. For birdwatchers the best habitat is at either end of this 5½ mile long lake as the water here is sheltered and has areas of reedbed on its fringe for cover. The south end around High Nibthwaite is perhaps the best locality on the lake as access is difficult and the area has, as a consequence, less disturbance. The eastern shore is well wooded, the oak wood here covering the fellside over the top to the Grizedale Forest. Also on this shore, about halfway along its length, is a small islet covered with Scots Pine known as the Fir Island. This is the main Cormorant roost site for the lake. The southern part of the western shore has easy access as the A5084 runs along its length. Beyond this is Torver Back Common, a popular area for resident and migrant birds of the open countryside. The rest of this shore is occupied by Torver Common Wood and Coniston Hall and its large camp site.

Species

This is a good lake for wildfowl, particularly in winter when numbers of Teal, Wigeon, Tufted Duck, Pochard, Goldeneye and Goosander join the resident population of Little Grebe, Canada and Greylag Geese and Red-breasted Merganser. The lake is also popular with gulls with a Black-headed and Common Gull roost reaching around 5,000 birds at its peak. Torver Back Common and the woods around Coniston Hall are a good area to see early passage migrants like Wheatear, Redstart, warblers and Tree Pipit. These woods, as well as the woods around Coniston and Monk Coniston, hold Nuthatch, woodpeckers (including the elusive Lesser-spotted Woodpecker), Jay, Redpoll, Siskin, Crossbill and the locally common Hawfinch.

A walk from Coniston up into the Coniston Fells can be productive as birds of higher altitudes like Peregrine, Short-eared Owl, Ring Ousel, Stonechat, Raven and Twite may be found. A Chough appeared in the area around Dow Crags recently, probably one of the stragglers from the Manx population that occasionally turn up in Cumbria. More unusual species have been seen on the lake from time to time including all three Divers, Red-necked and Slavonian Grebe and Ring-necked Duck. The Osprey has been seen on migration here.

Timing

Early morning is the time to see migrant passerines on Torver Back Common. Early in the day is also the best time to locate wildfowl even in the winter months as the lake is popular with yachts and windsurfing enthusiasts all year round. The south end is the most undisturbed area. Avoid visiting at Bank Holiday periods and mid-summer weekends. Woodland specialities like Lesser Spotted Woodpecker and Hawfinch appear more frequently in spring and early summer.

Access

Western shore: There are car parks at southern end of the A5084 at Brown Howe (SD 290910) and at Waterhead at the north end, a mile from Coniston just off the B5285 (SD 315978). A footpath up through the arboretum at Monk Coniston Hall leads over the fell three miles (5 km) to Tarn Hows.

Eastern shore: Many car parks along the length of this shore line, many in the woodland area. Best views of Nibthwaite area can be had from the car park (NT) at southern end (SD 297910). A track on to the Coniston Fells and the summit of the Old Man of Coniston starts at the mountain rescue post in Coniston at SD 300976.

Calendar

All year: Little Grebe, Cormorant, Heron, Greylag and Canada Geese, Teal, Tufted Duck, Red-breasted Merganser, Sparrowhawk, Buzzard, Peregrine, Snipe, Woodcock, gulls, woodpeckers, Grey Wagtail, Dipper, Nuthatch, Jay, Raven, Siskin, Twite, Redpoll, Crossbill and Hawfinch.

November/March: Great Crested Grebe, Wigeon, Shoveler, Pochard, Goldeneye, Goosander, Water Rail, Jack Snipe, Waxwing, winter thrushes, Brambling and flocks of mixed finches. Unusual species and rarities recorded in recent times include all three divers, Red-necked and Slavonian Grebe, Ring-necked Duck, Scaup, Long-tailed Duck with Hen Harrier, Merlin, Chough and Snow Bunting at higher levels on the fells.

April/October: Shelduck, Oystercatcher, Ringed Plover, Dunlin, Curlew, Redshank, Common Sandpiper, Common Tern, Tree Pipit, Redstart, Ring Ousel, warblers, Spotted and Pied Flycatcher, storm-blown seabirds, e.g. Fulmar, Gannet, Shag and Kittiwake. Recent unusual summer visitors include Osprey, Arctic Tern and Golden Oriole.

14 GRIZEDALE FOREST
(FORESTRY COMMISSION)

Habitat

Grizedale Forest lies between Coniston Water in the west and Esthwaite Water in the east. It covers around 8,000 acres (3,240 hectares) from Hawkshead south to the village of Satterthwaite. Although large expanses of conifers clothe most of the higher ground in the area the native oakwoods have been preserved for hardwood timber production covering around 750 acres (300 hectares). This is a relatively new forestry area and the Forestry Commission have applied a multi-purpose policy for the forest's use, encouraging wildlife conservation and recreation as well as general timber production practices. The large upland coniferous areas are now important for deer, fox, badger and red squirrel as well as many species of birds. An unsuccessful attempt was made to re-introduce the Capercaillie to the area in the early 1970s.

There are several nature trails through the forest, all starting at the wildlife centre. The longest trail, of 9½ miles (15 km) length, is called the Silurian Way, named after the underlying rock formation. Through the centre of the forest runs a strip of rich agricultural farmland along the course of the Grizedale Beck. There are also several man-made lakes within the forest in created clearings. These attract wildfowl and some waders as well as providing a source of water for deer and other animals, while insects such as dragonflies and butterflies are found in good numbers.

Species

The area is a stronghold for breeding Crossbill, Nuthatch and Hawfinch, all of which are uncommon birds in Cumbria. The coniferous woodland also have breeding Redpoll, Siskin and the odd pair of Long-eared Owls.

Crossbill

In the established oakwoods, woodpeckers, Redstart, Pied Flycatcher, Tree Pipit, Wood Warbler and Chiffchaff join the commoner species such as Spotted Flycatcher, Coal and Marsh Tits, Treecreeper and various finches. Woodcock are fairly common in this area but the Nightjar, once regular, has all but disappeared. In the open boggy clearings by the various tarns, Teal, Tufted Duck, Pochard, Goldeneye and Red-breasted Merganser occur from time to time, while Snipe, Curlew and Redshank appear in the boggy sites. Birds of prey also feature strongly in the forest, including Sparrowhawk, Buzzard, Peregrine and Barn, Little and Tawny Owls, with the odd sighting of Goshawk and Honey Buzzard.

Timing
The more unusual woodland species, for example Lesser Spotted Woodpecker, Crossbill and Hawfinch are most likely to be seen on a regular basis in early spring from February to April. Early morning is the best time to visit to see most of the woodland birds, although an evening visit will give a better chance of finding Nightjar and Woodcock.

Access
The main access route to Grizedale Forest centres on the minor road through the area from Hawkshead to Satterthwaite. From Hawkshead take the road to Newby Bridge and a mile (1.3 km) south of the village (SD 354976) turn right up the hill to Grizedale and Satterthwaite. Three miles along this road is the village of Grizedale and the Grizedale Forest Visitor Centre. Here there is parking, an information centre with guides to the various nature trails, hides and other access within the forest. A campsite is also situated here. Care must be taken when walking in the forest as it is easy to get lost, even with a local map. Extraction roads are constantly being added to and extended which can cause confusion, obscuring the right of way and reducing visibility to landmarks. A compass is necessary for freestyle wanderers.

Calendar
All year: Grey Heron, Gadwall, Teal, Sparrowhawk, Buzzard, Peregrine, Snipe, Barn Owl, Long-eared Owl, Woodcock, Black Grouse, woodpeckers, Grey Wagtail, Dipper, Goldcrest, Nuthatch, Treecreeper, Jay, Siskin, Redpoll, Crossbill, Hawfinch.

November/March: Tufted Duck, Goldeneye, Red-breasted Merganser, Water Rail, Jack Snipe, Short-eared Owl, Waxwing, Stonechat, winter thrushes, Raven, Brambling.

April/October: Shelduck, Oystercatcher, Curlew, Redshank, Common Sandpiper, Nightjar, Tree Pipit, Yellow Wagtail, Redstart, Whinchat, Wood Warbler, Spotted and Pied Flycatchers. Recent less common visitors have included Honey Buzzard, Red Kite, Hen Harrier, Goshawk, Rough-legged Buzzard, Osprey, Hobby, Turtle Dove, Wryneck, Water Pipit, Firecrest, Golden Oriole and Great Grey Shrike.

15 LAKE WINDERMERE AND ESTHWAITE WATER

OS Maps 90 and 97
SD 38, SD 39

Habitat

Windermere, which is 10½ miles (17 km) long, is the largest lake in England. It is also one of the most beautiful with the head of the lake to the north lying amongst the craggy volcanic mountain ring of the central Lake District. The shoreline of the southern half is well wooded in hardwood giving spectacular autumn colour at the end of the year. The lake appears to be in two halves, but is in fact divided by a group of islands of which Belle Isle is the largest. Although the lake is very popular with holidaymakers and tourists, they are mainly attracted to the towns of Bowness-on-Windermere and Ambleside. You can still find peace in the area in the summer months either in the woodlands of Claife Heights on the western shore or on the high pastures of the opposite side with magnificent views. On the western shore there are several secluded bays with reedbeds and these, together with the various islands, give sanctuary to a wide range of waterfowl during the winter months. Goldeneye in particular can be found in good numbers on Windermere. Information of current natural history activities around the area of the lake can be obtained at the National Park Centre at Brockhole.

Esthwaite Water with its large reedbeds is a better-known site for wildfowl and often attracts more unusual species.

Species

The winter months and migration times attract numbers of wildfowl, gulls and other water birds to the lake. Because the lake lies from south to north it is used as a regular flight lane by passage geese and often is host to storm-bound seabirds from nearby Morecambe Bay. Pink-footed Geese use this flight lane regularly as part of their movements between the Ribble estuary and the Solway during the winter. With the lake varying in depth throughout its length, wildfowl often choose regular sites in which to feed. Diving duck are to be found at either end of the lake at Fell Foot and Waterhead, and in the shelter around the islands near the ferry. These areas often attract more unusual species like Divers, Grebes, Scaup, Smew, Long-tailed Duck and Common Scoter along with small groups of Whooper Swan. Numbers of Cormorant seem to be slowly increasing over the years and now it has become a winter stronghold for the bird in the Lake District. The local feral population of Greylag Goose is occasionally joined by other species and the large gull roost between Belle Isle and Millerground has also gained Little Gull, Common and Black Tern.

The summer months attract occasional breeding pairs of Shelduck with Red-breasted Merganser, Tufted Duck and Mallard. Goldeneye are often found throughout the summer. Of the shoreline birds, the reed attracts Reed and Sedge Warblers and Reed Bunting in summer and Water Rail in winter.

Common Sandpiper are summer visitors to the open shoreline and are joined by passage Dunlin, Redshank and Greenshank from time to time.

Odd migrant waders like Sanderling, Turnstone and Purple Sandpiper have been recorded during or after bad weather conditions. Seabirds too are particularly evident after autumn gales and have included Storm and Leach's Petrels, Gannet, Fulmar, Shag, Grey Phalarope, Kittiwake, terns, Guillemot and Little Auk.

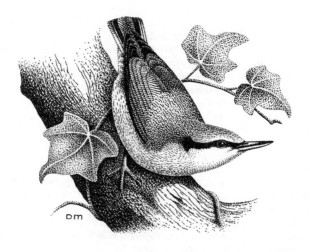

Nuthatch

The oak woods on the western shore hold breeding Nuthatch, Redstart, Pied and Spotted Flycatchers, Tree Pipits, Wood Warbler and Hawfinch, while the conifer stands on Claife Heights have Redpoll, Siskin and Crossbill. Buzzard, Sparrowhawk and Peregrine are to be seen here and rarer raptors like Honey Buzzard, Goshawk, Montagu's Harrier, Hobby and Osprey have all been reported. In 1977 a pair of Fieldfare bred in this area.

The lake is also well known for other forms of wildlife as the woodlands have deer, badgers and red squirrel whilst in the deep waters char and pike attract fishermen from a wide area.

Esthwaite Water is a breeding site for Great Crested Grebe and Reed Warbler, both scarce in the county, while in winter rarer wildfowl like Red- and Black-necked Grebes, Long-tailed Duck, Scaup, Common Scoter and Ring-necked Duck have all been recorded in recent years. Bittern have been found in winter in the reedbeds, which are also a favourite haunt for Water Rails.

Timing

Winter and early spring is the best time to watch the lake and walk the local woods and fellsides. The deep water areas at Fell Foot and between the Ferry and Belle Isle are favourite locations for divers, grebes and diving duck. The large gull roost is at its peak in mid-winter and can be viewed from either shore. During spells of keen frost the lake freezes over, and the restricted deep-water areas then focus the numbers of wildfowl and gulls. After autumn and winter storms look out for weak and lost seabirds.

Access

On the eastern shore the A592 and A591 follow the length of the lake and there are numerous car parks or viewpoints along its length. Noteworthy among them are the Fell Foot Country Park (SD 380870) run by the National Trust. The car park here is open all year, offering good views of the southern reedbeds and tail of the lake. Cockshot Point (SD 397965) is a vantage point for viewing the area near the ferry and around the islands. Brockhole (NY 390001), the National Park Centre, is only open from April to October. Waterhead, Ambleside (NY 375032) is useful for viewing the head of the lake.

On the western shore, Wray Castle (NT) at NY 375001 offers an area of oak wood and shoreline paths with all-year access. Take the A593 from Ambleside and at Clappersgate take the B5286 to Hawkshead. After 1½ miles (2.5 km) take a minor road left to High Wray and after a further mile (1.3 km) the imposing arched gateway to Wray Castle is on the left. Drive through the arch and down to the Castle. The car park and start of the various paths are at the north side of the Castle.

There are numerous walks through the woods on Claife Heights, several passing the tarns on the summit which can hold wildfowl in winter (Moss Eccles Tarn has a Black-headed Gullery in early summer). The recognised approach to Claife Heights is from Harrowslack (SD 387965), which is half a mile (1 km) along a minor road from the B5285 at Ferry House. At this point there are several routes over the Heights or alternatively you can take the Claife Shore Walk of 1½ miles (2.5 km) with its views to Belle Isle and beyond.

Esthwaite Water may be viewed along its length from the B5285 Hawkshead to Ferry Road. A car park at SD 364953 gives views of the reedbeds at the southern end of the lake.

Calendar

All year: Great Crested Grebe, Cormorant, Grey Heron, Greylag Goose, Tufted Duck, Red-breasted Merganser, Buzzard, Peregrine, Woodcock, gulls, woodpeckers, wagtails, Dipper, Goldcrest, Willow Tit, Nuthatch, Raven, Brambling, Crossbill, Siskin, Hawfinch, Reed Bunting.

November/March: Red-necked Grebe, Whooper Swan, Wigeon, Pochard, Long-tailed Duck, Goldeneye, Goosander, Water Rail, Kingfisher, winter thrushes.

April/October: Shelduck, Gadwall, Common Scoter, Oystercatcher, Dunlin, Curlew, Redshank, Common Sandpiper, Little Gull, terns, Tree Pipit, Yellow Wagtail, Redstart, warblers (including Reed and Grasshopper Warblers), Pied Flycatcher. Unusual and storm-bound birds have in the last ten years included divers, Slavonian Grebe, Fulmar, Storm and Leach's Petrels, Gannet, Shag, Bittern, Red-crested Pochard, Ring-necked Duck, Ruddy Duck, Montagu's Harrier, Goshawk, Osprey, Sanderling, Purple Sandpiper, Whimbrel, Greenshank, Turnstone, Grey Phalarope, Kittiwake, Little Auk, Golden Oriole and Nutcracker.

42

The River Kent is unique not only in that it is England's shortest river but also in that it is the fastest flowing one in the country. There are several good bird haunts along its length, the most notable being the slow moving upper reaches with alder- and willow-lined banks and small meadows between Staveley, Bowston and Burneside. On the northern outskirts of Kendal, the River Kent is joined by the River Mint, forming a large pool with long shingle banks. This area is locally known as Sandy Bottoms. At the southern end of Kendal the river passes Kendal Sewage Works at a pace before slowing down again in the wooded bends at Watercrook with its stands of alder. The river narrows and surges over limestone outcrops as it falls dramatically through Low Sizergh. Noteable of the falls here is Force Fall, a local salmon leap. On passing under the A591, the river is subdued once more as it meanders through Levens Park. Here there are shallow gravel banks and limestone outcrops hanging with ivy and other scrub. Beyond Levens Hall at Sampool the river is joined by the River Gilpin. These are the upper reaches of the Kent estuary, with sand and gravel banks and some reedbeds, where the river becomes tidal.

Species

Typical river birds like Common Sandpiper, Kingfisher, Sand Martin, Grey Wagtail and Dipper breed along the rivers length. Added to these are a few pairs of Red-breasted Merganser, Goosander, Oystercatcher, Redshank and Yellow Wagtail. There is a small heronry near Staveley and the Cormorant is a frequent winter visitor. Also in winter the deep water areas around Kendal and in Levens Park hold Little Grebe, Pochard, Tufted Duck, Goldeneye and occasionally Smew, waders such as Ringed Plover, Dunlin, Snipe and Green Sandpiper occur and there have been records of Little Ringed Plover, Jack Snipe and Wood Sandpiper. Gulls regularly move in good numbers along the length of the river with Kittiwake, Mediterranean Gull and Common Tern sometimes appearing.

The wooded and scrub areas along the river have breeding pairs of Little Owl, woodpeckers (with the odd pair of Lesser Spotted) and Nuthatch in Levens Park, Sedge and Garden Warblers, Whitethroat and Chiffchaff. Buzzard, Sparrowhawk and Peregrine often hunt along the river. In winter, Merlin may visit from the fells. Ravens are seen moving between the Lake District and Howgill Fells and Greylag and Pink-footed Goose use the valley as a north–south flight lane. A flock of post-breeding Greylag gathers on the saltmarsh near Sampool from August onwards. Whooper Swan sometimes appear here too, as do wintering Green Sandpiper.

In the alders and birch at Burneside, Watercrook, Low Sizergh and Levens Park can be found wandering flocks of Siskin and Redpoll. Small mixed flocks of tits sometimes include wintering Blackcap and Chiffchaff and the occasional Nuthatch. Goldfinch and Brambling are also regular winter visitors.

In spring and autumn there is a regular steady migration through the valley with the open sites of Sandy Bottoms, Watercrook, Sampool and Kendal Sewage Works being particularly attractive. Often large numbers of hirundines, Swift, gulls, Starlings, corvids, winter thrushes and finches use the valley on passage movements. Oddities have appeared from time to time including Night Heron, Temminck's Stint, Pectoral Sandpiper, Bee-eater and Wryneck.

Timing and General Access

Cold weather movements in winter, particularly when the surrounding fells are snow-covered often finds the lower reaches of the river clear due to the influence of Morecambe Bay. Early morning is the best time to visit during the periods of migration.

The main trunk routes along the River Kent are the A591 from the M6 to Kendal and beyond to Staveley. The A590 Levens Bridge to Gilpin Bridge and the A6 at Levens Bridge.

16A SAMPOOL

OS ref: SD 476843
SD 48

The junction of the River Gilpin and River Kent with a tidal influence, sand and gravel banks and some reedbed attract Cormorant, Grey Heron, Greylag Goose, Shelduck, Red-breasted Merganser, Goosander, Sparrowhawk, various waders, gulls and wagtails, Sedge Warbler and Reed Bunting. In the winter months come Little Grebe, Mute and Whooper Swan, Wigeon, Teal, Tufted Duck, Goldeneye, Green Sandpiper, Peregrine, Dipper and Kingfisher. Occasional visitors are Canada and White-fronted Geese, Scaup, Long-tailed Duck, Smew, Hen Harrier, Water Rail, Little Ringed Plover, Wood Sandpiper and various terns. Oddities include Temminck's Stint and Pectoral Sandpiper. Take the minor road to Foulshaw off the A590(T) at Sampool Bridge. At SD 470848, a footpath follows the River Gilpin to Sampool.

16B LEVENS PARK

OS ref: SD 503858
SD 48

Levens Park lies on the other side of the A6 from Levens Hall. It is an area of open parkland with a famous avenue of ancient oaks and stands of mature elms and beech. Herds of Bagot goats and the black or dark race of Roe Deer roam the parkland. Many of the trees are old and broken offering plenty of sites for hole-nesting birds like Redstart, tits, woodpeckers (including Lesser Spotted) and Nuthatch. The River Kent meanders through these 100 acres (40 hectares) of parkland and birds like Kingfisher, Sand Martin, Dipper, Heron, Red-breasted Merganser and Goosander can be found here. In winter the central area of box and laurels, which is Pheasant cover, is home to a very large finch roost. Greenfinch, Chaffinch, Brambling, Siskin and Redpoll use this site. Occasional visitors include Shelduck, Long-tailed Duck, Smew, Osprey, Pied Flycatcher and Hawfinch. Levens Hall is situated 5 miles (8 km) south of Kendal on the M6.

16C Sizergh Castle (NT)

OS ref: SD 498879
SD 48

The estate of Sizergh covers 1,600 acres (720 hectares) from the west bank of the River Kent over Sizergh Fell to the Lyth Valley. Part of the estate is Brigsteer Park (SSSI) and Low Sizergh Wood which is near the river. The farmland is devoted to cattle and sheep rearing and the fields are not large with many drystone walls and hedges. Breeding species include Little Grebe, Buzzard, Sparrowhawk, Curlew, Green Woodpecker, Grey Wagtail, Redstart, Siskin and Hawfinch. Oddities have included Gannet, Osprey, Corncrake, Bee-eater, Ring Ousel, Firecrest and Great Grey Shrike. Brigsteer Park attracts very early spring migrants and holds a large corvid roost in winter. Sizergh Castle is located 3½ miles (5.5 km) south of Kendal. Take junction 36 off the M6 for Barrow, take the A590 at the first junction and the first left for Sizergh Castle just beyond this junction. Footpaths to Brigsteer park and other points start from the Castle car park. Details are available from the ticket office at the Castle on open days.

Hawfinch

16D Kendal

SD 48

The fact that the River Kent is its central feature makes the town of Kendal attractive to birdwatchers. Two sites, Watercrook, where the river slowly bends around a Roman Fort on one bank and the Kendal Sewage Works on the other, and Sandy Bottoms to the north of the town, an open site where the River Mint joins with the River Kent are the favourite locations for birds. Breeding birds include Common Sandpiper, Kingfisher, Dipper, Grey Wagtail and Sand Martin. In winter, Little Grebe, Tufted Duck, Goldeneye, Red-breasted Merganser, Goosander, Redshank, Dunlin, gulls, Blackcap, Siskin and Brambling appear regularly. Oddities have included Black-throated Diver, Black-necked Grebe,

Night Heron, occasional Smew, Water Rail, Kittiwake, Blue-headed Wagtail and Black Redstart. Access is relatively simple as a footpath follows the river on its western side right through Kendal. For Watercrook a footpath at Helsington Garage through Scroggs Wood on the A6 (SD 508907) leads to the river; a footpath to Burneside along the river starts amongst the houses at Kentrigg (SD 515944).

16E Burneside/Bowston

OS ref: SD 503963
SD 48

At Burneside the riverside footpath leads along the eastern shore of the River Kent eventually to Staveley. It is tree-lined with alder, willow, elm and ash along its length. Several weirs have dammed the river along the stretch for the various mills here, one of the best deep water areas being at Bowston Mill. Grey Heron, Goosander, Kingfisher, Dipper and Grey Wagtail frequent the area. Oddities on this part of the river have included Bittern and Red Kite. Access to the footpath can be at Burneside Mill, the large paper mill in Burneside at SD 507958 or at the northern end at the bridge at Bowston Mill at SD 498967.

THE CUMBRIAN COAST

17 Workington Harbour
18 Siddick Pond
19 St Bees Head
20 Ravenglass and District
21 Duddon Estuary

22 Hodbarrow
23 Walney Island
24 Cavendish Dock
25 Foulney Island

The coastline of Cumbria from Workington to Barrow-in-Furness is not generally associated with natural beauty. More often it is regarded as a polluted part of Britain's coast affected by the nuclear, chemical and coal industries which feature here. However, it has a great range of habitats ranging from the red sandstone cliffs of St Bees Head in the north, which is the point where the vast estuary of the Solway merges with the Irish Sea, to the low lying estuarine area around Walney Island in the south.

South of St Bees, the coastline becomes a little uninspiring as the fields and hedgerows end on low muddy cliffs and a shingle shoreline. Here the skyline is marred by the dominant building of Sellafield Nuclear Power Site, beyond which the shoreline changes to the large sand dune systems of Drigg and Eskmeals at Ravenglass. Here estuaries of the Rivers Irt, Mite and Esk meet to form a large estuary surrounded by dune slacks. From Eskmeals the narrow coastline runs close to the southern tip of the Lake District mountains with the high bracken covered fells of Black Combe coming close to the sea at Silecroft. Beyond Kirksanton, another sand dune system starts surrounding the large estuary of the River Duddon. On the northern side of the estuary the dune slacks protect Haverigg and the man-made Hodbarrow Lagoon. The inner estuary with its large saltmarshes is very important ornithologically. On the southern shore the large slacks of Sandscale Haws and North Walney are divided by the Walney channel which isolates Walney Island from the mainland. The tern colony on Foulney Island is important, as are the deep waters of Cavendish Dock adjacent to the Bay for its diving duck and as a moult site for Mute Swans.

Habitat and Species

The harbour at Workington lies at the mouth of the River Derwent. Although the docks are still active with coasters, fishing boats and a small marina, the surrounding area has lost all the large foundries and slag banks associated with the steel industry and has been landscaped. Access to the old pier on the southern side of the harbour gives good views over the whole area as well as along the local coastline and out to sea. From the shelter of the old light station at the end of the pier one can watch Purple Sandpiper and Rock Pipits feeding amongst the concrete block breakwater. Further out more regular divers, sea duck, auks, gulls and terns can be found with occasional visits from Manx Shearwater, Shag, Arctic and Great Skuas, Mediterranean, Little and Glaucous Gulls. Along the shoreline, waders such as Ringed Plover, Dunlin, Knot and Sanderling are to be found while the newly landscaped area attracts passage Wheatear, Stonechat, Whinchat, Meadow Pipits and occasionally Black Redstart. The northern shoreline at low tide exposes shingle

Glaucous Gull

and sandbanks where Curlew, Godwits, Knot, Dunlin and Turnstone feed and the larger gulls come to roost. Look out for Glaucous Gulls here in winter.

Access

From Workington Railway Station take the minor road over the railway to the harbour. This road meanders round the railway yards and British Leyland factory complex to the Marina, where it follows the estuary of the River Derwent to the pier and coastguard lookout (NY 985298). The pier is popular with sea anglers.

18 SIDDICK POND (ADC)

Habitat

Siddick Pond lies between the northern bank of the River Derwent and the village of Siddick. It is an area of open water and reedbed surrounded on the northern shore by an old colliery waste tip while a railway embankment bounds the western and southern fringes. To the east a large timber yard of the local Board Mill and the main Carlisle to Workington road form the boundary. The pond lies in an ancient channel of the River Derwent and is shallow in nature being between nine and ten feet (about 3 m) deep at the deepest point. A culvert under the railway lets the water flow to another smaller pond. The whole area is fed by a small stream known as Ling Beck.

A major feature of the site is that its fringe is predominantly reedbed mingled with patches of rush, sedge and areas of waterlily. In summer the water level falls, exposing areas of mud popular with passage waders. The embankments behind the reedbeds are covered with bramble, gorse and hawthorn, while at the southern end a small thicket of willow gives shelter to passerines and birds of prey.

Species

During the winter months a wide selection of waterfowl are normally present including Whooper Swan, Wigeon, Teal, Shoveler, Pochard, Tufted Duck and Goldeneye with Great Crested Grebe, Shelduck, Gadwall, Pintail, Long-tailed Duck, Goosander and Red-breasted Merganser appearing from time to time. During periods of winter gales or prolonged frost conditions rarer species like Red-throated Diver, Black-necked Grebe, Bewick's Swan, Scaup, Common Scoter and Smew have been recorded. Gulls use the pond all year to bathe and preen with Cormorant also being a regular visitor. The reedbed is a roost for Starling in winter and they are predated by Sparrowhawk, Tawny Owl and occasionally Merlin, Barn Owl and Long and Short-eared Owls. Bittern and Water Rail have also been recorded at this time of year.

During spring and autumn passage waders, for example Little Stint, Curlew Sandpiper, Dunlin, Ruff, Jack Snipe, godwits, Greenshank and Sandpipers have been found along with Goldeneye, Black Tern, hirundines (which gather in large numbers), wagtails, warblers including Grasshopper and Reed (which is scarce in the north), Lesser Whitethroat and other passerines. In 1981 an irruption movement of fifteen Bearded Tits was recorded here and 1982 a singing Savi's Warbler was found. Rarities and sub-rarities seen here in recent years include Leach's Petrel, Spoonbill, Ruddy Duck, Marsh Harrier, Long-tailed Skua, Barred and Yellow-browed Warblers, Firecrest and Little Bunting. Breeding species include Little Grebe, Tufted Duck and Reed Warbler.

Access

Allerdale District Council are to provide a hide near the timber yard (on the A596) during 1992. Good views of the northern end of the pond can be had in the small car park across the road from the hide. Permits to walk along the railway on the west bank of the pond may be obtained through British Rail, Carlisle, but please note that the railway is private property and the permits are limited.

Calendar

All year: Little Grebe, Cormorant, Grey Heron, Teal, Shoveler, Tufted Duck, Water Rail, Barn Owl, Reed Bunting.

November/March: Whooper Swan, Wigeon, Pochard, Goldeneye, Red-breasted Merganser in cold weather. Goosander, possibly Bewick's Swan and Red-throated Diver, Sparrowhawk, Merlin, Peregrine, the occasional Hen Harrier, Long and Short-eared Owls, Snipe, Jack Snipe, gulls including possibly Glaucous and Kittiwake, Kingfisher, Grey Wagtail, Stonechat, winter thrushes, Blackcap, Starling roost, finch roost, mainly Chaffinch, Greenfinch with a few Brambling, Goldfinch and Linnet.

April/July: Garganey, lingering winter wildfowl, the odd passage Osprey and Marsh Harrier, migrant waders, a few terns including Common, Arctic, Little, Sandwich and Black, landbird migrants including pipits, swifts, hirundines, Grasshopper, Sedge and Reed Warblers.

August/October: Returning winter wildfowl and migrant raptors. Waders include Little Stint, Curlew Sandpiper, Ruff, Greenshank, large hirundine roost, Pied Flycatcher, warblers, Wagtail roost.

19 ST BEES HEAD (RSPB)

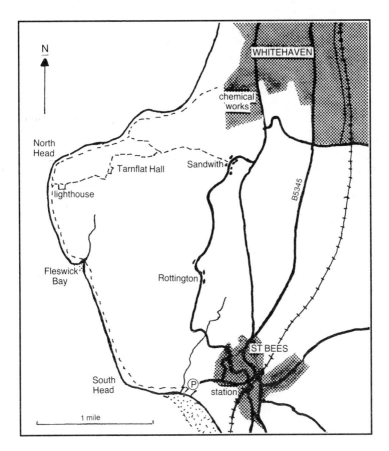

Habitat
The magnificent red sandstone cliffs at St Bees Head dominate the
Cumbrian coastline. The North Head with its lighthouse is the highest
point. A coastal path follows the clifftop from St Bees to Workington.
Inland from the cliffs are large fields and drystone walls with little cover
for birds. The only feature along the cliff path is Fleswick Bay which is
half-way between North Head and South Head. This is a small sheltered
bay behind which a steep sided valley extends inland with good gorse
and bramble cover and a small stream tumbling down to the shore. The
farm at Tarnflat Hall is behind the North Head and is part of the RSPB
recording area.

Species
The cliffs of St Bees hold around 5,000 breeding seabirds: the largest
colony on the west coast of England. The bulk of this colony is made up

Black Guillemots

of Guillemot, Razorbill and Kittiwake, with a few pairs of Puffin and Black Guillemot. This is the only breeding site in England for the latter species. Several thousand pairs of Herring and Lesser Black-backed Gulls breed, as do a few Greater Black-backed Gulls. Surprisingly, neither Cormorant nor Shag have been recorded as a breeding species here.

During spring and autumn migration sea-bird passage and passerine passage over the cliffs are notable. Divers, grebes, sea-ducks, 'grey' geese, skuas and terns are all noted here. Mid-summer sees a regular movement of Manx Shearwater, Fulmar and Gannet while in late autumn there is a good possibility of seeing Storm and Leach's Petrels.

Passerine passage along the cliffs can be heavy in early spring with good numbers of Skylark, pipits, chats and warblers. Hirundine and Swift movements can be noteworthy from time to time. All the small birds attract birds of prey like Sparrowhawk, occasional Merlin and Peregrine. Little Owls breed in the area. Late autumn movements of corvids, for example Carrion Crow, Rook and Jackdaw have been known to include the odd Chough or Hooded Crow, probably from the not so distant Manx population. The Raven is a breeding species here.

In winter the sea still holds interesting species such as Red-throated Diver, Great Crested Grebe, Eider, Common Scoter and the odd over-wintering auk. The feral pigeons on the cliffs keep Peregrine in the vicinity while the clifftop fields hold flocks of winter thrushes, Skylark, pipits, Starling and mixed finch flocks. Corn Bunting and the occasional Black Redstart or Stonechat occur in these flocks.

Bottle-nosed Dolphins and seals add to the wildlife interest of this stretch of coast.

Timing

Breeding seabirds are present from March to mid-July. Although most activity occurs early in the day many of the auks sit on the sea near the cliffs. Black Guillemot and Puffin tend to feed away from the bulk of the other birds and are often nearest to the cliffs. A visit early in the day is best when looking for spring and autumn migrants particularly in the 'valley' of Fleswick Bay and the fields and low hedgerows behind the North Head around Tarnflat Hall.

Access

From the north follow the A595(T) from Whitehaven to the outer edge of the built up area of Mirehouse, approximately two miles (3 km), where a minor road to the right to Sandwith village crosses the valley and the B5345. In Sandwith leave your vehicle near the Post Office and walk along the private road to St Bees Head, starting at NX 965147. It is approximately two miles (3 km) to the lighthouse and the cliff path via Tarnflat Hall. Although it is an uphill walk it is fairly easy. From the lighthouse take the cliff path south to St Bees. The best views of the breeding cliffs are between the lighthouse and Fleswick Bay.

From the south you will find the start of the cliff path in the car park in St Bees at NX 961118. Stout footwear is recommended.

Calendar

All year: Fulmar, Cormorant, gulls, Grey Partridge, Kittiwake, Stock Dove, Little Owl, Rock Pipit, Stonechat, Raven, Corn Bunting.

March/May: Divers, Manx Shearwater, Gannet, Common Scoter, Eider, Red-breasted Merganser, Pink-footed Geese, waders including godwits, Whimbrel, Greenshank and Common Sandpiper, Arctic and Great Skuas, terns, breeding seabirds from mid-March (see below). Migrant raptors including Merlin. Landbird migrants including chats and the occasional Ring Ousel, and warblers, particularly Whitethroat and Lesser Whitethroat.

June/August: Breeding species include Fulmar, Guillemot, Razorbill, a few pairs of Puffin and Black Guillemot, Kittiwake and larger gulls, feral pigeons, Rock Pipit and Raven. Offshore, there are occasional movements of Gannets, Manx Shearwater and terns and the odd Arctic and Great Skua.

September/November: Seabird movement, particularly during westerly gales. Rarer species like Sooty Shearwater, Storm and Leach's Petrel can be expected. Passerine passage on the cliffs can bring Pied Flycatcher, Black Redstart, Firecrest and other sub-rarities. Chough and Hooded Crow have appeared at this time.

December/February: Divers, sea-duck including Velvet Scoter and Long-tailed Duck, one or two Fulmar, auks and Kittiwakes, raptors such as Merlin, Peregrine and the occasional Hen Harrier, Purple Sandpiper and Turnstone, and a wide range of gulls with the odd Great Skua. Landbirds include flocks of Skylark, Meadow Pipit and Starling, winter thrushes, Stonechat and Barn Owl. Rarer species in recent years have included Great Shearwater, Red Kite, Quail, Long-tailed Skua, Mediterranean Gull, Wryneck, Red-backed Shrike and Chough.

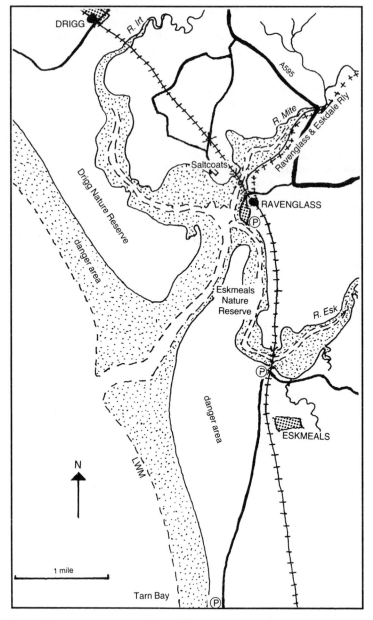

Habitat and Species

The historic village of Ravenglass is situated on an estuary where the rivers Irt, Mite and Esk meet then flow into the sea through a channel in a large sand dune system. The north shore is protected by the dunes of Drigg, once the largest Black-headed Gull colony in Europe, and the south shore by the dunes of Eskmeals Nature Reserve. The three inner estuaries provide shelter and feeding habitat for a large number of wildfowl, waders, gulls and terns. During the winter the Greylag Geese, which are resident here, increase their numbers to over one hundred birds with Shelduck, Wigeon and Teal gathering in good numbers too. Smaller numbers of Whooper Swan, Pintail, Common Scoter, Goldeneye and Red-breasted Merganser also occur. Waders at this time include Ringed and Grey Plover, Knot, Dunlin, Snipe, Curlew, Redshank, the odd Greenshank and Turnstone.

The gull colony on the Drigg reserve dwindled away in the 1980s and the Tern colony there disappeared in 1977.

In spring a small flock of Common Scoter gather off the Eskmeals dune system, as do numbers of Red-throated Diver, Cormorant and auks. Amongst the dunes grow good patches of Sea Buckthorn whose fruit attracts winter thrushes, finches and other passage migrants. Eskmeals Dunes are also a site of importance for a wide range of fauna and flora as well as a thriving Natterjack Toad colony. Down the coast three miles (5 km) south of Eskmeals reserve and the MOD Gun Range is a small headland with a coastguard station at Selker. In the last few years this has become a local sea watch point particularly in spring and autumn. A good range of passage seabirds have been recorded during periods of October gales in which numbers of Manx and Sooty Shearwater, Storm and Leach's Petrel, Gannets, auks, gulls and skuas have been recorded.

Access

The central confluence of the three estuaries can be seen quite well from the village of Ravenglass with viewpoints of the upper reaches of the River Irt accessible from Drigg Station down a track off the minor road at SD 064983. The upper area of the River Mite can be seen from the A598 at Thornflatt Hill at SD 092971 and the minor road at the Esk railway viaduct at SD 086943 gives good viewpoints along the inner Esk estuary.

Eskmeals Dunes Nature Reserve is also accessible at the latter grid reference by the Esk viaduct: permits are obtainable from the CWT Warden. Wear suitable footwear as the area is very muddy.

For the Drigg Dunes Nature Reserve, take the B5344 at Holmrook for Seascale and in the village of Drigg take the minor road left to Drigg Station and to the coast two miles (3 km) beyond. Permits are required from Cumbria County Council, and care must be taken to observe the warden's instructions as to access on this site as it is in an MOD Danger Area.

At Tarn Bay, Bootle, the car part on the coast south of the Eskmeals Gun Range (SD 080907) is excellent for passage seabirds and coastal wildfowl, waders and gulls.

To reach Selker Coastguard Station, take the minor road westwards to Bootle Station off the A595 in the village of Bootle. At the station turn left along a minor road which becomes a track to Broadwater Farm. Continue past the farm to the Coastguard Station where the sea can be watched from the hill top.

Calendar

All year: Cormorant, Grey Heron, Greylag Geese, Shelduck, Teal, Red-breasted Merganser, Sparrowhawk, Buzzard, Peregrine, Oystercatcher, Ringed Plover, Dunlin, Snipe, Curlew, Redshank, gulls, Barn Owl, Little Owl, Stonechat.

March-May: Divers, Manx Shearwater, Gannet, Common Scoter, over-flighting Pink-footed Geese, godwits, Whimbrel, Greenshank, Sanderling, Common Sandpiper, Arctic Skua, terns, some migrant raptors, landbird migrants including hirundines, chats and warblers.

June-August: Breeding waders, gulls and terns. Offshore movements of Shearwaters, Gannets, auks, terns and occasional skua.

September-November: Seabird movement brought by autumn's south-westerly gales include shearwaters, petrels, auks, gulls, terns and skuas. Passage waders and returning winter wildfowl are also to be seen, as are migrant Short-eared Owl and small passerines.

December-February: Divers, sea-ducks, Whooper Swan, 'grey' geese, Wigeon, Goldeneye, Goosander, waders, gulls. Landbirds include flocks of Skylark, Meadow Pipit and Starlings with smaller numbers of winter thrushes and finches. Occasional small parties of Twite and Snow Bunting. Of the scarcer species seen over the estuaries in recent years birds of prey figure high. Red-necked and Slavonian Grebes, Spoonbill, Red Kite, Rough-legged Buzzard, Goshawk, Marsh Harrier, Osprey, Stone Curlew, Red-necked Phalarope, Black Tern and Hoopoe have all been recorded.

21 DUDDON ESTUARY

Habitat

The Duddon Estuary or Duddon Sands is a long wide area of saltmarsh, sands and channels running from Duddon Bridge south eight miles (13 km) to Sandscale Haws on the south shore of the estuary and Haverigg Point on the north. Several large grassland saltmarshes on the inner estuary provide winter feeding sites for 'grey' geese whilst the shoreline hosts a good range of waders. South of the town of Millom is the Nature

Reserve at Hodbarrow. This is an area of scrub and marsh around a large freshwater lagoon.

The outer estuary is dominated by the dune systems of Haverigg to the north and the very impressive sand systems of Sandscale Haws to the south. Behind the Sandscale Haws systems are areas of wet slack which have a rich flora as well as good breeding sites for wetland species. Haverigg Point is a sea watch point. Both these dune systems are SSSIs, having a wealth of fauna and flora.

Species

During the winter the Duddon Estuary attracts a wide range of both wildfowl and waders. The large saltmarsh areas of Millom Marsh and Angerton Marsh attract good numbers of grazing Greylag Goose along with smaller numbers of Pink-footed Goose. Teal, Wigeon and Shelduck are regular and Pintail have increased in numbers in recent years. The waters of the central estuary hold Goldeneye and Red-breasted Merganser with the occasional small party of Great Crested Grebe, Red-throated Diver, Eider, Common Scoter and Scaup. There are several large high water wader roosts in the estuary with Oystercatcher, Ringed Plover, Curlew, Redshank, Dunlin and a few Turnstone frequenting Millom Marsh, Borwick Rails, Angerton, Dunnerholme Point and Askam. The upper reaches around Lady Hall regularly hold a few Green Sandpiper and Greenshank while, around Askham and Sandscale Haws, there are good numbers of Knot, Grey Plover, Bar-tailed Godwit and Sanderling. Odd numbers of Ruff, Snipe, Black-tailed Godwit and Spotted Redshank also occur around Borwick Rails and Dunnerholme Point. Black-headed and Common Gulls appear in large flocks along with the larger gulls. The odd Glaucous Gull can be found around Redhills tip (near to Borwick Rails) and Iceland Gull has also been recorded. Sparrowhawk, Merlin and Peregrine regularly hunt the estuary for prey which also attracts the occasional Hen Harrier. Cormorant and Grey Heron are a regular feature in winter with Kingfisher sometimes even on the upper reaches. Other smaller birds include Rock Pipit and Reed Bunting feeding on the tideline while on the outer estuary, along the dune systems, tideline Twite, Snow Bunting and in recent years, the odd Lapland Bunting have been found.

Spring sees the departing wildfowl and waders replaced by small numbers of Whimbrel, Greenshank and Common Sandpiper whilst the flock of Golden Plover on Kirksanton Haws increases, sometimes adding the odd Dotterel to its number. Sandwich, Common, Arctic and Little Terns return to feed in the estuary which in turn brings in Arctic Skuas to predate them. The odd Black Tern and Little Gull are seen and Gannet also come to feed in the shallow waters of the outer estuary, as do small groups of Common Scoter. Wheatear and Yellow Wagtail can be found on the open saltmarsh while the boundary hedgerows and reed-fringed ditches hold passage Redstart, Whinchat, Stonechat, Sedge Warbler, the odd Grasshopper Warbler, Whitethroat, Lesser Whitethroat, Willow Warbler, Goldcrest and Spotted Flycatcher. Of the breeding birds seen in summer Shelduck, Oystercatcher, Curlew, Redshank are the most noteworthy.

Autumn passage brings the return of the wintering wildfowl and waders and often more unusual species, for example Little Stint and Curlew Sandpiper, while in the outer estuary the flocks of feeding terns and Kittiwake attract Arctic and Great Skua.

Timing

The estuary is best viewed in the hour before, and during, high tide, when the feeding waders and wildfowl emerge out of the vast expanse of sand and mud flat onto the high tide roost sites. Sea-duck and other seabirds are often drawn in with the tide. Early morning is recommended in spring and autumn for passage migrants.

Access

See under individual sites for road access. Access is possible by rail to Green Road Station, Foxfield and Kirkby for Angerton Marsh and to Millom for Borwick Rails, using the regular Barrow-Workington-Carlisle service.

21A LADY HALL

OS ref: SD 193859

From Broughton-in-Furness take the A595 west over Duddon Bridge to Holme at SD 196874 where a minor road turns to the left and Lady Hall. At Lady Hall a track to the saltmarsh ends near the railway viaduct. A good site for Greenshank and Green Sandpiper throughout the year.

21B GREEN ROAD STATION

OS ref: SD 189840

From Duddon Bridge take the A595 to Hallthwaites Church. At this point take the road to Millom (A5093) as far as the village of The Green. Follow the minor road to the left through the village to Green Road Station and cross the level crossing to the embankment on the saltmarsh. Here there is a good view over most of Millom Marsh. This is the best area for grazing geese and wildfowl in winter.

21C ANGERTON MARSH

OS Ref: SD 215835

Access to this marsh is either from Kirkby-in-Furness Station or from Foxfield Station two miles (3 km) to the north (SD 209855). Take the A595 from Barrow-in-Furness north towards Broughton-in-Furness and at Sandside take the minor road left to the station. Behind Kirkby station runs a stream, Kirkby Pool. A footpath across Angerton Marsh to Foxfield starts at the station with a footbridge over Kirkby Pool. From the north, Foxfield is 1½ miles (2.5 km) south of Broughton-in-Furness, on a minor road. At the station, access to the marsh is gained by crossing the level crossing.

21D ASKAM/DUNNERHOLME

OS Ref: SD 210785

A peninsula into the estuary at Askam-in-Furness, locally known as Askam 'pier' can be reached by taking the minor road at the railway station to the golf course. The 'pier' is to the left on reaching the shore at the golf course. Follow the shore north past the golf course to Dunnerholme Point. Sea-duck and auks are often found in this part of the estuary, also waders such as godwits and Sanderling.

21E SANDSCALE HAWS

OS ref: SD 200757

This large dune system at the mouth of the estuary is an SSSI owned by the National Trust. It is very rich in fauna and flora. The flooded mines to the east of the dune slacks are a good wetland habitat to add waterfowl to the range of birds found on the site.

Heading south on the A590, turn right at the roundabout at Furness Abbey, between Dalton-in-Furness and Barrow, for Ormsgill Industrial Estate. After a mile (2 km) take the second minor road on the right over the railway to Roanhead. Follow the road past the flooded mines to Roanhead Farm where there is a car park behind the dunes. The National Trust warden is Peter Carty, 135 Sharp Street, Dalton-in-Furness (tel. Barrow (0229) 62855).

21F BORWICK RAILS

OS ref: SD 190795

This is the old harbour area of Millom, most of which has been infilled. It is a good watchpoint for resident and passage wildfowl, waders, gulls and terns, providing views of most of the estuary and Millom Marsh, and is especially rewarding on a good rising tide. The road from Millom station past the town square ends after a mile (2 km) at Borwick Rails. Rare passage birds and weather-bound coastal migrants include Leach's Petrel, Little Egret, Spoonbill, American Wigeon, Osprey, Kentish Plover, Mediterranean Gull and Nightingale, many of which were recorded in and around the area of Hodbarrow (see next site).

22 HODBARROW

Habitat and Species

This RSPB Reserve is important on two counts: firstly as a passage site for wildfowl and waders, particularly for the large moulting flock of Red-breasted Merganser, and secondly as a breeding Sandwich Tern colony with a few pairs of Common, Arctic and Little Terns in most years.

Although part of this former industrial site is now a holiday complex with caravans and water sport facilities, the main part of the area has become a first rate reserve. The lagoon and smaller pools are an important habitat, and the surrounding derelict landscape, which has become overgrown, is a good refuge for passage migrants on this site at the mouth of the Duddon Estuary. The various lime waste tips are important for flora and the whole reserve has a good insect and mammal population. It is also a Natterjack Toad site. Resident bird species include Great Crested Grebe, Tufted Duck, Red-breasted Merganser, Sparrowhawk, Peregrine, waders, gulls, Stock Dove and Barn Owl.

Red-breasted Mergansers

During the winter this site hosts divers, grebes, Whooper Swan, Wigeon, Teal, Pochard, Scaup, Long-tailed Duck, Goldeneye, raptors, and gulls (including Glaucous). Regular waders include Golden Plover, Sanderling, Dunlin, godwits, Greenshank, Spotted Redshank and Turnstone. During storm conditions, the site is a refuge to sea-duck and other seabirds. Amongst the migrant passerines have been White Wagtail, Black Redstart, Ring Ousel, Grasshopper Warbler, Lesser Whitethroat and Pied Flycatcher.

In autumn the moult flock of Red-breasted Merganser can number 250 birds. Other migrants at this time can include Garganey, Little Stint, Curlew Sandpiper, Ruff, skuas, Little Gull and Black Tern. Rarer species recorded in the last few years have included Temminck's Stint, White-rumped Sandpiper, Richard's Pipit and Icterine Warbler.

Timing

A visit coinciding with a high tide on the Duddon is best, particularly an early morning visit as the site is popular during the day with dog-walkers and strollers from nearby Millom.

Access

Take the A5093 from Broughton to Millom. Turn left over the railway along Devonshire Road into the centre, then on Mainsgate Road take the right-hand turning signposted Hodbarrow Nature Reserve. Follow this road and park between the lagoon and access to the rubbish tip. Alternatively, you can approach on foot from Haverigg via the entrance to the caravan site. There are also bus and rail services to Millom. The reserve warden is Douglas Radford, 29 Mainsgate Road, Millom (tel.no. Barrow (0229) 77381).

23 WALNEY ISLAND

Habitat

Walney Island is situated at the south-west corner of Cumbria and is the westernmost point of Morecambe Bay. The central part of the island is the residential area serving the shipyards across the Walney channel. The north and south ends of the island are the key bird sites. At the north end is a large dune slack system forming the final part of the Duddon estuary. The Walney channel running to the east of the island has a muddy shoreline here and is attractive to waders. Walney Aerodrome has an area of scrub known as 'Willow Woods' which attracts migrant passerines. On the coastal dune slack there are a few freshwater pools. The south end of the island is most important for birds. It is a nature reserve of Cumbria Wildlife Trust and an active Bird Ringing Station and observatory. The terrain is a mixture of inter-tidal mudflats, saltmarsh and dune systems with flooded gravel workings. It is home to one of the largest gull colonies in Europe and is a key sea watch point in the area.

Species

This is the most productive site in the county for passage sea fowl with up to twenty Red-throated Divers in the area during the winter period, along with a few other Diver species and Great Crested Grebes. Other Grebe species are also to be found, the most regular being Red-necked. Seabird passage usually starts in March and lasts through to October, the peak being in August and September. Good numbers of Fulmar, Gannet, Manx Shearwater, auks and Kittiwake can be seen. During the 'high' autumn migration, rarer species of shearwater and Storm and Leach's Petrels have been found. Also notable are passage Commom Scoter which also bring odd Velvet Scoter and Long-tailed Duck. All four skuas have been recorded, Arctic and Great being the most regular. Other wildfowl peak in winter with around 500 Shelduck, 1,000 Wigeon, and 500 Teal. Pink-footed Geese are recorded flighting over on passage during the winter. Other winter wildfowl include Whooper Swan, Greylag and a few Brent Geese, Pintail, Shoveler, Tufted Duck, Scaup, Goldeneye, Red-breasted Merganser and the odd Garganey on spring passage.

Eider

Of the birds of prey, Sparrowhawk, Kestrel, Merlin and Peregrine have been recorded throughout the year with Marsh Harrier, Osprey, Long and Short-eared Owls, Barn, Little and Tawny Owls being resident.

Walney is an important wader site with a winter peak of 12,000 Oystercatcher, 10,000 Knot and 3,000 Dunlin. Other waders to be found in number include Ringed, Golden and Grey Plover, Lapwing, Curlew, Redshank and Turnstone. Smaller numbers of Sanderling, Purple Sandpiper, Snipe, godwits, Greenshank and sandpipers are also present.

The south end of Walney is well known for its large breeding colony of large gulls, numbering some 20,000 Herring and 30,000 Lesser Black-backed Gulls during recent breeding seasons. Around 60 pairs of Great Black-backed Gulls also breed.

Numbers of spring and autumn passage of passerines through Walney are not outstanding but it has proved to be excellent in the variety of species recorded. Occasional 'falls' of chats, pipits and warblers have occurred, with Meadow Pipit movement being particularly strong in early spring. Among the rarer passerines recorded on passage are Hoopoe, Wryneck, Richard's and Tawny Pipits, Icterine, Melodious, Subalpine, Barred and Yellow-browed Warblers, Firecrest, Red-breasted Flycatcher, Lapland and Snow Buntings.

Access
In North Walney, coastal waders and wildfowl may be viewed at Earnse Point car park (SD 170700). For access to the North End dunes and North End Marsh in Walney channel take the shoreline track from this point north past Walney Aerodrome. Do not enter or cross the airfield at any point. Alternatively, access to Willow Woods and Walney Channel can be gained by turning right off Walney Bridge along the channel promenade following the signs to the Aerodrome at North Scale. At the Aerodrome boundary leave the car and follow the footpath across the fields to Willow Woods and Walney channel.

The car park at the end of the coast road at Biggar Bank SD 183664 is excellent for observing coastal movement of wildfowl and waders as well as being a good seabird watch point.

To reach South Walney Bird Observatory (SD 220620), turn left on crossing Walney Bridge and continue for half a mile (1 km) towards Tummer Hill. Turn left at Tummer Hill Marsh or beyond the housing estate along the coast road to the village of Biggar. Go past the village and the refuse tip to the South End Caravan Site, where you drive along a track past South End Farm to South Walney Nature Reserve. A modest admission charge is levied, but this allows the use of three excellent, well-placed hides for watching local bird movement and sea-watching.

Timing
The best time to visit Walney Island is during autumn migration from August to late October, although visits during the spring and winter can often be very rewarding. Early morning is the best time for passerine passage, particularly if light winds from the south or east predominate. Sea watching is best during September and October; following a south-west 'blow', there is a good possibility of seeing Leach's Petrel, shearwaters and skuas. May and September are the best months for seeing wader flocks gathering at South Walney and there is the chance of spotting an unusual one on the gravel pit pools on the reserve.

Calendar
All year: Shelduck, Eider, Red-breasted Merganser, Peregrine, Oystercatcher, Ringed Plover, Dunlin, Snipe, Greenshank, Turnstone, large gulls, Barn and Little Owls, Meadow Pipit, Skylark and Linnet.

April-July: Breeding visitors include Sandwich, Common Arctic and Little Terns, Yellow Wagtail, Stonechat, Whinchat, Sedge Warbler, Lesser Whitethroat, Spotted Flycatcher. Spring passage birds include all three divers, Great Crested Grebe, Fulmar, Manx Shearwater, Gannet, 'grey' Geese, the occasional Garganey, Common Scoter, Goldeneye, the odd Marsh or Hen Harrier, Osprey, Merlin, Golden and Grey Plovers, Knot, Sanderling, Black and Bar-tailed Godwits, Whimbrel, sandpipers, Arctic and Great Skuas, auks, Turtle Dove, Black Redstart, warblers and other small passerines.

August-October: Passage birds include Sooty Shearwater, Storm and Leach's Petrel, Shag, Whooper Swan, 'grey' Geese, Wigeon, Pintail, Shoveler, Scaup, Velvet Scoter, Merlin, the occasional Hobby, and waders. Also likely are Little Stint, Curlew Sandpiper, Ruff and Spotted Redshanks, skuas, various gulls including Little Gull, Black Tern, Short-eared Owl, Swift, hirundines, wagtails, chats, winter thrushes, warblers (with possibly Melodious and Yellow-browed), Flycatchers, passage corvids, finches including Twite, Snow Bunting.

November-March: Red-throated is the commonest diver with small numbers of Black-throated and Great Northern. Other interesting winter species include Red-necked and Slavonian Grebes, Brent Goose, Wigeon, Teal, Pintail, Pochard, Tufted Duck, Scaup, Long-tailed Duck, Goldeneye, Merlin, Peregrine, Water Rail, waders including Jack Snipe, Woodcock in severe weather, Greenshank, large gulls (including Glaucous), Short-eared Owl, Rock Pipit, winter thrushes, corvids, Brambling, Twite, the odd Lapland and Snow Buntings.

Rarities on Walney Island in recent years have included Black Stork, Cory's and Great Shearwater, King Eider, Common Crane, White-rumped and Buff-breasted Sandpiper, Greater Sand Plover, Wilson's Phalarope, Ring-billed Gull, Richard's and Tawny Pipits, Desert Wheatear, Paddyfield Warbler, Subalpine, Pallas's and Bonelli's Warblers, Red-breasted Flycatcher, Woodchat Shrike, Nutcracker and White-throated Sparrow.

Reference

Walney Bird Observatory Report is an Annual Report covering the whole of the island. Contact address: Tim Dean, Coastguard Cottage, South Walney Nature Reserve, Walney Island, Barrow-in-Furness, Cumbria, LA14 3YQ.

24 CAVENDISH DOCK, BARROW

OS Map 96
SD 26
(See map on p. 65)

Habitat and Species

This is an important site for wildfowl as the redundant dock is used by the local Power Station for a warm water outflow, thus keeping the water ice-free in winter. It is a local moult site for Mute Swans with a peak of 150 birds in July and August. Concentrations of wildfowl are notable throughout the winter period with good numbers of grebes (Great Crested and Little), Wigeon, Pochard, Tufted Duck, Goldeneye and Red-breasted Merganser. Coot numbers also increase at this time of year. A central barrier across the dock provides a roost platform for Redshank and Cormorant, the latter often numbering up to 200 birds. Gulls in large numbers use the dock to wash and preen and occasionally to feed.

On the east side of the dock is an area of phragmites. This wet area attracts small passerines and some waders during spring and autumn. It also holds a few breeding pairs of Sedge and Reed Warblers. Beyond the seawall of the dock are Roosecote Sands which expand southwards to the Westfield Gas Terminal and beyond to Roa Island. This area has concentrations of wildfowl, for example Eider, Wigeon and Shelduck with flocks of Greylag Goose sometimes appearing in bad weather. Good numbers of waders are to be found here, with Ringed, Golden and Grey Plovers, Dunlin, Redshank, Bar-tailed Godwit and Curlew reaching good figures. Peregrine, Merlin and Short-eared Owl regularly harass the sometimes very large wader flocks.

The area around Cavendish Dock has recorded sightings of a fair number of unusual species including Red-necked, Slavonian and Black-necked Grebes, Red-crested Pochard, Ferruginous Duck, Temminck's Stint, Pectoral Sandpiper, Lesser Yellowlegs, Water Pipit and Lapland Bunting.

Access

From Barrow Town Hall take the A5087 to Ulverston beyond the roundabout. At the first bend, by St George the Martyr Church, turn right down Cavendish Dock Road. Follow this over the railway, through Buccleugh Dock to the British Nuclear Fuels terminal where Cavendish Dock is visible on the left. Alternatively follow the A5087 a further half-mile (1 km) under the railway bridge to the Catholic Church on the right, turn right down St Luke's Avenue, across the road junction under the railway bridge and park. Cavendish Dock is over the embankment on the right. There is a footpath right round the dock area.

25 FOULNEY ISLAND (CWT)

Habitat and Species

This small shingle island is connected to the mainland by a granite block walkway. It is a nature reserve owned by the Cumbria Wildlife Trust who warden the large tern colony present here in the summer months. It extends along the eastern side of the Walney channel out into Morecambe Bay and is an excellent watch point for wildfowl, waders, seabirds and passerines.

In winter it shares the Eider population with Walney Island (Site 23) according to weather and tide. Other wildfowl at this season include Brent Geese, Teal, Wigeon, Shelduck, Goldeneye, Red-breasted Merganser with smaller numbers of Red-throated Diver, grebe species (including Great Crested), Scaup, Long-tailed Duck and Common Scoter. Wader numbers are important here too. At the Rampside Marsh area with its saltmarsh cover of grasses and sea lavender, good numbers of Dunlin, Snipe, Bar-tailed Godwit, Curlew and Redshank gather whilst further out on the island are Ringed and Grey Plovers, Oystercatcher and Turnstone. Passage waders include Knot, Sanderling, Black-tailed Godwit, Little Stint, Curlew Sandpiper, Jack Snipe, Whimbrel, Spotted Redshank and Greenshank. Various auk species and Glaucous Gull may also appear in the winter, while small groups of Brambling, Twite and sometimes Snow Bunting forage on the tideline. Merlin and Short-eared Owl often cover the long grasses in the middle of the island. During the breeding season Black-headed Gull and four tern species occupy the nesting area at the tip of the island. At this time Roseate and Black Tern can appear along with Little Gull, Arctic and Great Skua. Spring and autumn passage have produced a crop of unusual species including Hobby, Temminck's Stint, Mediterranean Gull, Ring-billed Gull, Pomarine Skua, Shore Lark and Bluethroat.

Brent Geese

Access

Take the A5087 from Barrow-in-Furness to Ulverston as far as the village of Rampside. At the roundabout follow the route marked Rampside through the village and on to the causeway to Roa Island. Halfway along this causeway (SD 234657) you can park at the start of the track out to the island. The best time to visit is an hour or so before high tide, ideally during calm conditions as it has become a popular site for wind surfing.

MORECAMBE BAY

26 Leven Estuary
27 Flookburgh Marshes
28 Kent Estuary
29 Leighton Moss

30 Carnforth Marsh and Hest Bank
31 Heysham Harbour and Power Station
32 Lune Estuary
33 Wyre Estuary

The 120 square miles (300 or so square kilometres) of sand at Morecambe Bay covered at high tide by a shallow sea form Britain's most important site for estaurine birds, recognised as of international importance for twelve species of wildfowl and waders. The Bay is the common estuary of a number of swift-flowing rivers including the Wyre, Lune, Keer, Kent, Leven and Crake. The sand flats, which contain molluscs and worms sought by many shore waders, are broken here and there by areas of dark, seaweed-covered rocks called skeers where gulls and Oystercatcher feed on mussels. Much of the coastline is fringed with grazed saltmarsh, but here and there outcrops of limestone or red sandstone provides elevated viewpoints. The RSPB protects 6,200 acres (about 2,000 hectares) of mudflats and saltmarsh to the west of the estuaries of the Kent and Keer.

Morecambe Bay is internationally important for a number of shore-birds. Coordinated counts have produced totals of around 140,000 waders spread over a number of favourite roosting spots. Wildfowl numbers are more difficult to estimate as they can disperse at high tide on the surface of the sea. Two species should be mentioned however: Shelduck, of which 15 per cent of the British population has been recorded in winter on the Bay; and Eider, whose breeding colony on Walney Island is the only one on the west coast of England. All in all it is estimated that some 22,300 (January 1990 total) wildfowl use the Bay in winter. Other species use the vast feeding grounds of the Bay and there are several very large gull roosts, in particular on the Kent estuary.

The southern saltmarshes of the Wyre and Lune estuaries are also internationally important, particularly in winter for Greylag and Pink-footed Geese.

Timing

Any tide of 30 ft (9.2 m) or over will drive the birds off their feeding areas on to traditional roost sites high up on the saltmarsh. In severe winter weather many Knot and Dunlin move to the more sheltered areas around Walney Island. In gale conditions the Shelduck and Pintail flocks congregate behind Humphrey Head into the Kent estuary. Watch out during these conditions for windblown sea-birds. Obtain a local tide-table and do not venture out on the sands on a rising tide as it is swift and dangerous.

Habitat and Species

This large river estuary is divided in two by a railway viaduct. The Greenodd Sands and upper estuary to the north of the viaduct have good numbers of wildfowl in winter with Teal, Wigeon, a few Pintail, Shelduck and Goldeneye, the latter gathering in flocks of fifty or more in late spring near Greenodd. Occasional 'grey' Geese use this area. It is also the haunt of waders such as Golden Plover, Dunlin, Curlew, Redshank and a few Greenshank. South of the viaduct the vast expanse of sand and mud is some 3½ miles (5.5 km) across at its widest point between Bardsea on the west shore and Sandgate Marsh opposite. In its midst runs the Ulverston channel and a small limestone outcrop, Chapel Island. Wildfowl gather in large numbers here particularly Mallard, Pintail, Wigeon, the odd Shoveler, a few Scaup, Goldeneye and Red-breasted Merganser. Red-throated Divers, grebes, Whooper Swan, 'grey' Geese including Bean and White-fronted, Barnacle Geese, Eider and Long-tailed Duck visit from time to time.

Chapel Island supports a strong high tide wader roost with Oystercatcher, Ringed Plover, Dunlin, Curlew and Redshank. Another Redshank roost on the old slag banks at South Ulverston occasionally has Spotted Redshank, Greenshank and Turnstone present. This is also a good site for early and late migrants and passerines.

Sand Gate Marsh holds a Gull roost mainly of the larger gulls and is always worth looking at. Peregrine, Merlin, the odd Hen Harrier and Short-eared Owls often hunt the estuary marshes. Among the more unusual species recorded are Red-necked and Slavonian Grebes, Storm Petrel, White Stork, American Wigeon, Stone Curlew, Collared Pratincole and Golden Oriole.

Access

The west shore has easy access from Ulverston which has both rail and 'bus services. For Canal Foot take the minor road parallel to the Ulverston Canal to the large Glaxo Chemical Works. Follow the road past the works entrance to the Bay Horse Inn at Canal Foot. The canal at this point in recent winters has had Red-necked Grebe, Chiffchaff and Waxwings. Access to the South Ulverston slag banks is from the rear of the Glaxo works car park (SD 307775). A shoreline footpath between Conishead Priory, Wadhead Scar (locally known as Priory Point) and Bardsea can be reached by two minor roads off the A5087. Good views of the wildfowl and wader roosts around Chapel Island can be had from the shore here. Bardsea Country Park is an SSSI which includes Sea Wood, an oak woodland on the shore of Morecambe Bay. Access is easy here as the A5087 runs through the site with many parking areas.

North of the viaduct, parking areas off the A590 at Greenodd and near Arrod Foot (SD 308809) give good views across the Greenodd Sands. On the eastern shore of the estuary, views of the upper reaches can be had at Low Frith. Take the A590(T) to Haverthwaite and then the B5278 towards Cark and Grange-over-Sands. After $4\frac{1}{2}$ miles (7 km), having passed through the woodland of Holker Moss, take the minor road to Old Park and Low Frith at SD 355780. This straight avenue of walnut trees leads to Old Park Farm and beyond to Park Head car park. A short walk will give good views of the estuary from the viaduct to Low Frith. For Sand Gate Marsh continue further along the B5278 through Cark village to the square at Flookburgh, turn right and follow the road out of the village to the shore at Sand Gate Farm.

27 FLOOKBURGH MARSHES

Habitat and Species

The vast expanse of tidal sand and mudflats between the Leven Estuary and the limestone headland of Humphrey Head are best viewed when there is a good high tide bringing the waders and wildfowl up on the equally vast salt marshes of East and West Plains.

The West Plain is the largest salt marsh stretching for 3 miles (5 km) between Cowpren Point on the Leven Estuary to the Ponderosa Holiday Complex at East Plain Farm. It is one of the most important high tide roost sites for waders on Morecambe Bay and in peak migration period can hold 12,000 Oystercatcher, 15,000 Dunlin and 3,000 Curlew. According to tide, weather and disturbance, many of these birds will also use East Plain or, just to the east, Out Marsh. This was formerly a roost for large flocks of Knot and Bar-tailed Godwit but in recent years numbers have dwindled.

The Flookburgh marshes also hold good numbers of Shelduck with a few Wigeon and Pintail. Ringed and Grey Plovers, with Golden Plover, gather on Cark Airfield behind East Plain Farm. Birds of prey regularly hunt here including Peregrine, Merlin, Sparrowhawk, the odd Hen Harrier and Short-eared Owl. West Plain has a Cormorant roost of over 200 birds and a large gull roost of all species; 'grey' Geese also visit. More unusual species on the marshes have included Leach's Petrel, Spoonbill, Crane, Dotterel and Glaucous Gull.

Access

Access to the salt marshes is a little difficult. West Plain can be viewed from Cowpren Point which is reached by walking, either along the shore from Sand Gate Farm (see Site 26) round Lenibrick Point or from the embankment of the Ponderosa Holiday Complex. To reach this take the minor road to Cark Airfield from the square at Flookburgh. Park at West Plain Farm at the end of the straight road by the airfield and walk towards the sea along the grass embankment. For the Out Marsh (East Plain) take the B5277 for Grange-over-Sands from Flookburgh. After 1½ miles (2.5 km) turn right for Humphrey Head, follow the minor road over the railway crossing, turning left at the junction for the headland. This road leads to the shore under the limestone cliffs. A short walk along the shore to the west brings you to Out Marsh.

Timing

This area is obviously best visited during peak high tides in spring and autumn. Obtain a tide-table from a fishing tackle shop in Kendal, Grange, Ulverston or Barrow and visit just before high tide.

WARNING *Do not venture on to the mudflats.* Keep to the grass saltflats as there are quicksands and the rising tide comes in very quickly. There have been fatalities here through carelessness.

Habitat and Species

The Kent Estuary has become a popular site with local birdwatchers and as such has produced a good range of birds in recent years. The estuary stretches from Humphrey Head across to Silverdale on the Lancashire shore and is tidal upstream as far as Levens Hall estate. The towns of Grange-over-Sands and Arnside are on the west and east shores respectively and, as in the Leven Estuary, a railway viaduct divides the area in two.

Beyond the viaduct the upper estuary has some important salt marshes at Brogden, Arnside Marsh, Foulshaw and Halforth Farm. Near the latter point the River Gilpin joins the River Kent and is a site for Greylag Geese in winter (see also under Site 16A). This area has had the odd interesting wader on passage. The 'grey' Geese use the mosses at Foulshaw and Brogden and have in recent years been joined by a few Pink-footed, White-fronted, Bean and Barnacle Geese. Waders visiting the shore here include Ringed and Golden Plover, Dunlin, Ruff, godwits, Whimbrel, Curlew, Spotted Redshank, Greenshank and sandpipers. These birds quite often move around the upper estuary visiting Arnside Marsh or over the viaduct to Meathop Moss when disturbed. In the upper estuary, post-breeding Lapwings gather in autumn in a large flock often exceeding 1,500 birds. At this time there is also a very large gull roost of some 8,000 birds, mainly Common and Black-headed Gulls, with just a few larger gulls. Little, Mediterranean and Glaucous Gull along with Kittiwake and Great Skua have been found occasionally at this roost.

The river around the viaduct and Arnside Marsh is more disturbed and deeper round the viaduct piers and diving duck with the odd grebe or seabird can be found feeding here. During autumn high tide periods, pools formed on Arnside Marsh can attract waders like Sanderling, Little Stint, Curlew Sandpiper, Wood Sandpiper. The county's first record of Baird's Sandpiper, an American vagrant, was made here.

The shore opposite Arnside is Meathop Marsh. This saltmarsh runs from the viaduct to Holme Island at Grange-over-Sands. Good numbers of Greylag Goose, Pintail, Teal, Wigeon and Red-breasted Merganser feed and roost here with Oystercatcher, Redshank and Curlew. The shoreline from Holme Island to Humphrey Head includes the promenades at Grange-over-Sands and Kents Bank. By the causeway to Holme Island is an area of spartina grass which attracts Redshank, Snipe, the odd Jack Snipe and, in winter, mixed finch flocks with Reed Buntings. The mud-flats around Grange are known for a high population of Pintail and Shelduck. Wildfowl counts here often exceed a thousand for each species. The channel at Kents Bank railway station is particularly favoured by these ducks, especially in stormy conditions as it is sheltered by Humphrey Head. This area often attracts grebes, the odd diver, Goldeneye, Long-tailed Duck, Scaup and Common Scoter. Storm Petrel, Manx Shearwater, Fulmar, Gannet and Kittiwake have been seen during autumn gales.

Access

A good part of this estuary has easy access as good views can be had from the promenades at Kents Bank, Grange-over-Sands, Sandside and Arnside.

For Brogden and Foulshaw marshes, take the A590 from the M6 Motorway at Junction 35 and follow the road for Barrow past Levens Bridge to the Derby Arms, Witherslack (SD 443828). At this point take the minor road to Ulpha. After two miles a footpath at SD 450812 for Sampool Bridge leads down to the estuary at Crag Wood. Look across the fields from the sluice for geese and in the channel and estuary beyond for waders.

Halforth Farm is reached from the A6 at Heversham taking the lane left at SD 485840 past College Green to the farm. Park in the yard and view from the gateway on the embankment.

Timing

Autumn and winter are the best periods to visit, particularly in or after stormy conditions as the estuary is a sheltered site. Choose a period on or around high tide as the wildfowl, waders and gulls come in off Morecambe Bay with the tide. Remember that certain tides here have a strong bore, the water rushing in on large waves similar to the Severn Bore.

Habitat

Formerly an inlet of Morecambe Bay, Leighton Moss was claimed from the sea and drained, but flooded again, this time with fresh water, in 1917. Now an RSPB reserve of 321 acres (130 hectares), it lies between the villages of Yealand Redmayne on the east and Silverdale on the west, close to the eastern corner of Morecambe Bay. The reserve lies between limestone hills and comprises largely phragmites swamp with invading willow scrub and shallow, open pools frequented by otters as well as a rich avifauna. Artificial scrapes and islands are overlooked from hides.

Meadow Rue is an uncommon plant growing at the edge of the marsh and the spikes of Marestail protrude from shallower pools. The valley sides are clothed in woods of Ash, Oak, Yew and Birch which conceal Red and Roe Deer. Purple Hairstreak butterflies frequent the crowns of oak and ash trees and High Brown Fritillaries may be seen on the grassy slopes.

Species

Leighton Moss has long been famous for its breeding Bitterns and Bearded Tit, both species closely tied to large beds of phragmites, a scarce habitat in north-western England, and recently joined by Marsh Harrier. Up to 15 pairs of Bittern have nested in recent years either here or at the adjacent Haweswater. Bearded Tit first bred in 1973 and have increased to some 30 pairs. Breeding waterfowl include Teal, Shoveler, Pochard, Tufted Duck and Gadwall. Garganey are occasionally seen during the summer, but proof of breeding is still awaited. Water Rail, though common here, are very elusive, as is their scarcer cousin the Spotted Crake which has also bred here. Shingle islands on the main mere have attracted breeding Oystercatchers and Common Terns as well as raucous Black-headed Gulls. Scrubby areas hold nesting Common and Lesser Whitethroats, Grasshopper and Sedge Warblers, Reed Buntings and Redpolls, while Reed Warblers, here approaching the northerly limit of their range, prefer the cleaner stands of reeds. Heron fly in to feed on the abundant eels. All three woodpeckers, a few Nuthatches and elusive Hawfinches inhabit local ashwoods and Buzzards float overhead. Woodcocks rode at dusk in spring and summer and Marsh Tits are plentiful.

Marsh Harriers

Unusual migrants may occur in both spring and autumn. Marsh Harriers often arrive in May and recent springs have produced Osprey, Purple Heron and Spoonbill. Black Terns and Little Gulls hawk over the meres before moving on to the east. Wader passage in spring or especially autumn brings the occasional Ruff, Wood and Green Sandpiper, Spotted Redshank or Greenshank and, at dusk, Starlings, Pied Wagtails, Swallows and Sand Martins mass to roost in the reed-beds. Sparrowhawks and Barn Owls all prey here and Merlin, Peregrine and Hobby all dash in from time to time to snatch a Starling or Swallow.

Winter ducks include up to 1,000 Mallard and Teal with smaller numbers of Pintail, Shoveler, Wigeon, Pochard, Tufted Duck and

Goldeneye. Skeins of gibbering Pink-footed and honking Greylag Geese pass overhead but seldom land unless the meres are frozen. Resident Mute Swans are joined at times by small parties of Whooper or Bewick's Swans. Hen Harriers cover the reedbeds on the lookout for unwary mammals or birds such as the Snipes and uncommon Jack Snipe that crouch in the marsh.

Timing

The marsh is at its liveliest in spring and summer when Black-headed Gulls bring a sense of urgency to the proceedings and singing warblers and other marsh birds are visible from the paths between hides. Bittern are difficult to see except in frosty weather when the pools freeze rapidly, forcing the birds to feed in the open. However they tend to be more bold in May when feeding young and may then be glimpsed briefly as they flap low over the reeds. Water Rail are also easier to see in frosty weather. Autumn and winter visits should be timed to allow a dusk watch over the passerine roosts to see hunting predators.

Access

Leighton Moss can be reached from the A6 north of Carnforth through Yealand Conyers, Yealand Redmayne to Myers Farm near Silverdale railway station. There is an information centre, with a bookshop, at the farm. Permits are available on payment at the shop and allow access via clearly marked paths and walkways to the hides. The reserve is closed on Tuesdays, but there is a public causeway running across the north end of the reserve which allows free access to two public hides.

Habitat and Species

These two saltmarshes are formed either side of the estuary of the River Keer and as such provide one of the most important roost sites for waders, wildfowl and gulls on the south side of the Bay. They become particularly important during the winter and spring peak high tides, when numbers are large having moved out of smaller roosts at lower levels. Greylag Goose, Shelduck, Wigeon, Teal and Pintail gather in large numbers along with a few Shoveler and Goldeneye. Ten thousand Oystercatcher can be found on a peak tide here along with over 5,000 Knot and Dunlin. Lapwing, Golden Plover, Bar-tailed Godwit, Curlew and Redshank can also reach large numbers here.

On Carnforth Marsh several pools, scrapes and embankments have been formed by the RSPB to make an excellent habitat which is overlooked by two hides, the Allen Hide and Eric Morecambe Hide (see map on p. 79). Several hundred pairs of Black-headed Gulls nest here but the visiting birdwatcher can expect to see something a little different here at any time of year. In the last few years this has included rarities such as Little Egret, Black Stork, Red-footed Falcon, or Wilson's Phalarope mixed in with more regular passage birds like Garganey, Marsh Harrier from nearby Leighton Moss, Ruff, Greenshank, sandpipers, Mediterranean and Little Gulls and Black Terns.

To the south end are several large slag banks which are remnants of a long gone iron industry in Carnforth. These are now good vantage points over the Bay and Keer estuary and provide shelters for passage migrants particularly in hard winter weather for birds such as Snow Bunting, Twite and the odd Lapland Bunting. Early migrant Wheatears are often found here.

At Hest Bank Saltmarsh, to the south of Carnforth, large flocks of Ringed Plover, Knot, Dunlin, Redshank and Turnstone can be seen, along with Shelduck and larger gulls.

Access

For Carnforth Marsh follow the road for Warton, past Carnforth railway station, under two bridges, after a mile turn left to Silverdale. At the first sharp right hand bend keep straight on to Cote Stones Farm at SD 487715. Follow the footpath from this point to the slag banks which provide a good observation point.

Hest Bank Saltmarsh is very easily accessible as most of it can be viewed from the shore car park at the railway crossing or from the northernmost point of the Morecambe Promenade at the Cinderella Home.

From Morecambe take the A5105 along the Promenade over the railway to Hest Bank. Turn left over the level crossing by the signal box and park on the grassy ridge overlooking the marsh. This area is within the RSPB Reserve and a small parking fee may be required, but the car is an excellent hide.

31 HEYSHAM HARBOUR AND POWER STATION

OS Maps 97 and 102
SD 35, 36, 45, 46

Habitat and Species

Heysham Harbour has become recognised as an excellent seabird watch point. It is probably the only mainland site which regularly produces Leach's Petrel in autumn. The ideal conditions for this phenomenon occur during September and October after a sustained period of South-West to Westerly gales. These conditions blow passage seabirds into the Bay and the harbour provides an excellent vantage point to see these birds, many at close quarters, struggling back out to sea. Other birds caught in these conditions can include sea terns and Black Tern, Kittiwake, Little Gull and occasionally Sabine's Gull, skuas, auks and Grey Phalarope.

The Power Station 'outflows' are worth checking in these conditions also as they are a favoured feeding site for terns and gulls. Both sites can be rewarding during the winter months as divers, grebes, sea-duck, auks, gulls (including Little Gull) and skuas appear with regularity. During the winter months the harbour is a favourite site for Purple Sandpiper. Spring brings the return migrants with Fulmar, terns and skuas. Only a few Manx Shearwater and Gannet are seen annually here, as elsewhere on Morecambe Bay they are scarce.

Sabine's Gull

At the back of the two Nuclear Power Stations is an area of gorse and thorn scrub with a pool surrounded by phragmites and willow. National Power have opened a viewpoint and display in an observation tower here and a nature trail and ringing station have been set up by local ornithologists. This is an excellent site for passage migrants with good numbers of hirundines, chats, winter thrushes and warblers to be seen on passage. Autumn falls can be good with species like Reed Warbler (scarce in the north), Marsh, Barred and Yellow-browed Warblers and Firecrest appearing. Other rarities on passage in spring or autumn here have included Spotted Crake, Bee-eater, Wryneck, Melodious Warbler, Woodchat Shrike and Ortolan Bunting.

The area of shore to the south of the Power Station is known as Red Rocks. This is a good wader roost with Ringed Plover, Dunlin, Knot, Bar-tailed Godwit, Curlew, Redshank and Turnstone along with Shelduck, the odd Eider and Red-breasted Merganser. Brambling, Linnets and other finches may appear on the shore here in severe winter weather conditions.

Access

Follow the A589 south through Heysham turning right at the traffic lights for Heysham Harbour. At the next set of traffic lights, at the Moneyclose Inn, turn left over the railway bridge along Moneyclose Lane. The next right takes you to the Observation Tower Car Park and the ringing station where information of recent sightings is chalked up on a board. For the Power Station outflows continue to Ocean Edge Caravan Park. On entry to the park turn sharp right and follow the drive to the shore. This is the Red Rocks site. Follow the sea wall round the Power Station to the outflows and a metal container hide. For the north Harbour wall turn right at the traffic lights to the Heliport. Take the road left and right round the Helipad and follow the sea wall to the end at the harbour entrance.

Timing

For seabirds, visit one hour before high water and during periods of prevailing westerly winds. During September and October in periods of westerly gales, Leach's Petrels and other unusual seabirds are seen. Spring and autumn passage passerines are usually seen around the Observation Tower area in the morning, the earlier the better.

Habitat and Species

As with the other river estuaries on Morecambe Bay, the Lune has several important roost sites for wildfowl and waders. The prime roost sites are Pilling Marsh, Cockerham Sands, around Glasson Dock at Conder Green and Middleton Sands on the north shore.

The fields in the area of Cockerham Moss hold good numbers of Pink-footed Goose from February to April, often peaking at around 5,000 birds. These birds roost on Pilling Sands and may bring stragglers of other species with them including White-fronted, Barnacle and Brent Geese. Good numbers of Golden Plover and Lapwing are to be found in these fields in winter, often being molested by preying Sparrowhawk and Peregrine. Breeding species include Partridge, Whitethroat, occasional

Lesser Whitethroat and Corn Bunting, the latter a bird which is rare north of the Lune.

Middleton Sands to Sunderland Point on the north shore of the estuary is fairly difficult for access and, as a result, is not watched as closely as other areas of the estuary. However, the monthly wader counts reveal good numbers of Ringed Plover, Knot, Dunlin, Sanderling and Redshank. Around Sunderland Point there are Grey Plover, Bar-tailed Godwit and Greenshank. This headland sees a movement of passage passerines with winter thrushes in cold conditions and pipits in spring and autumn. Richard's Pipit was recorded here in 1980 and Water Pipit in 1982.

The south shore of the estuary has much easier access as the old railway embankment from Glasson Dock to Lancaster carries a well maintained footpath with parking facilities provided at Conder Green. Apart from the regular wildfowl and waders Conder Green, with its creeks and mudflats, has been visited by a few notable birds such as White-rumped and Buff-breasted Sandpipers.

Travelling south of Glasson Dock into the Flyde towards Pilling Sands you pass Cockerham Point with its prominent sandstone Abbey before coming to the vast expanse of sands of Cockerham and Pilling. A Pacific Golden Plover was found here in July 1990. Here amongst the scarcer shorebirds seen on this length of coast have been Little Egret, Spoonbill, Little Ringed Plover, Little Stint, Curlew and Wood Sandpiper, Ruff, and odd Little Gull and Arctic Skua and occasional Lapland and Snow Buntings in winter. Just inland from this area Quail have been heard in summer and in 1987 a Crane was seen.

Access

For Middleton Sands take the A589 in Heysham to the traffic lights at High Heysham continuing straight on down the minor road to Middleton. In the village take the first right to Middleton Tower Holiday Campsite following the road to its end at Patts Corner, where good views of the sands can be had. For Sunderland Point, pass through Middleton for Overton where you turn right for Sunderland. Park in the village and walk to Sunderland Point. Beware of high tides as the road crosses the saltmarsh at several points and is flooded twice a day.

To reach Conder Green take the A588 from Lancaster. At Conder Green village turn right at the Stork Inn and park in the foreshore car park by the railway embankment. For Cockerham Point turn right off the A588 a mile (2 km) further south, at Thurnham and follow the road to the Abbey. Good views of the sands can also be had from the car park placed on the new flood prevention embankment near Pilling Hall off the A588 five miles (8 km) south of Cockerham (SD 416495).

33 THE WYRE ESTUARY

Habitat and Species

Fleetwood which is situated at the head of the Wyre Estuary, forms the southernmost point of Morecambe Bay. Its prominent position makes it not only an interesting place to watch wildfowl and waders but also a very rewarding site during migration periods for seabirds and passage passerines. The prime watch point is at the head of the promenade at Rossall Point. Here can be found offshore flocks of Common Scoter and Red-breasted Merganser while the flocks of common waders often contain both species of godwit, Purple Sandpiper and Sanderling. During migration periods, auks, Kittiwake, terns, Arctic and Great Skua can be seen. In autumn gales, Manx Shearwater, Leach's Petrel, Grey Phalarope, Sabine's Gull and Pomarine Skua have all been recorded here. During the winter months occasional Red-throated Diver, Twite and Snow Bunting can be found.

On the Wyre Estuary, the pools around the ICI works and Power Station attract grebes, Tufted Duck, Pochard, Wigeon, Teal, Goldeneye and a summer peak of moulting Mute Swans. Little Stint, Curlew and Wood Sandpiper, Little and Mediterranean Gull have been recorded on passage.

Knott End on the opposite shore holds common waders with good numbers of Redshank and Turnstone. Occasional Eider and Scaup may venture up the estuary here and Glaucous Gull have been seen here as in other sites around Fleetwood in winter. The Wyre Estuary has long been noted for migrating flocks of Black-tailed Godwit.

Access

Rossall Point to the Lifeboat Station on the Wyre has easy access as viewing can be done from any point along the promenade.

The pools near the Power Station and at the ICI Chemical Works can be reached by following the A585, by-passing Thornton to a roundabout at the Cala Gran Caravan Park. Turn right and then left down a minor road to the Waste Recycling Centre. View the ICI pools from the railway bridge where the Fleetwood Nature Reserve is sited on the opposite side of the road. The Power Station pools are half a mile (1 km) further down the road.

NORTH LANCASHIRE

34 Marton Mere
35 Forest of Bowland
36 Stocks Reservoir
37 Pendle Hill

North of the Ribble, the Pennine Hills sweep closer to the west coast so that the lowland plain, including the area known as the Fylde, narrows northwards. In the far north of the region lie the reedbeds and shallow meres of Leighton Moss, close by Morecambe Bay. The agricultural Fylde attracts geese in winter, while waders frequent the coastline. Marton Mere, lying behind Blackpool, attracts its share of oddities – as befits the town!

The Pennines themselves hold breeding moorland species on the higher plateaux, while Goosanders are spreading on hill streams. The whaleback ridge of Pendle Hill stands above lower hills and valleys where walled and hedged fields are grazed by sheep.

34 MARTON MERE, BLACKPOOL

OS Map 102
SD 33
SD 343353

This mere on the outskirts of Blackpool is an area of open water, marsh and reedbed which is a local Nature Reserve. It holds breeding Little and Great Crested Grebes, Sedge and Reed Warblers. It is best known for its migrant waders which regularly include Little Ringed Plover, Jack Snipe, Green and Wood Sandpipers. Other migrants include Little Gull, Glaucous Gull, sea terns, Black Tern and Short-eared Owl. In winter it holds good wildfowl numbers particularly Wigeon, Teal, Shoveler, Pochard, Tufted Duck, Goldeneye and Ruddy Duck. Bewick's Swan, Garganey, Scaup and Common Scoter have also been recorded here. Scarcer visitors have included Red-necked Grebe, Marsh Harrier, Osprey, Turtle Dove, Wryneck and Black Redstart.

An American Bittern stayed during the winter 1990/91.

Access
From Preston take the M55 to Junction 4 and then the A583 to Great Marton. Turn right for Stanley Park and after half a mile (1 km) turn right again down Lawson Road. Half way down the road, walk across the football pitch to Marton Mere.

35 FOREST OF BOWLAND OS Maps 102 and 103SD 55, 64 and 65

Habitat
The Forest of Bowland is an upland area of great scenic beauty with its
narrow valleys and steep sided fells punctuated by small pastures,
drystone walls and small areas of mature woodland. On the western side
is Wyresdale surrounded by Tarnbrook Fell to the north and
Hawthornthwaite Fell to the south. Through the valley flows the upper
part of the River Wyre from its source and it is joined by several streams
and becks to form a lake at Abbeystead before continuing its journey
westwards to the sea. Passing through the upland Trough of Bowland the
heather moorland reverts to a scene of upland grassland and fell farm-
steads. At Dunsop Bridge the River Dunsop joins the River Hodder to flow
southwards through the lower part of the Bowland Forest to meet the
River Ribble at Little Mitton. This is an Area of Oustanding Natural Beauty
with its fine stands of beech woodland and heather covered hills. To the
north east, amongst the open grass upland, is Stocks Reservoir and the
large conifer stands of Gisburn Forest beyond.

Species
A very large gull colony centred in the Tarnbrook area holds some 5,000
Herring and Lesser Black-backed Gulls. A large part of the high open fells
are well stocked with Red Grouse. On the high tops one can expect to
encounter the odd Merlin and Hen Harrier with Golden Plover, Curlew,
Dunlin, Short-eared Owl and, on the rocky crags, Raven, Ring Ousel and
Twite. Lower down, the fellside streams have their resident Dippers,
wagtails and in some areas Stonechat added to in summer by breeding
pairs of Wheatear and Whinchat. In the valley bottoms amongst the
wooded riversides there are Oystercatcher, Snipe, Woodcock,
Red-breasted Merganser and some Goosander. Some river embankments

Golden Plover

have Sand Martin and Kingfisher and on the woodland fringes there are still the odd pair of Blackcock with Buzzard and Sparrowhawk hunting overhead in places. The beech woodland has Redstart, Pied Flycatcher, Wood Warbler, Little and Tawny Owls and a few pairs of Long-eared Owls with the occasional Green Woodpecker and Nuthatch. Amongst the more unusual species recorded in the Bowland area recently are Rough-legged Buzzard, Golden Eagle, Opsrey and Hobby with Wood Sandpiper at Abbeystead Reservoir. Winter brings good passage numbers of winter thrushes and Brambling with a few Snow Bunting on the highest tops and flighting Greylag and Pink-footed Geese.

The lake at Abbeystead is part of a private estate but a footpath below the dam gives a general view. Regular birds here include Great Crested Grebe, Canada Geese, Teal, Oystercatcher, Dipper and Grey Wagtail. Migrants include Pochard, Tufted Duck, Goldeneye, Cormorant, sandpipers and hirundines.

Access

Make Dunsop Bridge the centre point. Take Junction 33 off the M6 and follow the A6 to Galgate, then taking the minor road for Dolphinholme and Abbeystead which continues through the Trough of Bowland for Dunsop Bridge. Access to the summits of Tarnbrook Fell and Brennand can be gained by turning left beyond Abbeystead for Grizedale Bridge at SD 566554. Turn right along the valley to Tarnbrook where a footpath takes you to the top of Tarnbrook Fell and Wolfhole Crag. From the east, Dunsop Bridge can be reached from Clitheroe taking the B6478 via Newton Fell and Newton or the more scenic route from Clitheroe via the B6243 to Edisford Hall. Turn right for Bashall Eaves and Whitewell for Dunsop Bridge.

36 STOCKS RESERVOIR (NORTH WEST WATER)

OS Map 103
SD 75

Habitat and Species

Stock Reservoir is some 700 ft (220 m) up amongst the grouse moors near Slaidburn and the North Yorkshire border. It covers some 344 acres (140 hectares) and is visable from the road and picnic site provided by the NWWA. The central island is a refuge and breeding site for Canada and Greylag Geese, Teal, Tufted Duck and waders including Oystercatcher, Ringed Plover, Snipe and Redshank. Around 500 pairs of Black-headed Gull also breed here. In winter the reservoir holds a large gull roost and wildfowl numbers increase with Whooper Swan, Wigeon, Pochard, Goldeneye, an occasional Smew and Goosander to add interest. Also at this time have been recorded Hen Harrier, Golden Plover, Dunlin, winter thrushes and Great Grey Shrike. Ring-necked Duck have been recorded twice here in winter.

The reservoir is part of a notable trans-Pennine migration route and as such produces some interesting passage migrants in spring and autumn. These have included Shelduck, Scaup, Common Scoter, Osprey, Little Ringed Plover, Little Stint, Curlew Sandpiper, Ruff, Black-tailed Godwit, Greenshank, sandpipers, Arctic Skua, Little Gull and Common and Black Terns.

On the northern edge of the reservoir lies the large expanse of Gisburn Forest, a Forestry Commission plantation which holds good woodland species like Sparrowhawk, Long-eared Owl, Tree Pipit, Redstart, Wood Warbler, Siskin, Redpoll and a few Crossbill.

Access

From the A65 Kendal to Skipton road take the B6478 at Long Preston for Slaidburn. Some eight miles (13 km) on, having passed through the villages of Wigglesworth and Tosside, turn right at the crossroads on Stephen Moor (SD 748543) for Stock Reservoir and Clapham. A further 2½ miles (4 km) will bring you to the north bank of the reservoir and the car park. Good views of most of the reservoir can be obtained here or along the road. From the west, travel through the Trough of Bowland to Dunsop Bridge and Slaidburn where the B6478 will take you to the crossroads at Stephen Moor.

Timing

The area is important for both breeding and passage wildfowl and waders. Spring and autumn can produce the unexpected while in winter the large gull roost and the increase in wildfowl numbers are the main attractions.

93

37 PENDLE HILL

Habitat
The summit of Pendle Hill is occupied by grass moor with some sparse heather. The rocky slopes are covered with bracken in places, and below these there are pasture fields bounded by stone walls or hedges. Fast-flowing streams are home to riparian birds.

Species
Pendle is best known as a spring passage haunt of Dotterel, which crouch on the barren, windswept top of this rounded hill. The first birds arrive in mid-April, but most are present in early May prior to a mass departure in mid-month. In 1988, for example, 32 birds were counted. Greenland Wheatear often pass through around this time.

Earlier in the spring Golden Plover and Curlew flock in lower-lying pastures before dispersing to breeding territories, and Snipe and a few Redshank return to rushy fields which later attract Yellow Wagtail. The hill itself still holds small numbers of resident Red Grouse and a few Golden Plover, but these latter birds resent disturbance from ramblers. Twite return in April, and remain through the summer, forming small parties in August. Ring Ousel in March and Whinchat in April are as likely to be passing through as holding territory, but Wheatear breed on the rocky slopes.

Redstart favour the lower, bracken-clad slopes with scattered bushes or trees. Where old hedgerow trees and semi-derelict barns stand together, listen for the curlew-hoot of Little Owl. Grey Wagtail are numerous along hill streams, where Dipper also breed. Goosander have bred locally too.

94

Dotterel

This tall, isolated hill attracts predators, for example Merlin and Short-eared Owl, and all Pennine hills may occasionally produce exciting birds in winter. Snow Bunting are irregular visitors, but in winter 1989–90 a flock of 25 spent some weeks here, feeding on moorland grass seeds. Overgrown thorn hedges attract berry-eating thrushes and, in invasion years, Waxwing.

Timing
The area generally is popular walking country, but the chief bird season is from March to May. Dotterel enthusiasts concentrate their efforts in the first two weeks of May. The summit itself is often relatively crowded on fine weekends.

Access
The most direct route to the summit follows a stepped path up from minor roads north of Barley, but there are numerous footpaths, particularly around the lower slopes. Dotterel favour the flat summit around the triangulation point at the Barley end.

Calendar
All year: Red Grouse on moors; Little Owl on farmland; Dipper and Grey Wagtail on streams.

March-May: Ring Ousel, Golden Plover and other moorland species on passage; Redshank, Snipe and Curlew in pastures; Dotterel on tops in early May. Twite, Redstart and other migrants arrive during April.

SOUTH LANCASHIRE, MERSEYSIDE AND GREATER MANCHESTER

38 South Ribble Marshes
39 Martin Mere and the South Lancashire Mosslands
40 Mere Sands Wood
41 Sefton Coast
42 Seaforth Nature Reserve and Crosby Marina
43 Bolton Area and the West Pennine Moors
44 Wigan Flashes
45 Pennington Flash
46 Elton Reservoir, Bury
47 Mersey Valley

The shallow coastline of South Lancashire is marked by wide, sandy beaches which, together with the estuaries of Ribble and Alt, attract thousands of waders. The beaches are fringed to landward by extensive dune systems, lost to development in places, although many of the surviving dunes are now protected. The low-lying mosslands between the Ribble and Liverpool have been drained to create rich farmland. The Wildfowl and Wetlands Trust reserve at Martin Mere and the Ribble Marshes National Nature Reserve together attract vast numbers of wild-fowl which fly out to feed on farmland elsewhere.

A legacy of the industrial revolution, much of which was concentrated in south Lancashire and what is now Greater Manchester, is a variety of rich ornithological sites which arose accidentally as a result of industrial development. The Seaforth Dock Pools in Liverpool and the coal-mining subsidence flashes at Leigh and Wigan are good examples. Fast-flowing streams off the Pennines were harnessed to power textile mills. As the population grew, larger drinking water reservoirs were constructed to supply the cities. The cluster of reservoirs around Bolton attract a wide range of birds, but all such reservoirs are worth a look on occasion.

Few heather moors remain, but Twite still nest commonly on grass moors towards the Yorkshire border.

For many urban birdwatchers, especially in Greater Manchester, the network of river valley walkways provides opportunities close to home. Hundreds of thousands of young trees were planted along the Mersey and other valley corridors by the former County Council and its constituent boroughs. Where this maturing woodland coincides with wetlands, as at Sale Water Park, uncommon birds are now being discovered with some regularity.

The Ribble Estuary, with its associated marshes, is of international importance for wildfowl and waders. Wide, sandy outer shores merge with the tourist beaches of Southport to the south and Lytham St Annes to the north. Further into the estuary there are extensive saltmarshes. Concentrations such as 35,000 Wigeon, 60,000 Knot, 7,000 Sanderling and 16,000 Bar-tailed Godwit have been counted. At times over 100,000 waders and 50,000 wildfowl have been present. The richness of the site for wildfowl is largely due to its hinterland. The damp mosslands between Southport and the Liverpool suburbs attract Pink-footed Goose, swans and dabbling ducks which fly out to the coast to roost. Grazing land adjacent to the marshes supports geese, swans and Wigeon, and provides safe roosting sites for waders on the highest tides. Many birds commute between the marshes and Martin Mere.

Habitat

The Ribble Marshes National Nature Reserve was established following a threat of agricultural destruction of its wildlife potential in 1979. Banks and Crossens Marshes now form the bulk of 5,430 acres (2,182 hectares) of reserve, with 300 acres (120 hectares) added at Hesketh Out Marsh. Some wildfowling is permitted, chiefly for Wigeon and Pink-footed Goose, but wildfowl numbers have increased since the establishment of the reserve.

The marshes consist of mud-banks and saltmarsh, the latter grazed by cattle during the summer. The wet fields at Marshside and Crossens are frequented by wildfowl and waders, especially at high tide. Southwards from the Marshside sand workings, the expansive beach is largely free of vegetation and backed by small dunes behind the road. The coast is exposed to autumnal gales, which may drive seabirds over the marshes or onto the sheltered marine lake at Southport.

Species

Wildfowl frequenting the marshes peak between late November and March. Whooper and Bewick's Swans both number several hundred, and often mingle, allowing direct comparison of two species which can pose identification problems when seen alone. Pink-footed Goose flocks sometimes total 10–15,000 birds. Other goose species are often represented by stragglers, picked up on the journey in from Iceland or Greenland. Sooty Greenland Whitefronted, pale Greylag or brown, orange-legged Bean Geese are not so easily spotted as Barnacle Goose or the occasional Snow Goose. This last, rare species has accompanied the Pink-footed in several winters. Parties of Eurasian Whitefronted Goose have occasionally settled. White-breasted Pintail drakes are conspicuous among the Wigeon flocks, although more careful scrutiny is required to detect the grey females. Shelducks are numerous, both on the marshes and on the beaches beyond. Mallard and Teal sit around the pools on the marsh, flying inland towards dusk to feed. Brent Goose are infrequent on this coast. Take careful note of the race to which any birds seen belong. Dark and pale-bellied races both occur.

At high tide, rafts of dabbling ducks float on the sea at the edge of the marsh. Small parties of Scaup and a few Merganser or Eider occasionally drift in with the tide. The highest tides may flood the saltmarsh, driving a few Water Rail from cover.

The grazing marsh at Crossens and Marshside is a favourite haunt of Golden Plover, with 3–4,000 present. Over 1,000 Black-tailed Godwit may roost at high tide, and parties of Curlew may be seen. Shorter-legged Bar-tailed Godwit and Grey Plover prefer the beaches. As the tide rises, packs of Knot swirl over the Southport beaches before settling to roost. Sanderling, Turnstone and Ringed Plover may also be seen, with the inevitable Dunlin and piping Oystercatcher. Tiny numbers of Little Stint and the occasional Spotted Redshank or Greenshank may be seen in winter. Ruff are more usual, with perhaps 20 or 30 feeding with Redshank in the damp fields.

Sanderling

Spring passage brings a variety of marshland waders to the Marshside pools in late April and May—few in number but smart in plumage. Ruff have been seen gathering at this season. There may still be thousands of Knot on the beaches, and northward passage may bring several hundred Arctic Ringed Plover to Marshside.

White Wagtail are a feature of spring passage all along the coast in April and early May, but Yellow Wagtail are fewer than formerly. Wheatear are frequently present during April, many of them also bound for Iceland. Whinchat pass through in early May. A Marsh Harrier may appear, floating low over the marsh, at almost any time from spring to autumn. A Garganey may be seen on the pools in spring or early summer.

The marshes are nationally important for breeding species. Several hundred pairs of Common Tern, a few Arctic Tern, and several thousand pairs of Black-headed Gull breed, as do up to 500 pairs of Redshank. Lapwing, Ringed Plover and Oystercatcher also breed, and Dunlin have done so. Several hundred pairs of Lesser Black-backed and Herring Gulls nest, with a few Great Black-backed. Yellow Wagtails and a few

Stonechats breed around the inner edge of the marsh, and Partridge are numerous in neighbouring fields where the jangling song of Corn Bunting may be heard. Shelduck breed in good numbers, and a few pairs of Shovelers are worth looking out for. Other ducks, such as Teal, Pintail and Tufted Duck, linger into the summer and sometimes attempt to breed.

By August the estuarine waders are starting to build up again. Several thousand Black-tailed Godwit may be present by the end of the month. This is also the most likely time to encounter Curlew Sandpiper or Little Stint and such species as Green or Wood Sandpiper, on muddy pools. Ruffs again reach double figures.

September gales may blow seabirds over the Marine Drive, but this is not a recognised seawatching site—at low tide the absence of the sea at Southport is legendary! However both Grey and Red-necked Phalaropes have appeared on sheltered pools after autumnal storms. Towards the end of the month the first Pinkfooted Goose arrive on north-westerly winds from Iceland. October sees the return of the winter predators. Several Hen Harriers hunt the marshes throughout the winter, as do Merlin and increasing number of Peregrine. Short-eared Owl numbers vary, but there are often ten or more of these birds scattered along the coastline.

During the winter Reed Bunting, Linnet and Greenfinch feed along the tideline around the sand workings at Marshside. Twite are often present, recognised by their abrupt flight call and the diagnostic twang after which they are named. A Black Redstart has been seen here on several occasions. Stonechat too are often present, as are Rock Pipit. Lapland Bunting feed out on the marsh, but are unlikely to be seen except in flight, when a knowledge of their calls is essential. Brambling numbers vary from year to year.

The Southport Marine Lake is a regular haunt of Cormorant, Goldeneye, and a few Merganser, and provides a haven for storm-blown sea-duck, and the odd Shag or diver. Snow Bunting sometimes feed around its shoreline, or along the beach nearby.

Timing

At low tide the saltmarshes look almost deserted, but they liven up rapidly as the tide pushes birds in. High tides between late August and mid-April are best. During the winter there are always interesting birds to be seen on the grazing marshes. There is some shooting between 1 September and 20 February, but this seldom detracts from birdwatching. The highest tides in winter (32 ft (10.5 m) or more) may flood the marsh and flush out Water Rail or Jack Snipe.

Access

Marshside, the area most popular with birdwatchers, lies adjacent to Crossens Marsh. Both can be viewed from the Marine Drive which runs north from the Southport pleasure beach past the Marine Lake up to the A565 Banks roundabout. Stopping along the Marine Drive is prohibited, but it is possible to pull off at various points, and there are car parks adjacent to the marine lake and by the sand-washing plant at Marshside. Trees opposite Crossens sewage works often hold Bramblings in winter. Crossens Out Marsh may also be viewed by turning first left on reaching the Banks roundabout, crossing the river then walking left along the footpath which follows the top of the sea-wall. This embankment also provides vantage point over Banks and Hesketh Out Marshes. A further embankment path runs from Hundred End around Ribble Bank Farm, turning in beside the River Douglas to Hesketh Bank.

During onshore gales, seawatching from the end of Southport Pier may be worthwhile.

CLIFTON MARSH

OS ref: SD 465285

This stretch of saltmarsh may hold large herds of wild swans when they are absent from Marshside or Martin Mere. The usual saltmarsh predators (Hen Harrier, Merlin, Peregrine, Short-eared Owl) may be seen. Access is difficult, but viewing is possible across the river from the embankment on the south shore. Access at various points in Higher Penwortham or Bottom of Hutton.

WARTON MARSH

OS ref: SD 400270

From Warton Marsh village take Bank Lane which runs past the end of the airfield. This lane narrows into a rough track where parking is difficult. Muddy footpaths lead east and west along the raised inner edge of the marsh, fringed in places by thorn scrub. In winter, flocks of Tree Sparrow, Linnet and other seed-eaters frequent this scrub, flying onto the strandline to feed on saltmarsh seeds. Twite and Brambling are sometimes present. On the highest spring tides the marsh may flood, driving Water Rail from cover. To the east this path is also accessible off Naze Lane East to the south of Freckleton village.

LYTHAM ST ANNES

OS ref: SD 375270

The main A584 runs along the front at Lytham. Walk east from the lifeboat station past the windmill to view the saltmarsh. Linnet congregate along the strand line in winter with other finches, buntings and larks. The Lytham beaches attract many waders, notable Sanderling in May and early autumn. Black-tailed Godwit may exceed 1,000 in autumn, along with thousands of Knot, hundreds of Dunlin and smaller numbers of other species. A mile (2 km) west of the lifeboat station take Marine Drive which leads past Granny's Bay to Fairhaven Lake (SD 340273). The bay attracts many waders at high tide. Small numbers of diving ducks and Cormorant frequent the lake, with a possibility of storm-blown seafowl.

Habitat

The mosslands of southern Lancashire comprise an extensive area of former peatlands, now converted to rich, arable farmland. The area generally is low-lying and flat, with narrow, reedy drainage ditches and small scattered woodlands. Many fields hold shallow puddles in winter.

The Wildfowl and Wetlands Trust reserve at Martin Mere covers 363 acres (150 hectares) of damp pastureland, shallow pools and scrapes which attract wildfowl and waders. It is a RAMSAR site, EEC Special Protection Area, and SSSI for ornithological and botanical interest. There is a large collection of penned wildfowl from around the world.

Species

Martin Mere in winter is probably the best site in the region for watching wild geese. Up to 34,000 Pinkfooted Goose have been counted on the mosses in early winter, and there are regularly several thousand visible from the hides at the Trust centre. Careful searching through the flocks will often reveal odd birds of other species, perhaps a family group of White-fronted or a solitary Bean, Brent or Snow Goose. Wild Greylag and Barnacle Geese also occur in small numbers, but identification is made confusing by the presence of feral birds. A decreasing flock of semi-tame, fully-winged Barnacles is present throughout the year (numbering 11 in 1990), and up to 300 Greylags feed on the reserve outside the nesting season, with smaller numbers during April to July. A very few pairs breed. These geese, and a flock of around 30 feral Pinkfooted which consort with them all year, fly out from Scarisbrick Hall. Canada Goose are numerous only during August when up to 200 freshly moulted birds visit the mere. In some winters, tiny, small-billed Canada Goose of one of the small races with a high-pitched, cackling voice have accompanied the Pinkfooted – perhaps genuine vagrants from North America. Lesser Whitefront has also been recorded. Slightly injured or old Pinkfooted Goose and wild swans occasionally stay over the summer. While scanning through the Pinkfooted, check for white plastic rings with black numbers which can be read through a telescope, and report any sightings to the staff.

Pink-footed Geese

Provision of grain attracts concentrations of wild swans into the grounds. Up to 400 Whoopers and 500–600 Bewick's Swans are present at peak times, although these often commute to the Ribble marshes. Up to 20 Mute swans are on the mere in winter. Teal and Mallard are present in their thousands, and Wigeon have exceeded 25,000. Pintail, though highly mobile and erratic in their appearances, may top 3,000 in early winter. Gadwall have increased considerably since the Trust established their collection here, perhaps aided in part by collection-reared birds which, having flown free up until the early 1980s, now behave as wild birds. Up to 50 or so may be seen scattered amongst the Mallard and Teal. A similar number of Shoveler, particularly in autumn or early winter, show a clearer preference for the company of their own species. Up to 250 or more Shelduck feed around muddy pools in late winter. All the regular freshwater ducks appear from time to time. Recently dredged areas of the mere have held up to 100 Pochard, a similar number of Tufted Duck, and a few Goldeneye, with occasional Scaup, Goosander or Ruddy Duck. Ferruginous Duck and Common Scoter have also occurred. North American stragglers, sighted in several recent winters, are one or two Green-winged Teal and American Wigeon among their Eurasian counterparts.

Small feral populations of several duck species have established themselves. The Trust now takes greater care than formerly to ensure that such birds do not fly from the pens. Nevertheless in 1990 some 30 Goldeneye, 7 Goosander, 15 Mandarin and 10 Wood Duck were living ferally around the grounds. Some of these birds breed on site.

Ducks nesting in a wild state include Shelduck, Gadwall, many Mallard (400 pairs in 1988), Shoveler and Pochard. Wigeon and Teal in small numbers spend the summer here. Garganey are occasional visitors in spring or autumn.

The abundance of nesting waders gives some idea of the productivity of the mosslands in general before they were drained. Some dozens of pairs of Lapwing and Snipe nest, as do a few pairs of Redshank. Oystercatcher attempt to do so, and both Little Ringed Plover and (at least once) Ruff have been known to do so. Non-breeding Black-tailed Godwit may be present in numbers through the summer, with up to 1,000 at passage times. Autumn brings a fair variety of waders to the pools. Curlew and Dunlin, Ringed and Little Ringed Plovers regularly reach double figures, while Snipe are numbered in hundreds. Many other species occur less predictably and in small numbers. Several Pectoral Sandpiper have been recorded while Collared Pratincole, Lesser Yellowlegs and other rarities have occurred.

Thousands of Lapwing and Golden Plover flock during autumn and winter in the damp, rushy pastures, where they are joined by many Ruff. A hundred or more of these often red-legged, hunch-backed waders may be present. Gulls visiting the mere in winter have included such rarities as Franklin's, Ring-billed, Mediterranean, Glaucous, Iceland and Yellow-legged. Spring wader passage, during April and May, is again dominated by Black-tailed Godwit, but Spotted Redshank, Greenshank and others may visit.

Short-eared Owl, Kestrel and Hen Harrier are quite likely to be seen during a winter afternoon's watch from the hides. Merlin and Peregrine too will take Snipe, and the larger falcon may tackle a duck. A Barn Owl is sometimes seen hunting mice or small passerines along the rough grass of field edges. These scarce, white owls breed on the reserve.

Within the pens of the wildfowl collection, Moorhen and Collared Dove help themselves to the inmates' food, as do Corn Bunting in winter. Although this species is declining in the region, this remains a fairly reliable site to see the birds. A flock overhead sounds rather like a bowl of 'rice crispies' – appropriate for a grain-eating species! Starling may roost in their thousands, attracting raptors as the light fades, and Tree Sparrow regularly flock here in mid-winter.

While summer is often regarded as the quiet season at Martin Mere, there is still much to be seen. Spring passage of hirundines brings flocks of Sand Martin, while parties of White and Yellow Wagtails scurry along the mere edge. The occasional Black Tern or Little Gull may hawk over the water. One or two Marsh Harrier generally appear at this season and there is a possibility of sightings throughout the summer. Some 35 pairs of Sedge Warbler nest, while slightly fewer pairs of Reed Bunting and Meadow Pipit breed. Skylark are also common, and have bred on the turf roof of the entrance building. Up to 20 or so Grey Heron fish the pools at any season. Several Spoonbill and once a Little Egret have been recorded.

Although nowadays geese are generally present on the reserve in winter, some watchers still tour the lanes across the more southern mosslands to seek flocks which often feed in carrot-fields. Fields beside the lanes at Plex Moss, Halsall Moss and Altcar Moss at times hold thousands of geese, with Wigeon, Pintail and other ducks in damper areas. Grey Partridge and Pheasant are numerous throughout the area, with a few Red-legged Partridge too. There is also a chance of seeing raptors – the same species as at Martin Mere itself – attracted by the mixed finch and bunting flocks which venture from thorn hedges into the stubbles. Tree Sparrow too are common here.

Mossland Birchwoods beyond the reserve hold a sprinkling of nesting, Woodcock, Turtle Dove and Long-eared Owl – the last two both increasingly scarce and hard to locate. Barn Owl frequent old farm buildings and there is a healthy population of Little Owl. Wader passage in both seasons brings a range of marshland species to flooded fields. A feature of spring passage in most years is the appearance of groups of Dotterel in the flat fields, most regularly at Altcar Moss, although they may occur anywhere in ploughed fields. Plex Moss is often good for Whimbrel. Marsh Harrier sometimes favour Altcar Moss in summer.

Access
Martin Mere (SJ 423143) is conspicuously signposted for miles around, even from the M6. The reserve is open from 9.30am till dusk or 5.30pm, whichever comes sooner, throughout the year except for Christmas Eve and Christmas Day. There is an admission fee for non-members of the Wildfowl and Wetlands Trust, currently £3 for adults, £2 OAP, £1.50 children. Coach parties should book in advance (tel. 0704 895181) – concessionary rates may be claimed for parties of more than twenty.

The mosslands to the south are best explored by car. Goose flocks are wary and highly mobile, so it is often necessary to tour the lanes for some time before a flock is located. Scan carefully from the cover of a vehicle if possible to avoid flushing the birds. Plex Moss Lane is often particularly good.

The area lies between the A5147 to the east and A565(T) to the west. All transverse lanes between the B5195 and the A570 are worth exploring, as is the area to the north of Bescar Lane Station (SJ 396145).

Calendar
All year: feral wildfowl including Greylag Goose; Grey Partridge, Barn Owl, Little Owl, Collared Dove, Corn Bunting, Tree Sparrow.

December/February: Whooper and Bewick's Swans, Pink-footed and other geese; Shelduck, Wigeon, Teal, Gadwall, Mallard, Pochard and Tufted Duck; good chance of a rarer duck or goose; predators include regular Hen Harrier, Merlin, Short-eared Owl, perhaps Peregrine; large plover flocks with many Ruff and Snipe; finch and bunting flocks visit pens at Martin Mere, or stubbles elsewhere.

March/May: winter wildfowl and raptors depart from March: Garganey and a sprinkling of waders on spring passage; Black-tailed Godwit may be numerous. White Wagtail pass through, and Sedge Warbler arrive. Snipe, Lapwing and other waders in display flights. Dotterel on mosslands in May. Small passage of Marsh Harrier.

June/July: wader display tails off. Duck and feral goose broods hatch. Perhaps the quietest time of year, although waders start to trickle through in July, and Black-tailed Godwit numbers peak soon after. Possible breeding Marsh Harrier.

August/November: ducks in drab plumage in August, starting to resume smart plumage by end of the period. Wader passage now more diverse, with Greenshank, Spotted Redshank, Green and Wood Sandpipers regular. Pinkfooted Goose start to return in mid-September, as duck flocks gather. Usually five or six individual Marsh Harrier on passage, and a few Garganey. Predators more in evidence from October.

40 MERE SANDS WOOD

Habitat

Mere Sands Wood at Rufford is managed by the Lancashire Trust for Nature Conservation. The reserve covers some 105 acres and contains a number of disused, flooded sandpits in a wooded, heathland setting. There are extensive areas of birch and oak woodland, and plantations of Scots Pine. Red squirrels occur around the car park. The site is a geological SSSI.

Species

The woods hold a variety of common woodland species, such as Redpoll, Nuthatch, and Coal and Willow Tits, with Blackcap, Chiffchaff, Willow and Garden Warbler in summer. Linnet and Yellowhammer frequent the more open areas. Little Ringed Plover have bred in the pits, where a wader scrape attracts Snipe, Green Sandpiper and other passage species such as Ringed Plover and Common Sandpiper. Feral Goldeneye which flew from Martin Mere in the early 1980s may be seen throughout the summer and have bred. Ruddy Duck, Great Crested and Little Grebes also breed. By August a wide variety of eclipse-plumaged ducks on the reserve may include Gadwall, Wigeon and Shoveler.

Winter brings much larger numbers of wildfowl. Gadwall have topped 100, with over 1,000 each of Teal and Mallard at times. A few dozen Pochard and Tufted Duck are generally present.

Access

Mere Sands Wood lies off the B5246 between Rufford and Holmeswood, only a few minutes drive from Martin Mere. The reserve is signposted (at SJ 448162) along a track to the car park set in the wood. The LTNC information centre lies close to one of the hides overlooking the flooded workings of the old quarry. There is a charge of £1 per car for non-members of LTNC. At weekends and Bank Holidays access is restricted to Trust members.

Circular walks lead around the pools and direct visitors to a series of public hides which provide good views of the water areas and wader scrape.

Between Southport and the northern suburbs of Liverpool lies an area of wide, sandy beaches backed by a dune system of outstanding botanical and entomological interest. The extensive sand flats linking those of the Ribble to those of North Wirral and the Dee are feeding and roosting grounds for large flocks of waders. Breeding birds include Shelduck, Whinchat, Stonechat and Grasshopper Warbler. The dunes shelter a wide range of migrants in both spring and autumn.

The Sefton Coast is used intensively for recreation, with much of the area wardened by Sefton Council's Coast Management Scheme, which aims to harmonise recreation with the natural interest of the area. Other sections are managed by the National Trust and the Nature Conservancy Council.

It is difficult to split the area into separate birdwatching sites. Indeed the whole area is contiguous with ornithologically outstanding coastline to both north and south. The following access points are suggested.

41A ALT ESTUARY AND HIGHTOWN DUNES

OS ref: SJ 297908

The River Alt emerges at Hightown, past a small saltmarsh and reedbed, meandering across mud and sand flats. Access to the north shore is restricted by the presence of the Altcar rifle range.

The dunes between Hightown and Crosby include areas of stunted poplar, willow and sycamore scrub which hold migrants at the appropriate seasons.

Species

The Alt estuary is internationally important for Knot, Bar-tailed Godwit and Sanderling, and nationally important for Grey Plover. Other waders, Shelduck, terns and gulls also occur in good numbers. At high tide small parties of Turnstones, Ringed Plovers and Sanderlings may roost on the south side amongst the bricks and rubble of the shoreline. As the tide ebbs, these birds are joined by others which fly in from the main roost (at Formby) to feed on the newly exposed mud.

While the estuary waders are present from late summer to spring, marshland species also appear on spring and autumn passage, preferring the muddier areas near to the river. Greenshank, Common Sandpiper, Little Stint and Curlew Sandpiper may appear. Rarities have included Kentish Plover.

In winter a few Merganser, Scaup and Goldeneye dive in the river channels. Little Gull are frequent and may number as many as fifty or more in spring. Mediterranean, Glaucous and Iceland Gulls have also occurred. In fact the range of species mirrors the pattern at Seaforth Docks (Site 42). For example Common Tern are numerous offshore in August, with smaller numbers of Sandwich, Little and Arctic Terns.

Meadow Pipit nesting in the dunes are sometimes parasitised by Cuckoo. Other nesting species include Skylark (with one of the highest concentrations in the county), Redpoll, Willow Warbler, Whitethroat, Grasshopper Warbler and Stonechat. In both spring and autumn passage warblers and chats appear in the stunted sycamore and poplar thickets. Regular coverage has turned up less common species such as Barred Warbler and Red-backed Shrike.

Access

Take the road from Hall Road Station (on the northern outskirts of Crosby) down to the seafront, turn right and park by the Coastguard Station (SJ 298895). This car park forms a useful vantage point for seawatching during onshore winds, although a wide beach is exposed at low tide. Walk north from the car park, checking weedy areas for pipits or buntings. Bushes, especially the larger clumps towards Hightown, should be checked for migrants. From the dunes above the moorings of the sailing club, scan the estuary for wildfowl and waders. The wader roosts can be seen gathering in the distance as the tide rises.

Access is also possible from Hightown. Cross the station road bridge and turn right at the roundabout up Lower Alt Road. A footpath at the end gives access to the salt-marsh and dunes (SJ 296037).

41B Formby Point

OS ref: SJ 267068

An area of dunes backed by woodland of pines and poplars, Formby is a noted haunt of passerine migrants and of interest for other wildlife too. Red squirrels, introduced from the continent, may be seen throughout the area, but most easily at the National Trust's squirrel reserve at Victoria Road, Freshfield. At high tide the Point provides good seawatching. At low tide the Formby Channel area is an important feeding ground for waders. It is also a major high tide roost. The Cabin Hill National Nature Reserve is sandwiched between Raven Meols LNR and the Altcar Rifle Range. On clear days it is possible to see along the North Wales coast to Anglesey.

Species

Seawatches can be exciting at any time of year. In winter Red-throated Diver and Great Crested Grebe fish offshore, with other divers or grebes on occasion. Common Scoter are often present, varying in numbers between a few dozen and several hundred. Other sea-ducks, such as

Firecrest

Eider, Long-tailed Duck, Red-breasted Merganser or Velvet Scoter are occasionally present. Little Gull visit the Formby Channel in spring and during onshore winds. Gannet and Fulmar appear during summer storms, when Kittiwake may be numerous. Manx (and, rarely, Sooty) Shearwaters occur in August/September. But it is autumnal westerlies that bring the greatest variety of birds with Leach's Petrel, Arctic and Great Skuas and Guillemot being typical. Long-tailed and Pomarine Skuas, Sabine's Gull and Grey Phalarope have all been reported during storms.

At high tide one of the region's major wader roosts gathers near the rifle range at Formby Channel. From September to March, Knot are counted in their tens of thousands, Bar-tailed Godwit and Dunlin in the thousands, and Oystercatcher, Grey Plover, Redshank and Sanderling in the hundreds. Smaller numbers of various other species are also expected. Sanderling and Ringed Plover are more numerous on spring and autumn passage in May and August/September. At low tide these birds are scattered over the flats, with some flying to feed along the North Wirral shore or in the Dee estuary. Common Tern fish in the Channel on spring passage in May, often joined by a few Little and Sandwich Terns. From July to September there are regularly several hundred Common Tern, with smaller numbers of Sandwich and Little and, rarely, Arctic or Roseate.

West coast passage stations seldom attract the range of landbirds seen at their east coast counterparts. In spring, White and Yellow Wagtails, Willow and Sedge Warblers, Whitethroat, Wheatear and a few Whinchat are staple birds, with other warblers, chats and flycatchers in smaller numbers. A similar range of species migrates through in the autumn, when there is an increased chance of rarities. The first British Eleanora's Falcon to be recorded was watched at Cabin Hill in July 1977. Other highlights have included Melodious and Barred Warblers, Bearded Tit, Red-breasted Flycatcher, Rough-legged Buzzard, Osprey, Golden Oriole, Great Grey Shrike, Wryneck and Greenland Redpoll. Yellow-browed Warbler have occurred in October, when Goldcrest may be numerous.

Access

From Formby take the road past the main station or the parallel Raven Meols Road which converge and become Lifeboat Road. There is a free car park at the end (SJ 275065). The sea can be scanned from various points straight out from or to the north of the car park. Numerous footpaths enable exploration of bushes behind the dunes for migrants. Cabin Hill NNR lies a mile to the south of the Point, beyond Raven Meols LNR.

The road past Freshfield Station in the northern outskirts of Formby leads down to a National Trust car park (parking charge) adjacent to the squirrel reserve (SJ 274083). There are good areas of bushes on either side, but especially to the south of this track.

41C Ainsdale and Birkdale Hills

OS ref: SJ 300115 and 310138

North of the National Trust's holding at Formby Point, although largely separated by the Formby golf course, lie the 1,216 acres (243 hectares) of

111

Ainsdale National Nature Reserve. Dominated by high dunes, the habitat is similar to the adjacent Ainsdale and Birkdale LNRs but with the addition of areas of tall pines, with breeding natterjack toads (in the damp slacks) and sand lizards. Red squirrels are found in some numbers.

On the LNRs, berries of sea buckthorn and hawthorn provide food for migrant birds in autumn. Insects are concentrated around the dune-slacks where they are sought by hirundines and warblers. Just outside the Ainsdale LNR is a saline boating lake. This is generally too busy for good bird-watching in summer but may be more rewarding in winter.

Species

The range of nesting passerines is typical of the coastline, and includes a few Stonechat and Grasshopper Warbler. Ringed Plover and Oystercatcher have both been known to breed on the sand and outer dunes, and both are present through the winter when they are joined by Turnstone, Dunlin, Redshank, Bar-tailed Godwit and Curlew. Sanderling may gather in hundreds off Birkdale as the tide rises. During severe weather Stonechat feed along the tideline, and occasionally Shorelark and Snow Bunting are recorded.

Outside the breeding season Merlin and Peregrine visit on occasion, as do Short-eared Owl and perhaps a Hen Harrier. In autumn Fieldfare and Redwing feast on berries and are often hunted by a Sparrowhawk. A few Jack Snipe feed in the damp slacks, especially in October.

The Ainsdale Lake in winter attracts small numbers of waterfowl, and is always worth checking after storms for sheltering sea-ducks or perhaps a phalarope. Glaucous Gull have been seen at Ainsdale in every month of the year, and Mediterranean Gull appear with some regularity.

The pinewoods sometimes hold Crossbill and Siskin, and formerly Long-eared Owl.

Access

The Ainsdale and Birkdale Sandhills LNRs are administered by Sefton Borough Council. There is free parking near the boating lake at the end of the Ainsdale beach road (SJ 301129) – a walk of 1 mile (1.3 km) from Ainsdale railway station. Birkdale Hills lie to the North and Ainsdale Hills to the south of this road. The National Nature Reserve starts about 1 mile to the south. Footpaths are well marked. A permit is required to wander off these.

Timing

During the summer months the coast is very popular with trippers. Its interest is then primarily in plants and other aspects of natural history. Early morning visits are advisable at passage times, especially in spring. Autumn migrants may linger longer in busy areas. To see waders or seabirds, time visits around the high tide. Wader roosts begin to gather a couple of hours before the tide peaks. Seawatching at Formby Point can be productive in onshore gales. Watching is possible in greater comfort from the Hall Road car park, although the setting is not so good.

42 SEAFORTH NATURE RESERVE AND CROSBY MARINA

Habitat

Seaforth Nature Reserve comprises freshwater and saltwater pools bordered by overgrown piles of rubble with small numbers of recently planted shrubs. The area, lying within Liverpool Freeport and overlooked by the Radar Tower, appears unprepossesing, but it regularly supports impressive numbers of gulls, terns and waders, including the largest spring passage of Little Gull in the country. The area is owned by the

113

Mersey Docks and Harbour Company and managed as a reserve by the Lancashire Trust for Nature Conservation.

Crosby Marina, immediately adjacent to the north, is used extensively for watersports, but may hold birds when less disturbed. Quieter areas of the shoreline and surrounding grass attract waders during passage periods and gulls in winter.

Species

This reserve is of great interest for the gull enthusiast: regular observation here is clarifying the pattern of occurrence of several species in north-western England. Mediterranean Gull were seen on more than 200 days in 1989, in all months, with adults most frequent in March and September, and early summer concentrations of immature birds. Winter flocks of Little Gull have been present offshore in Liverpool Bay and the southern Irish Sea for many years, and birds from this population often visit the reserve, particularly during westerly gales when up to 100 have taken refuge on the pools. Generally, however, few birds are seen at this season. Spring passage to the east starts in late March, and peaks in mid-April with over 500 present at times. A small summering population of immature birds usually remains. Return passage may bring up to 50 birds in September and October, particularly with onshore winds.

Black-headed Gulls may exceed 10,000 but are much less numerous from April to the end of June. Common Gull number 5,000 or more at times in winter and spring. Lesser Black-backed Gull reach 1,000 in autumn, and Herring Gull may exceed 3,000. Great Black-backed are less numerous and appear in large numbers mainly in cold or windy weather.

Kittiwake are seen on most days, in largest numbers during strong winds when birds shelter on the reserve, but also during calm weather in summer when up to a hundred non-breeders may loaf on the causeway.

Sabine's Gull are seen annually during onshore gales in autumn. Iceland Gull are also annual in small numbers and have been recorded in most months, particularly during late winter and spring. Glaucous Gull are rather more frequent but follow a similar pattern to Iceland Gull. There are records of Bonaparte's and Ross's Gulls – two real rarities. Ring-billed Gull are now being detected among passage flocks of Common Gull. One bird wintered at Crosby Marina in 1987–8. Immature 'Yellow-legged' gulls are often found amongst the Herring Gull in summer, followed by adults in autumn.

Common Tern are the most frequent in their family, arriving in small numbers in April but reaching well over 1,000 in August. A few pairs have nested. Arctic and Black Terns are scarce, the former occurring mainly in spring and the latter in autumn. Sandwich and Little Terns are rather more regular, especially in August. Roseate Tern have appeared on a handful of occasions in autumn, while a Forster's Tern was a major find in March 1987.

Surface-feeding waterfowl are represented by moderate winter numbers of Mallard, Teal and Shelduck, with some Gadwall present most of the year. Diving species are more of a feature. Over 100 Cormorant are regular outside the nesting season and over 300 have been counted. In winter several dozen Pochard and fewer Tufted Duck feed on the pools, often joined at high tide by a small flock of Scaup. Goldeneye and Red-breasted Merganser are present in winter. Moderate flocks of Coot are to be seen from August to March and a few breed.

Any stretch of water on this coast will attract waders and at least thirty species have been recorded, including Temminck's Stint, Grey Phalarope and White-rumped Sandpiper. Ringed Plover and Lapwing breed regularly here and Oystercatcher, Redshank and Little Ringed Plover have done so. The high tide wader roost consists mainly of two species, Oystercatcher (up to 1,800) and Redshank (up to 1,000), with smaller numbers of Dunlin, Ringed Plover and Turnstone. Black-tailed and, in early summer, Bar-tailed Godwits have shown signs of becoming regular features. Whimbrel and Common Sandpiper are regular passage birds. Curlew Sandpiper, Little Stint and Sanderling occur chiefly in autumn in small numbers. The grass at Crosby Marina may be productive for these three species. A few Jack Snipe join good numbers of Snipe in winter. Shore waders on Crosby beach include Knot, Bar-tailed Godwit and the occasional Grey Plover.

Breeding landbirds are scarce, but include Skylark and Meadow Pipit. As planted shrubs mature this list should increase. Greater interest will undoubtedly focus on migrant passerines which should stop off in increasing numbers. To date the chief evidence of passage has been for those species which are not dependent on such cover. White Wagtail may pass through in hundreds in spring and Wheatear have exceeded a hundred in number. Yellow Wagtail are more prevalent in autumn, but bright spring males have included odd birds of the Blue-headed, Grey-headed and even Black-headed races. Black Redstart have appeared on fifteen or so occasions. Snow Bunting occur with some regularity in winter, more often on sand dunes around the Marina than the reserve.

Little Gull – first winter

During autumnal gales, numbers of Leach's Petrels and other seabirds may exceed those seen from New Brighton on the opposite side of the Mersey. Indeed, Seaforth's exposed position in the angle of the Lancashire and Wirral coasts makes it the ideal seawatching site in such conditions. Two hundred Leach's Petrel passed on 30 September 1978, 370 on 14 September 1987, and smaller, but still considerable numbers may be expected with any onshore blow in autumn. Storm Petrel are less

115

frequent, generally arriving with more westerly winds and more likely to appear in late summer. Skuas and shearwaters are also likely given suitable winds. In early October 1988 as many as 17 Long-tailed Skua were seen, with several Pomarine, Great and the commoner Arctic Skuas. Three Sabine's Gull and several hundred Kittiwake were seen during the same gales.

Timing

Wader roosts begin to form two to three hours before high tide. Gull numbers are less affected by tides, with late morning and afternoon being the best times.

Access

From the north end of the M57 take the A5036 dual carriageway south-westward, following signs for the Freeport. Park at the Freeport entrance, from where it is necessary to walk, following signposts to the reserve.

Two hides overlook the freshwater pool and the causeway where gulls, terns and waders congregate.

For seawatching, continue along the road past the hides up to the river, then turn towards the conspicuous Coastguard tower.

The reserve is closed on Bank Holidays. Entry is free during the week, but there is a 50p charge to non-members of LTNC at weekends.

Contact: 051-920 3769
Publications: Seaforth Bird Reports

43 BOLTON AREA AND THE WEST PENNINE MOORS

OS Map 109

The area to the north of Bolton consists largely of pastureland, rising to grass moorland with some heather moor on the highest ground. There are areas of young conifer plantations on the moors, and more mature conifers around the margins of the many water supply reservoirs which lie within the steep-sided Pennine valleys. Tracts of old oak woodland add to the diversity. A large part of the area is covered by a countryside warden service, who can advise on quieter areas to visit. Public footpaths are well maintained and signposted. Some of the better sites are detailed below, but there is plenty of scope for exploration.

43A ANGLEZARKE AND DARWEN MOORS

Limited areas of heather support Red Grouse (keepered on Darwen Moor) and a few breeding Golden Plover. Twite nest in small numbers,

117

with a few pairs of Wheatear on rocky slopes. Young conifer plantations may hold nesting Whinchat, and there is a possibility of Short-eared Owl. Snipe are numerous in rushy areas. In winter the likelihood of raptors increases, with perhaps a Hen Harrier or Merlin. Even a young Golden Eagle has visited. Snow Buntings are seen infrequently.

Access
Anglezarke Moor must be approached on foot, via one of the tracks that leave the minor road alongside the Anglezarke Reservoir north of Rivington. Darwen Moor is reached via footpaths westwards from the A666 at Cadshaw.

43B Belmont Reservoir
OS ref: SD 675167
Belmont lies at 262 m (800 ft) above sea level. Consequently it attracts only small numbers of dabbling ducks, although Teal may be more numerous here than elsewhere in the district, and a sprinkling of diving species is generally present. Quite a lot of mud can be exposed, and in spring a variety of moorland breeding waders visit the shoreline – Dunlin (which may display), Redshank and Common Sandpiper. In March and April there may be more than 100 Curlew in the pastures. Snipe drum conspicuously and Oystercatcher have bred. Other migrant species, such as Ringed Plover, occasionally visit. Wader passage in autumn may be more varied, with a trickle of birds, especially from late July to September. Dipper and Grey Wagtail frequent nearby streams. A Montagu's Harrier was seen in June 1988.

Access
Parking is difficult along the A675 clearway, but a minor road crosses the dam (SD 675164) and a footpath climbs the eastern shore.

43C Roddlesworth Woods

An extensive area of upland, broad-leaved woodland, the Roddlesworth Woods hold small numbers of Pied Flycatcher, Redstart and occasional Wood Warbler. Tree Pipit, Woodcock and resident Green and Great Spotted Woodpecker are other interesting woodland species. Redpoll may be numerous in winter.

Access
The woods lie alongside the A675 some four miles north of Belmont, just south of Abbey Village. One mile north from Belmont Reservoir, turn right onto a minor road for Tockholes. There is a car park and nature trail at Ryal Fold.

43D Jumbles Country Park Reservoir

OS Ref: SD 734145

Jumbles Reservoir, flooded in 1970, is surrounded by farmland and mixed, recently planted woodlands. Being in a country park, the reservoir is used for sailing and fishing, but there are quieter areas.

A range of common waterfowl occurs, including Great Crested Grebe, Teal, Tufted Duck and Pochard. Less often there may be Goldeneye or Goosander. Kingfisher hunt from perches overhanging the water and in streams. A variety of scrubland species nests in the planted woodlands, for example Bullfinch, Goldfinch and Redpoll. Fieldfare and Redwing may be abundant in October and November. A log-book of bird sightings is kept in the information centre, and the list of species recorded at the reservoir is growing steadily. Many of these are only fleeting visitors, but have included Spotted Sandpiper, Pomarine Skua, Little and Iceland Gulls, Black Tern and Hobby.

Access

The Country Park is signposted off the A676 Bolton to Ramsbottom Road (take the left turn at SD 737133). Alternatively there is a second car park at Ousel's Nest off the B6391 on the west bank, giving a more circuitous walk. Footpaths encircle the reservoir, and connect with Wayoh and Entwistle Reservoirs.

43E Wayoh Reservoir, Edgworth

OS ref: SD 733166

Lying a short distance to the north of Jumbles, at 147m (550ft) above sea-level, Wayoh is fringed for much of its circumference by mixed woodland. The northern inlet is very shallow with muddy, well vegetated margins.

Some 100 species have been recorded, including Bittern and Grey Phalarope. Common Sandpiper nest along the shoreline, and Little Ringed Plover have settled in briefly when the water level is low. Few waterfowl breed due to the fluctuating water levels, but Great Crested Grebe may gather to fish in late summer. In winter there is a strong likelihood of a party of Whooper Swan or a few Goosander. Scrubland habitats hold a variety of breeding finches and warblers, with Goldcrest and occasional Crossbill in the conifers. Sparrowhawks often hunt the smaller birds.

Access

From Edgworth crossroads (SD 741169) take the minor road to the north-west. After half a mile (1 km) take the very narrow road at SD 736175 (easily missed – look out for the little church on the left to Entwistle station). Park beyond the causeway which crosses the top end of the reservoir. A path leads around the entire reservoir and connects with Turton and Entwistle Reservoir. It passes through woodland and scrub habitats, with a good chance of Siskin in winter, and excellent views across the two wildfowl refuges.

43F TURTON AND ENTWISTLE RESERVOIR
OS ref: SD 720175

This is a stone-sided reservoir surrounded by mature conifer plantations which often hold Siskin and occasionally Crossbill. It attracts small numbers of diving waterfowl, notably Goosanders on occasion, and perhaps a party of 'wild' swans.

Access
A car park below the dam is accessible off the B6391 (turn right at SD 724168). A public footpath skirts the north shore.

43G WALKER FOLD CLOUGH
OS ref: SD 676124

Broad-leaved woodland to the south and conifers to the north give way to rough pasture and the heather moorland of Winter Hill with its Red Grouse, Twite and other moorland species.

Access
By the minor road between the B6226 and the A675. Footpaths lead north-westward onto the moor.

43H SMITHILLS HALL
OS ref: SD 700120

A nature trail through the woodlands offers a chance of Marsh Tit and Nuthatch, two scarce species hereabouts.

Access
By the minor road off the A58 between Doffcocker and Astley Bridge.

43I RIVINGTON, ANGLEZARKE AND YARROW RESERVOIRS

A chain of large reservoirs running north from Horwich, Rivington and Anglezarke are, like other reservoirs in the area, bounded by rocky shores with areas of mud restricted to the tops of inlets. Rivington in particular is heavily disturbed by visitors, especially in summer, and it is as a haunt of winter wildfowl that the reservoirs are best known. There are extensive woodlands however, and while those around Lever Park may swarm with picnickers, there are quieter areas to be found.

Dabbling ducks never reach the abundance in which they are encountered on lowland waters, although several hundred Mallard may be present at times. Most standard species do occur however. Diving ducks are better represented by Pochard, Tufted Duck and Goldeneye, with parties of Goosander at times. Smew and Merganser appear infrequently, with perhaps a Common Scoter or two at passage times. Scarce grebes and storm-blown divers find conditions to their liking and may stay for weeks following their rare arrival. Whooper Swan are often present.

There is a sizeable winter gull roost on the Lower Rivington Reservoir, which attracts 11,000 or more gulls, including many from the tips near Horwich. There may be in excess of 200 Great Black-backed Gull, and odd Glaucous and Iceland Gulls occasionally join the roost. A few Kittiwake may appear on passage in early spring, or after winter storms. Terns and Little Gull appear occasionally at passage times.

Goldeneye

Common Sandpiper nest around the margins, with Grey Wagtail and Dipper being found by inlet streams. A Spotted Sandpiper was a recent highlight.

Undisturbed oak woods hold a good range of common woodland birds, with Redstart, Wood Warbler, Tree Pipit and Pied Flycatcher in the better areas. Green Woodpecker favour the edge between woodland and moorland, and the odd pair of Lesser Spotted Woodpecker may nest in alders near the waterside. Woodcock rode in the twilight.

Access

The wider, southern end of Rivington is favoured by waterfowl and roosting gulls. It can be viewed from the A675 Bolton-Chorley road just west of Horwich (SD 626127), or by turning right off that road immediately after a small roundabout, following signs for the West Pennine Moors Information Centre. On this side viewing is best from the vicinity of the castle (SD 628130). Minor roads and footpaths provide viewing of Anglezarke from both banks. The causeway roads between reservoirs are also good vantage points.

There are interesting woodland areas at the north end of Anglezarke and between there and White Coppice. Dean Wood, accessible by permit only but skirted by a public footpath on its north side, is managed jointly by North West Water and the Lancashire Trust for Nature Conservation. From Anglezarke Quarry, take the minor road signposted to Belmont and · the wood lies on the right after almost a mile, just beyond Wilcock's Farm (SD 632155).

43J Rumworth Lodge Reservoir

OS ref: SD 678078

Rumworth has shallower margins than the other reservoirs – consequently it is more attractive to surface feeding waterfowl and to waders. It was formerly much favoured in winter by Whooper Swan, which still occur but in smaller numbers. Pochard, Tufted Duck and Coot may be present in large numbers, and Wigeon may graze with Canada Goose on neighbouring pastures. Cormorant often visit outside the breeding season. Small flocks of Shoveler sometimes gather in autumn. Uncommon visitors have included Great Northern Diver and Black-necked Grebe.

A flock of Lapwing often wanders around the shoreline from autumn to spring. Often they are joined by a few passage waders. Dunlin and Redshank are typical, but other species occur each year, and rarities have included Pectoral Sandpiper and Temminck's Stint. Snipe are common in the surrounding marsh, where they are joined by a few, elusive Jack Snipe.

Heron may generally be seen fishing in areas unoccupied by human anglers.

Access

Rumworth may be viewed from Beaumont Road (A58) to the east, where a short, dead-end public footpath gives views over the southern end (SD 680077). Continue westward and turn right at the lights into Junction Road for further viewing over the wall. On the south side take the cobbled Lock Lane between Chew Moor and Hunger Hill, walk up the private road to Tempest Court and follow a footpath marked by stiles to the right. This passes close to the southern edge of the reservoir at SD 676076.

43K Doffcocker

OS ref: SD 684103

Bordered on one side by a housing estate, Doffcocker Lodge is nevertheless extensively fringed by tall ruderal and marsh vegetation. It holds breeding Great Crested Grebe and possibly Ruddy Duck, with Reed Bunting and Sedge and other warblers in surrounding scrub. In winter it is visited by large numbers of waterfowl in better variety, with Snipe and Jack Snipe in the marsh.

Access

A causeway runs south from the A58 dual carriageway at SD 682104. Parking is easier, however on the minor road through the housing estate on the south side. This road starts from opposite the B6402 junction on the A58 (SD 681101).

Calendar

All year: Red Grouse and Short-eared Owl on the moors; Kingfisher, Dipper and Grey Wagtail along watercourses; woodpeckers and other common woodland species. (Nuthatch are scarce here.)

December/February Raptors on the moors, where Snow Bunting are a slim possibility; Whooper Swan, Goosander and other wildfowl on the reservoirs. Lower Rivington gull roost may contain an Iceland or Glaucous Gull.

March/May: Summer visitors include Wheatear and Twite from late March with Whinchat, Pied Flycatcher, Wood Warbler and Redstart a month later. Small passage of waders by reservoirs includes moorland breeders moving onto breeding areas.

June/July: Common Sandpiper and perhaps Little Ringed Plover by reservoirs. Generally a rather quiet time.

August/November: Wildfowl return; wader passage at Rumworth and elsewhere; large thrush flocks in Wayoh-Jumbles area.

Habitat

The Wigan flashes resemble Pennington Flash (Site 45) in that they are the result of coal-mining. Indeed their proximity to Pennington ensures a degree of interchange by birds between the two sites. A number of wetland habitats near the Leeds and Liverpool Canal further links the major flashes. A rubbish tip attracts gulls and corvids. Extensive scrub of sallow and other species supports a range of breeding finches and warblers, the latter also favoured by reed-bed and tall marsh vegetation.

Species

The Wigan flashes attract a range of birds similar to those at Pennington, although since they lack the protective management offered at the latter site, numbers of birds tend to be smaller. Breeding waterfowl include Little and Great Crested Grebes, and Tufted and Ruddy Ducks. Odd birds of other species, such as Teal, Shoveler or Pochard may linger into spring. Little Ringed Plover breed in the area, and Snipe and Redshank may do so. Common Sandpiper are present with such regularity on spring passage that they too are suspected of breeding intent. A single pair of Common Tern has bred in several years, as also have Black-headed Gull.

Scrubland species are better represented, with a good variety of finches, Reed Bunting and Yellowhammer, and warblers include Reed, Sedge, Lesser Whitethroat and Grasshopper breeding locally. Yellow Wagtail and Meadow Pipit also nest, the latter catering for young Cuckoo. Resident Kingfisher are a further attraction, and long-eared Owl have been seen in winter.

Waders pass through in small numbers, as also do terns in spring and autumn. Outside the breeding season, large numbers of wildfowl are generally present. Water Rail frequent marshy areas throughout the winter, and have been known to stay in summer and breed.

The rubbish tip to the south of Pearson's Flash attracts large numbers of gulls, including occasional Glaucous or Iceland.

Access

From Wigan centre take the A49 Warrington road. A mile (1.3 km) after passing under the railway bridge turn left onto the B5238, and after a further mile, park below the conspicuous tower of St James with St Thomas church. Poolstock (SD 578046). Cross the main road and walk south along the canal towpath. The canal is traversed by bridges and lock gates, with viewing of the various flashes to either side. Paths may be very muddy.

45 PENNINGTON FLASH

Habitat

Pennington Flash lies one mile to the south-west of Leigh (SD 638990).
Since 1981 its 170 acres (68 hectares) of water have been incorporated
into a Country Park of more than 1000 acres (400 hectares). The flash
owes its origin to subsidence following coal-mining at the adjacent
Bickershaw colliery which dominates the view to the north. Resulting
shallow marshes attract wildfowl, waders and other wetland species,
whose numbers have increased considerably since wardening reduced
shooting over the flashes to a minimum. Former spoil tips from the mine
have been landscaped and planted with trees which are beginning to
attract woodland species.

The Country Park is heavily used by anglers and a sailing club, as well
as the general public, but areas of shallow water and reedbeds are
reserved for wildlife and overlooked by hides.

Species

Waterfowl dominate the winter scene. Up to thirty Little Grebe and at
times dozens of Cormorant feed on fish, the latter often perching on
stumps below Sorrowcow Farm. Great Crested Grebe are present in
small numbers. Three species of diver and Red-necked, Black-necked
and Slavonian Grebes have been known to visit, especially in severe
weather. Bittern may lurk unseen in reedbeds and flooded areas, where
Water Rail are more conspicuous on frosty days. Two or three pairs of

126

Kingfisher are resident and may be seen on most days of the year.

Several hundred Mallard form the bulk of the dabbling ducks, with up to 200 or more Teal, small numbers of Pintail, Wigeon and Gadwall, with Shoveler in mild winters. Two hundred or so Pochard are normally present, with 600 or more in some winters. They are accompanied by lesser numbers of Tufted Duck, and often a few round-headed Scaup. Goldeneye increase to a maximum in late winter or early spring. Ruddy Duck are becoming more frequent. Scarcer diving ducks, such as Long-tailed Duck, Smew, Merganser and Goosander visit infrequently. Coot flocks vary in size from one winter to the next: in 1984 nearly 1,000 were present. Pennington is not a noted goose haunt. Parties of Canada Goose visit erratically, and skeins of Pinkfooted Goose pass overhead from time to time.

Large plover flocks frequent fields by the A580 to the south, where there may be hundreds of Golden Plover and several thousand Lapwing. Some of these visit the park, perhaps bringing an accompanying Redshank or other wader. A hundred or more Snipe are often present in dam areas, with a sprinkling of Jack Snipe around Pengy's Pond, where they generally crouch unseen.

There is a sizeable gull roost, often containing 4–5,000 Black-headed, and 1–2,000 Herring Gulls in late December, with smaller numbers of other common species. Determined scanning of these flocks may reveal a Glaucous or Iceland Gull.

Such species as the Great Spotted Woodpecker, Marsh and Coal Tit, and Nuthatch remain uncommon winter visitors due to the absence of suitable habitat, although this situation is changing as planted wood-lands mature. Any black-capped tit seen is almost certain to be one of the resident Willow Tit. Long-tailed Tit and Chaffinch are two other species just returning to the area: air pollution obliterated the mosses from which they build their nests, but industrial decline has reversed this trend. Siskin and Goldfinch are increasing as winter residents as planted alder begin to fruit.

Short-eared Owl roost within the park in some winters. As many as five have been noted hunting for voles. Merlin dash through on occasion. An even smaller predator, the Great Grey Shrike, has been recorded in several winters. Some dozens of Corn Bunting fly in towards dusk during the winter months, settling in bushes before dropping into patches of long grass to roost.

Early spring sees the departure of winter visitors and the return of breeding species. Great Crested Grebe build up to a peak of 40–50 birds, many of these displaying in front of the hides. In March, flocks of winter thrushes head north-east and parties of Bewick's Swan stop off briefly. Meadow Pipit return from mid-March, often with fresh-plumaged Pied Wagtail and Reed Bunting. Summer visitors drift in from the end of March, with more pronounced passage from mid-April. Hirundines swirl over the water, and parties of wagtails scurry over short turf at the water's edge. Both Yellow and White Wagtails reach a peak towards the end of April. Blue-headed Wagtail or a pink-breasted Water Pipit may add to the spectacle, with a few Common Sandpiper.

The shingle should always be checked for waders. At this season these include species prospecting for possible nest sites, such as Oystercatcher, Ringed and Little Ringed Plover, and such long distance migrants as arctic Ringed Plover, Sanderling and Turnstone. A few Dunlin are often present, and there is the possibility of odd individuals of several other species, Rarities have included Kentish Plover, Avocet, Temminck's Stint and Red-necked Phalarope.

A small passage of terns may be evident, most like Common or perhaps Arctic Tern, although Black Tern may well appear following easterly winds. White-winged Black Tern have appeared twice. Other scarce migrants have included Osprey on several occasions, Alpine Swift and Great Reed Warbler – the rewards of persistent watching.

By now breeding waterfowl have settled into their territories. Nesting ducks may include Gadwall, Pochard and Ruddy, as well as the more usual Mallard and Tufted. Good numbers of Little and Great Crested Grebes breed. Twenty to thirty heron feed by the flash in spring and summer. Common Scoter are infrequent passage migrants at this time. Little Ringed Plover breed within the park, and Ringed Plover and Redshank have done so. Common Tern have shown signs of breeding intent. Nesting passerines include Meadow Pipit, Sedge and Reed Warbler, Lesser and Common Whitethroats, and a few Yellow Wagtail. Reed Bunting and Linnet are common, with small numbers of Tree Sparrow, Goldfinch, Yellowhammer and Redpoll. Days with bad weather in June or July may see 1,000 or more Swift feeding over the flash, accompanied by fewer House Martin.

By August, Goldfinch flock to feed on thistle seed, and Mistle Thrush to strip berries from rowans. In late summer, Kestrel and their fledged young hover over rougher areas, returning Water Rail may be heard squealing from cover, and Lapwing flocks begin to increase.

Autumn wader passage is light since the shingle is then often occupied by anglers, although Greenshank are more likely to appear than in spring. Terns are less numerous at this season. A feature of autumn passage is the large gathering of hirundines. In some years up to 5,000 or 10,000 Sand Martins may roost in the reed-beds. There may also be several thousand Swallow at the height of passage in September, and up to 200 Yellow Wagtail may join the roost. There is a moderate diurnal passage of wagtails and pipits, and the occasional Whinchat, Redstart or perhaps Tree Pipit may settle in the plantations. In late autumn, Fieldfare, Redwing and Blackbird gather in the hedges to the south of the flash, with fewer grey, continental Song Thrush. Parties of migrant Chaffinch and Brambling may alight to join local finches in weedy arable fields. By this season the resident Partridge and Tawny Owl begin to call at dusk, advertising their territories.

Timing

Summer visits in fine weather are likely to be the least rewarding due to the popularity of the Country Park with day-trippers. During this season, early morning visits are advisable. At passage times, showery weather may cause migrants to drop in. Dusk visits are advisable in autumn to view hirundine roosts, which may attract predators. Storm-driven seabirds are a possibility following gales. Frosty weather may drive Water Rail from cover.

Access

The entrance to the country park lies on the A572 St Helens Road (SJ 646986). Park near the information centre, and explore the nature reserve area to the north from obvious footpaths. Paths along the south side of the flash are recommended in the autumn, and at the west end in winter.

Calendar

All year: Partridge, Kingfisher, Willow Tit.

December/February: good variety of waterfowl including Gadwall, Pochard, Tufted Duck, Goldeneye and Ruddy Duck. Gull roost may include 'white-winged' birds. Short-eared Owl in some years.

March/May: passage of pipits, wagtails and Reed Bunting in March/April; small wader passage continuing into June; breeding warblers arrive.

June/July: Swifts congregate in wet weather; breeding waterfowl have young.

August/November: rather quiet during August, but Swallow roost may be spectacular in September. Winter visitors arrive from October.

Reference

Wilson, J. D. (1985) *Birds and Birdwatching at Pennington Flash*, Pennington Flash Joint Committee.

46 ELTON RESERVOIR, BURY OS Map 109
SD 788094

Habitat
Elton Reservoir has gently shelving muddy and grassy banks on its north-western side, and a stone-lined eastern retaining bank. It is surrounded by pastureland with tall hedgerows. The reservoir is much disturbed by anglers, dog walkers and a sailing club, so is primarily a haunt of passage birds rather than long term residents.

Species
Passage at Elton is similar to movements at other inland waters in south Lancashire and Cheshire. Pipits and wagtails move through in April. There is a variable spring passage of terns and waders, and a more reliable autumn movement of these birds. Little, Sandwich and Black Terns have each been recorded on a number of occasions. There is a light passage of waders. Scarcer species have included Pectoral and several Wood Sandpiper.

Few waterfowl breed, other than Little and Great Crested Grebes and Mallard. However, Snipe, Redshank and Yellow Wagtail nest in damp fields nearby.

Most common duck species occur from time to time between autumn and spring, but watersports prevent any large flocks from gathering. Storm-blown seabirds have included Fulmar and Velvet Scoter, with several records of Red-breasted Merganser.

Timing
Elton is an ideal local patch, requiring persistent coverage, rather than a place for a one-off visit. Early morning visits are likely to be more rewarding than later in the day when the shoreline is increasingly disturbed.

Access
Various access points are available, the most straightforward being down Kitchener Street, to the east off the A58, signposted to the reservoir and Florence Nightingale Hospital. A track leads past the hospital to a car park at the north end of the reservoir. Footpaths lead around almost the entire shoreline, only skirting around the sailing club's compound.

The flood plain of the River Mersey between Stockport and the Manchester Ship Canal contains a variety of habitats – mature woodland and agricultural land, golf courses and playing fields, working and reclaimed tips and sewage works, 'natural' and canalised river. Many sites are managed for wildlife and recreation by the Mersey Valley Warden Service, and over 190 species have been recorded in the last decade, including such rarities as Caspian Tern, Crane and Black-throated Thrush. Some of the best sites for birdwatching are described below.

Timing

Convenience of access from the city and suburbs means that the Mersey Valley (and others in the network of Greater Manchester river valley access schemes) forms an excellent 'local patch' that will repay regular coverage.

Sale Water Park is worth a visit at any time of year, although hot summer weather produces more people and fewer birds. Chorlton Water Park is arguably at its best for waterfowl in winter.

47A CHORLTON WATER PARK

OS ref: SJ 820919

The attractively landscaped former borrow pit, from which material was taken for building the adjacent motorway, forms the centrepiece of the park. Two islands and several compounds containing marginal vegetation attract a range of species. In winter the lake is closed to boats and regularly attracts large numbers of wildfowl.

The Water Park also includes many acres of rough grassland and young tree plantations popular with passerines.

In winter there may be 1,000 or more Pochard and 200 or so Tufted Ducks on the lake, with a few Goldeneye and Great Crested and Little

Pochard

Grebes. Scarcer diving duck appear in with the Pochard from time to time. Scaup appear each winter in very small numbers, and Red-crested Pochard, Ring-necked and Ferruginous Ducks have occurred. Do not be misled by odd hybrids!

Parties of terns appear on both spring and autumn passage.

Access

Chorlton Water Park can be visited by turning off Barlow Moor Road (A5145) opposite Southern Cemetery (SJ 825925) into Maitland Avenue and proceeding to the car park at the south end.

Alternatively the site may be reached from Sale Water Park by walking up Rifle Road to Jackson's Bridge (SJ 810926), then turning right and following obvious paths beside the river for about a mile.

47B SALE WATER PARK AND BROAD EES DOLE NATURE RESERVE

OS ref: SJ 800930

Another large gravel pit dominates Sale Water Park. Its popularity for water sports and its depth limit its value for wildlife. Around the park are several mature hedgerows and substantial areas of rough grassland.

Lying between the lake and the River Mersey is Broad Ees Dole Nature Reserve, which has been developed by the Mersey Valley Warden Service since 1985. A hide overlooks a lagoon area popular with waders, a wet marsh and willow and alder scrub. The site is closed to the public, but excellent views can be obtained from the perimeter.

In winter Cormorant fly in from Rostherne to fish, and may perch on the electricity pylons after feeding. Great Crested Grebe are generally present. Up to 70 Teal join the Mallard on the reserve where over 100 Snipe probe for food. Jack Snipe often reach double figures, and with luck can be watched feeding, using their strange, bobbing, 'sewing machine' action. Up to a dozen Water Pipit also winter here, assuming fine plumage towards spring.

Little Ringed Plover and Common Sandpiper appear on spring pass-age, with a chance of other waders, although the variety is better in the autumn. Terns pass through at both seasons.

Whitethroat, Redpoll and other passerines breed in the scrubby areas. Herons roost by day on the Broad Ees Dole scrape.

Access

Sale Water Park lies between Junctions 7 and 8 of the M63. From Junction 8 follow Rifle Road to the north-east, turning very shortly into the drive to the park.

47C CHORLTON EES NATURE RESERVE

OS ref: SJ 811928

Occupying the site of a former sewage works, Chorlton Ees is a fine example of reclamation for wildlife. Young woodland, tall reedy grass-land and several ponds provide a range of habitats, in turn attracting a wide variety of species. A network of footpaths makes for easy exploration.

The reserve holds a range of commoner woodland species. Less common migrants such as Wood Warbler, Pied Flycatcher, Redstart and Whinchat pass through. Short-eared Owl and Great Grey Shrike have been recorded in winter.

Access

Cross the Mersey from Sale Water Park via Jackson's Bridge (SJ 810926) and turn left. The Ees lie directly across the river from the Water Park.

From the north side, turn south off the A5145 in Chorlton-cum-Hardy, onto Barlow Moor Road, into Beech Road then almost immediately into Reynard Road. This becomes Claude Road and, shortly after, Brookburn Road. There are car parks on Brookburn Road and along the cobbled road to the west.

47D CARRINGTON MOSS

OS ref: SJ 743916

Carrington Moss is an extensive area of arable land lying south of the Mersey. It is criss-crossed by a network of footpaths, many alongside mature hedgerows, and there are several areas of mature woodland, mostly closed reserves managed by the Cheshire Conservation Trust. Views can be obtained of the large wetland and scrub area within the Shell UK complex, an important site for wildfowl.

Willow Tit nest in the birchwoods, and there is a range of common farmland species. Wheatear passage can be large, with 50 or more present at times.

Access

From the A56 through Sale, take Carrington Lane (A6144) north-westwards from Ashton upon Mersey. At the crossroads with Flixton Road (B5158) turn left into Isherwood Road (SJ 745930). This deteriorates into the cinder track of Ackers Lane. Park here and follow footpaths to the right around the edge of the petrochemical compound.

47E FLETCHER MOSS GARDENS, STENNER WOODS AND MILLGATE FIELDS

OS ref: SJ 847903

These adjacent sites offer a variety of habitats within a surprisingly small area. Fletcher Moss Gardens provide excellent formal parkland, while Stenner Woods is an area of mature wet woodland dominated by willows and oaks. Millgate Fields includes a large hay meadow and pasture land popular with larks and Lapwings. In 1971 only two species of lichens were found growing on the trees here. Now there are at least 25 – a measure of both air pollution abatement and general wildlife habitat improvement.

Access

Via Millgate Lane off the A5145 Wilmslow Road in Disbury.

CHESHIRE AND WIRRAL

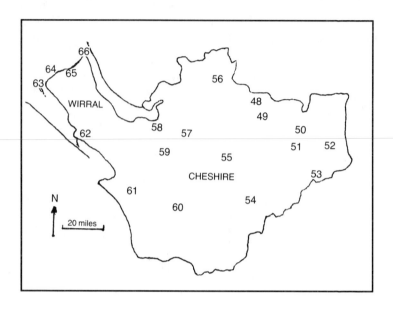

48 Rostherne Mere
49 Tatton Park and Knutsford Moor
50 Alderley Woods
51 Chelford Area Sand Quarries
52 Macclesfield Forest, Langley Resrs and Teggs Nose Country Park
53 River Dane Valley
54 Sandbach Flashes
55 Northwich Area
56 Woolston Eyes
57 Lower Weaver Valley
58 Frodsham Marsh and the Weaver Bend
59 Delamere Forest
60 Beeston Castle and Peckforton Hills
61 Eccleston and the Dee at Eaton
62 Gayton Sands and the Inner Dee Marshes
63 Hilbre Islands and the Dee Mouth
64 Red Rocks, Hoylake
65 North Wirral Shore
66 New Brighton

The Cheshire Plain is dotted with dairy farms and oak-lined hedge-rows. Many flooded marl-pits survive, but many more have been lost. The principal ornithological sites on the plain are the meres, many of them of glacial origin, and the flashes – shallow lakes created by the pumping of brine from underground salt-fields. Salt extraction has also provided a number of sludge-beds. These are now attractive to waders, although access is often difficult.

Dredging of the Manchester Ship Canal and the Weaver Navigation Canal has given rise to large, wet sludge-beds of great ornithological value. A few ancient woodlands are accessible to birdwatchers, the oak woods at Peckforton are particularly rewarding. Mature trees are com-mon in the parks of the stately homes which are particularly numerous in the north-east of Cheshire, although the Eaton Estate in the west is well wooded.

Little moorland survives on the eastern hills, and its characteristic birds are vulnerable to disturbance. On the plain, heathland has all but disappeared. Fragments survive around certain of the sand quarries (good bird habitats in their own right), especially in the Delamere area where the former heaths amd broad-leaved woods have been largely replaced by conifers. Other heaths survive on sandstone outcrops, for example at Bickerton and on the Wirral. The Wirral coastline is essen-tially a continuation of the vast tract of sand- and mudflats which extend down almost without interruption from Morecambe Bay. The peninsula's sand-dunes have been tamed almost completely.

48 ROSTHERNE MERE

Habitat

Rostherne Mere lies in a deep, natural hollow, the mere itself extends to some 120 acres (48 hectares) with a maximum depth of 100ft (30 metres). The banks shelve steeply for the most part and, while much of the mere is fringed by narrow reedbeds, there is little submerged vegetation and few waterfowl breed. A few muddy cattle drinks and sandy spits provide limited habitat for passing waders.

Extensive mixed woodlands run down to the mere edge for more than half of its circumference. Elsewhere it is bordered by pastureland. The mere, woods and pastures together comprise the Rostherne Mere National Nature Reserve. The mere is known mainly as a winter haunt of wildfowl which can be watched in relative comfort from the A.W. Boyd Memorial Observatory.

Species

From October to March hundreds of ducks line the edges of the mere, roosting amongst the reedbeds or on overhanging branches. Mallard predominate in autumn, but may be outnumbered by several hundred Teal in winter, Pintail are erratic visitors, Wigeon graze the pastures along with Coot and Canada Goose. Two or three hundred of these feral geese may be present, and the flock should always be checked for oddities. The proliferation of wildfowl collections has led to an increase in sightings of escaped birds and it is now not unusual to find one or two Barnacle Goose with the Canada. Snow, Lesser White-fronted and Bar-headed Geese have turned up from time to time, and hybrid birds of questionable parentage also occur. A few Shoveler generally remain through the winter although this species is better known as an autumn passage migrant. In the last few years flocks of 50 or more Gadwall have been present in late autumn.

Pochard form the bulk of the diving duck population. In recent winters a large flock of more than a thousand birds has based itself on the Mersey valley, spending part of its time at Rostherne. Several dozen Tufted Duck generally mingle with the Pochard and a few of the larger, heavier-billed Scaup arrive on occasion. A drake Ferruginous Duck returned annually from 1980 to 1986. In mid-winter 20 or more Goldeneye spread out across the back of the mere to feed, and for some years now Rostherne has been as good a place as any in Cheshire to see Smew – one or two red-headed females often rest under Gale Bog in the north-western corner of the mere. The introduced Ruddy Duck is increasing here as elsewhere in the region. Scarcer waterfowl, such as Goosander and the rarer grebes, turn up from time to time, and there have been records of Green-winged Teal and American Wigeon.

Severe weather concentrates wildfowl on the mere. Due to its depth Rostherne hardly ever freezes completely and remains open long after other meres and flashes have frozen, in mid-February 1979, when the Baltic Sea froze over, 1,350 Pochards and 700 Tufted Duck gathered on the mere. A similar occurrence in February 1986 brought still larger numbers: 2,050 Pochard and 1,030 Tufted Duck. Under such conditions

Cormorants

137

the ducks are crowded into a small pool of open water and the smaller birds, such as weakened Teal and Ruddy Duck, fall victim to marauding Great Black-backed Gull.

Great Crested Grebe reach a peak in late summer and a handful remains on the mere during the winter, when the odd Dabchick may be seen. Bewick's Swan visit occasionally and Whooper Swan more rarely. A Bittern is reported in most winters, but even when present this species is highly adept at concealing itself in the reeds. A particular feature of Rostherne is the roost of Cormorant, occupied from September to April, in poplars along the edge of Harpers Bank Wood. These birds, which exceeded 200 in the 1989–90 winter, fly out by day to feed in rivers, meres and flashes throughout eastern Cheshire and parts of southern Lancashire. From mid-afternoon onwards, ones and twos, or even lines of Cormorant come gliding back into the Rostherne hollow, and towards dusk take up their positions in the trees. During March and April many adults assume the distinctive white-necked appearance of the tree-nesting continental race.

The elevated position of the Observatory makes it ideally situated for watching diurnal cold weather movements. With the onset of severe frosts Lapwings may be seen flying west in V-formation, sometimes being overtaken by faster, pointed-winged Golden Plover. Skylark and thrushes also move south or westwards. At any time during the winter, but especially after frost and snow, skeins of Pink-footed Goose pass over the west Manchester suburbs to the north of the mere, either heading eastwards from the south Lancashire mosslands to The Wash, or north-westwards on the return journey. Only rarely do wild geese alight on the reserve.

Towards dusk in winter the number of birds on and around the mere increases rapidly. Plump, grey Woodpigeon line the tree-tops in enormous numbers when the acorn crop is good locally. Rook and Jackdaw congregate in smaller, though not inconsiderable numbers and Carrion Crow gather in dozens. Separation of the various corvids is not easy in fading light.

Up to 10,000 Black-headed Gull roost on the mere, with perhaps a few hundred of the larger gull species. Gull enthusiasts find a few 'white-winged' Iceland or Glaucous Gulls each winter, but less often than when Lindow Moss tip, near Wilmslow, drew much larger numbers of gulls to the roost. Iceland Gull sometimes roost with the more or less distinct flock of smaller Black-headed and Common Gulls. Common Gull may reach a thousand or two between January and March. Kittiwake are infrequent visitors after storms at sea.

From late summer to early winter thousands of Starling wheel over the mere at dusk before roosting in the reed-beds. In recent years these have often been harassed in spectacular fashion by a Peregrine or two, and Sparrowhawk are even more likely to appear, sometimes becoming entrapped in the swirling flocks.

Woodland birds move through the alder trees at the mere's edge giving views of Siskin, Goldfinch, woodpeckers and the occasional Marsh Tit. Nuthatch, Long-tailed and Coal Tit, and Jay will take food from a bird-table just below the Observatory.

The winter flocks of wildfowl disperse during March and the reserve then becomes relatively quiet for the summer months. Stock Dove displaying in front of the Observatory are one of the first signs of spring, and Lesser Spotted Woodpecker call and drum from mereside alders,

Curlews visit the pastures by day and at dusk Woodcock rode around the woodlands.

Passage in April and May brings a few Common Sandpiper and other waders to the shoreline. Far more conspicuous are the swirling flocks of hirundines and Swifts which feed over the mere. Parties of terns, Common, Arctic or Black, may visit at this time.

Breeding species include Kestrel, Sparrowhawk and Little Owl, with such woodland species as Blackcap, Nuthatch and Spotted Flycatcher. Grey Wagtail may be present along the inlet stream and a Kingfisher may perch on posts by the old boathouse. A well-studied population of Reed Warbler breeds in the reedbeds. Sedge Warbler are now breeding again after an absence of many years, and Cuckoo have begun to parasitise the Reed Warbler. Nesting waterfowl include Great Crested Grebe, and sometimes Tufted and Ruddy Ducks. The odd non-breeding Cormorant, Wigeon or Shoveler may spend the summer on the mere, and scores of feral Grey Lag Goose arrive in early June to moult with the Canada Goose.

Late summer and early autumn may see a build-up of Great Crested Grebe, resting in a flock out on the open water. Parties of drake Pochard may arrive in July from breeding waters, and Tufted Duck may be more numerous than at any other season (except for severe winter weather). Shoveler numbers reach a peak in September or October. A few terns and waders may pass through, and autumn gales may blow a shearwater or other seabird inland.

Timing

For general viewing of wildfowl a visit at any time of day will do. During the winter months however afternoon and dusk visits are recommended for roosting birds. Persistent frosts concentrate wildfowl, driven off other waters. Westerly or north-westerly gales at any time of year may blow in seabirds.

Access

Leave the M56 at Junction 7, turning south onto the A556(T). After a mile take the second turning on the left, continue along this winding road for three quarters of a mile, past the church, and park on the left opposite a T-junction, outside the warden's house, 'Rowans' (SJ 743837). Otherwise follow signs for the main, north entrance to Tatton Park (SJ 748827), and take the minor road northwards directly opposite the park gate.

Access to the mere is prohibited. Permits for the Observatory are readily available however, costing £3 per person, £5 for a family and £1 for OAPs. They are valid from 1 January to 31 December, and are available from D.A. Clarke, 1 Hart Avenue, Sale, Cheshire on submission of a stamped, addressed envelope. Cheques or postal orders should be made payable to the Manchester Ornithological Society. Directions from Rostherne village to the Observatory are given on the back of the permit. Limited viewing of the mere is possible from the churchyard.

Escorted tours are available for groups by arrangement with the Warden, NCC, 'Rowans', Rostherne, Knutsford, Cheshire, WA16 6RY.

Calendar

All year: Great Crested Grebe, Cormorant (non-breeding), Canada Goose, Tufted Duck, Sparrowhawk, Kestrel, Stock Dove, Little Owl, all three woodpeckers, Nuthatch, Jay.

December/February: Cormorant, Wigeon, Teal, Pintail, Pochard, Tufted Duck, Goldeneye, Ruddy Duck, perhaps Gadwall and Smew, other wildfowl. Golden Plover and Lapwing overhead in frosty weather. Gull roost may include Glaucous and Iceland Gulls. Woodpigeon and crows roosting. Siskin below the Observatory.

March/May: Gull roost vacated and wildfowl disperse. Curlew and Common Sandpiper, possibly other waders; Woodcock roding, Swift, hirundines and occasional terns over the mere.

June/July: Non-breeding waterfowl may include Wigeon, Shoveler and Cormorant. Few wildfowl breed but Greylag Goose join the Canada Goose in June for the moult, and Pochard and Tufted Duck increase in July. Reed Warbler numerous in reedbeds.

August/November: Great Crested Grebe, Shoveler and Tufted Duck at their most numerous. Occasional terns or waders.

49 TATTON PARK AND KNUTSFORD MOOR

OS Map 109/118
SJ

Habitat

Tatton Park, designed by Humphrey Repton, consists of open grassland with scattered clumps of trees and some larger mixed woods of oak, chestnut, beech and pine. Grazing by sheep, cattle and both Red and Fallow Deer prevents the development of a scrub layer in all but a few, fenced woods.

The smaller of the two meres, Melchett Mere, has boggy areas of rushes along its banks. It acts as a refuge for wildfowl when the main mere is disturbed (as it is on most days of the year) by boats and windsurfers.

141

Tatton Mere itself, dammed by the monks of Mobberley Priory in medieval times, has little marginal vegetation except at the southern end where carr woodland has developed on either side. An extensive reedbed separates the mere from Knutsford Moor pool, which lies outside the park. The mere is often heavily disturbed by water sports.

At the north-east corner of the park is a mill pool, backed by a large bed of sedges. The fast-flowing brook downstream from the mill attracts riparian species.

Species

Wildlife has received low priority in the management of the park and wildfowl numbers on the meres have declined steadily over the years, but the plentiful mature timber makes Tatton outstanding for characteristic parkland birds. All three woodpeckers breed regularly, the ground-feeding Green Woodpecker favouring the combination of permanent pasture and old trees. Nuthatch and Treecreeper are abundant, and Jackdaw, Stock Dove and Little Owl nest in holes in trees. Two pairs of Mandarin bred in 1990. Buzzards are occasionally seen and have attempted to nest.

Dog Wood, along the eastern side of Tatton Mere, has held both black-capped tit species. Marsh Tit, with their abrupt 'Pichuu' calls, favour the drier mature woodland with its oaks and chestnuts, while the 'big-headed' Willow Tit prefer the damper carr where they can excavate their nest-holes in soft stumps of alder and birch. Goldcrest nest in the scattered pines. Blackcap sing from the canopy over rhododendrons, and a few Garden Warbler may answer back from scrubbier areas. Wood Warbler are present in some springs and have bred.

An area of rough grassland and bramble scrub, just outside the park, borders Dog Wood to the south. Whitethroat dance above the scrub uttering their scratchy song before plummeting back into cover. Several pairs of Garden Warbler breed and Willow Warbler sing from the birches. There is just a chance of hearing the reeling of a Grasshopper Warbler on a spring evening.

On the fringe of the reedbed a pair or two of Sedge Warbler continue to nest, although this species is withdrawing from eastern Cheshire. Several pairs of Reed Warbler nest in the phragmites, and probably a pair or two of Water Rail, whose weird wailing and trilling 'song' may be heard as the light fades.

Curlew nest in the remoter areas of parkland, arriving in March as a vociferous flock, then splitting up as pairs establish territories. Lapwing tumble in wild display flights over rushy patches and a pair or two of Snipe may still nest, although the more important of their haunts have been drained. Woodcock rode along the northern edge of the park.

The reedy southern end of Tatton Mere was the most important site in Cheshire for nesting Tufted Duck. In 1979 29 broods were seen totalling 146 young, but opening up of the woodland has caused a deterioration, and few if any now nest. Shoveler are seen around the reedbed in most springs, but it is many years since they have been known to nest. Ruddy and Tufted Ducks also nest on the mill-pool where Grey Wagtail breed and Kingfisher are often seen fishing.

Other breeding waterfowl include Little and Great Crested Grebes. This may be the only place where Great Cresteds have nested in a blackcurrant bush, for the shrub grows wild here and a pair once built their nest amongst emergent stems at the water's edge. Canada Goose nest along the rushy fringes of the meres and even beneath trees up to 100 yards (100m) from the water. In several years escaped Barnacle Goose have paired with Canada Goose here and twice eggs have been laid, although to date no hybrid goslings have been hatched. In September, after the moult most of the Canada Goose in eastern Cheshire tend to gather here. Up to 1,500 may be present, with the customary sprinkling of feral Barnacles, Greylags and cross-breeds.

Winter wildfowl include Teal, Pochard and Goldeneye, with a chance of Smew, although this eastern species has occurred infrequently of late. Tufted Duck are always present. Cormorant fly in from Rostherne, and later haul themselves out on the banks of Melchett Mere to digest their scaly meals. As spring approaches the Goldeneye display regularly and their numbers increase as passage to the north east commences. Scarcer waterfowl are seen in most winters, perhaps a diver or rare grebe, but in the case of exotic ducks, birdwatchers should beware of the existence of a small wildfowl collection in the hall gardens. Recent records of Red-crested Pochard, Wood Duck and others are believed to refer to birds from this source.

Snipe and Jack Snipe winter in the treacherous marshes around Melchett Mere where elusive Water Rail are often present. Rail are more easily seen around the Moor reedbed, even from the railings beside the playing field in the centre of Knutsford where a motley selection of overfed ducks waits for junk food. Bearded Tit have occurred here.

In autumn the reedbed holds roosts of Pied Wagtail and Swallow, and in winter Redwing and Blackbird roost in birch scrub and rhododendrons nearby. A roost of Corn Bunting has dwindled in recent years as the species declines in the surrounding area. Also in winter Siskin and Redpoll feed in mereside alder and birch trees. Greenfinch and Chaffinch gather to stubble fields around the park, and Brambling often appear either there or under beeches.

March brings the first passerine migrants to the mereside when parties of Meadow Pipit, Pied Wagtail and Reed Bunting comb the short turf, and the odd Wheatear flits along the shoreline. During showery weather in April the flocks are joined by White and Yellow Wagtails and perhaps a Water or Rock Pipit. Common Sandpiper rise from the water's edge and fly away low across the mere. The first Sand Martin are seen in late March, to be joined by Swallow and then House Martin during April, and Swift by the end of that month.

Terns are recorded annually on either passage, with perhaps more chance of a young Little Gull in the autumn. Migrant parties of hirundines again appear over the meres in September and October, when their numbers may change markedly from hour to hour as flocks arrive in dribs and drabs from the north, feed for a while as they reassemble, then depart *en masse* to the south.

Timing

The park is open from 10am until dusk daily except for Christmas Day. Sunny weekends, Bank Holidays and special events days should be avoided. Morning visits are recommended as disturbance increases during the day and waterfowl may then leave the park and fly to Rostherne. Evening visits in spring can be rewarding. Showery weather at passage times produces most migrants, particularly when the wind is from a southerly quarter in spring.

Access

Three entrances allow access to Tatton, and the park is well signposted on all approach roads to Knutsford, but most birdwatchers enter through Dog Lodge.

Take the B5085 from the A537 out of Knutsford, pass a brick church, then pull into a loop behind a grass verge on the left and park (SD 754786). Continue walking in the same direction and turn left into the 'ducks' housing estate. Take the first left, cross the railway bridge, and the stile into the park will then be obvious. Knutsford Moor and scrub areas are visible to the left.

Otherwise park in the car park below the lower shopping street in Knutsford itself, from where the Moor with its hungry ducks can be seen. Cross the Moor, keeping the railings on the left, then follow a rough track to the left through the scrub. This track eventually leads through to Dog Wood.

On a short visit it is customary to walk up the east side of the mere inspecting the wildfowl and any migrants, then continue to Melchett Mere which can be scanned from the south-east corner. It is then possible to complete the circuit of the mere, perhaps following an avenue of mature beeches down the west side of the park to the Knutsford gate. On evening visits however this gate may be locked, so it is advisable to retrace one's steps.

Calendar

All year: Little Grebe, Great Crested Grebe, Canada Goose, Tufted Duck, Ruddy Duck; Woodcock; Stock Dove, Little Owl, all three woodpeckers, woodland species.

December/February: Cormorant, Teal, Pochard and Goldeneye on the meres, Water Rail, Snipe and Jack Snipe in marshy ground, Brambling under beeches, Redpoll in birches and Siskin in alders. Thrushes and perhaps Corn Bunting roosting at the Moor.

March/May: Goldeney display conspicuously; Shoveler frequent the reedbeds. Mixed flocks of pipits, wagtails and Reed Bunting should be checked for Water Pipit and White Wagtail. Wheatear and Sand Martin from late March, other hirundines in April and Swifts around the end of that month. Terns may appear from late April. Wood Warbler and Redstart may sing in Dog Wood from mid-April.

June/July: Broods of Tufted and Ruddy Ducks, Canada Goose and grebes. Curlew and Snipe may have young. Reed, Sedge and Garden Warblers nesting on the Moor with Willow Warbler and Whitethroat. Blackcap and Chiffchaff in woodlands, and Tree Sparrow in the Parkland. With luck young Water Rail may be seen at the edge of the reedbed.

August/November: Hirundines sometimes plentiful; terns, perhaps Little Gull occasional over the meres. Pied Wagtail and Swallow roost on the Moor. Wildfowl increase sharply from October.

ADDITIONAL SITE:

MOBBERLEY LAKE

OS ref: SJ 784796

This disused sand quarry beside the B5085 in Mobberley is always worth a scan en route to or from Tatton by visitors from the east. The bottom is shallowly flooded, and grazed by cattle. Muddy margins attract occasional waders. In 1989 such oddities as Garganey, Wood Sandpiper, Black-tailed Godwit, Black Tern and Spoonbill were recorded, and in 1990 Hobby and Wood Sandpiper.

50 ALDERLEY WOODS

Habitat

The Edge at Alderley is an escarpment of red sandstone which contains veins of copper ore, mined from prehistoric times until early this century. Evidence of these mining activities is widespread in the form of square-sided cuttings and tunnels.

The mature, planted woodland which covers much of the edge consists principally of oak, scots pine and birch, with some chestnut and beech on the thinner soils overlying rocky outcrops, and larch. Ground flora is rather sparse with wavy hair grass, bracken and brambles dominant. An extensive network of paths and bare, eroded areas around mine entrances give the woodland an open character.

On the site of the old west mine, where a spoil tip stood into the 1960s, an area of open heathland is developing into birch scrub. Stands of gorse and sallow here are attractive to small finches and warblers.

Species

During the winter months, the woods contain large tit flocks, generally accompanied by a few Goldcrest, Nuthatch, Treecreeper and the occasional Lesser Spotted Woodpecker. The black-capped Marsh and Willow tits are scarce here. Coal and Great Tits in particular feed on beechmast, and both species may outnumber the Blue Tit in winter. When there is a good mast crop they are joined under the beeches by Chaffinch and Brambling. Parties of Redpoll feed in the birches, a food sources also used by small groups of Bullfinch. Siskin too feed in the birches, moving into larches towards spring. Redwing move into the woods to feed on holly berries so long as these are available. Green Woodpecker are seen each winter, often remaining into April. As spring approaches their ringing 'yaffle' echoes through the woods with increasing frequency, but the birds usually disappear without nesting.

Great Spotted Woodpecker nest commonly in the less accessible reaches or the woods, a scatter of chippings at the base of a birch tree sometimes betraying the presence of a nest. In June the strident calls of the young birds also give the nest away. These calls have a remarkable resemblance to the clearer 'pee-pee-pee . . .' note of the Lesser Spotted Woodpecker which also nests here in small numbers.

In spring Wood Warbler are the chief attraction at Alderley. Up to thirteen males have been estimated in recent years, although accurate counting is difficult as individual birds may use widely separated perches to deliver their song – a shivering trill sometimes replaced or preceded by a series of clear 'peu' notes on a descending scale. The first Wood Warbler arrive in late April and soon after that the breathtaking display flight may be seen, in which the bird flies rapidly through the branches, changing directon with such speed and frequency that its flight is very difficult to follow.

A pair or two of Redstart also breed, and in some years Pied Flycatcher. Like the Wood Warbler, these are species which have a restricted upland distribution in the region. Several pairs of Tree Pipit nest, finding the numerous clearings to their liking. Treecreeper and

Nuthatch are both plentiful breeders, the latter even plastering up fissures in the exposed rock faces to nest. From the middle of May Spotted Flycatcher stammer their weak song while Chiffchaff, which arrived in early April, are still singing vigorously. Coal Tit nest in mouse-holes beneath the pines where the numerous Goldcrest hang their flimsy structures. Reports of Firecrest in recent summers are unsubstantiated though not improbable.

The heath and scrubland area at the West Mine site supports a quite distinct breeding community with Whitethroat, Garden Warbler, Linnet and Redpoll. Lesser Whitethroat and Grasshopper Warbler have occurred, but Yellowhammer, once plentiful, have undergone a rapid decline both here and elsewhere in eastern Cheshire in the last few years. Adjacent pastures support a few pairs of Lapwing – now primarily a bird of arable land hereabouts in the breeding season. A Kestrel often hunts the area.

Though not noted as a Woodcock site, one or two birds do rode over the woods in spring, passing over the main car park. In May the hoarse hunger calls of young Tawny Owl may be heard.

Timing

The woods are owned by the National Trust and attract many visitors so that at times, particularly at weekend and on sunny evenings in spring and summer, they may become too crowded for the liking of many birdwatchers. Early morning visits may then be advisable. In spring birdsong is at its best at this time of day, although evening visits generally give sufficient time to locate most species.

In winter timing is less important. Birds are not then on territory, so that if the woods are heavily disturbed, the flocks move to quieter parts.

Access

The woods straddle the B5087 Alderley Edge-Macclesfield road some two kilometres out from Alderley. Several lay-bys border the road and there is a large car park, which may be locked at dusk, just to the east of the Wizard restaurant (SJ 860773).

Numerous paths criss-cross the woods to such an extent that it should be no trouble for visitors ro remain on paths to avoid contributing to the erosion which is an increasing problem. Most of the woodland species can be located in that part of the woods lying to the north of the road. To reach the heathland area, enter the southern part of the woods by a track opposite an unmade car park some 200 metres to the west of the Wizard. Follow this main track past the conifer plantations until the gorse is reached.

Calendar

All year: Good range of common woodland birds.

December/February: Large mixed tit flocks roam the woods, accompanied by other woodland species. Green Woodpecker in winter residence. Redwing strip berries off hollies; Bullfinch and Redpoll, along with Siskin, take birch seed; and Brambling may join Chaffinch under beeches.

March/May: Summer visitors arrive during April and by early May most warblers will be present. Lesser Spotted Woodpecker may be conspicuous in March or April. Woodcock rode and by May young Tawny Owl call to be fed.

June/July: Residents and summer visitors busy with nesting duties, although unmated Wood Warbler continue to sing regularly. Tree Pipit, Redstart, Spotted and perhaps Pied Flycatchers present in woods with Chiffchaff and Blackcap. Redpoll and Linnet, Whitethroat and Garden Warbler nest on the heathland.

August/November: Wood Warblers slip away unnoticed as other migrants depart.

51 CHELFORD AREA SAND QUARRIES

OS Map 118
SJ

Habitat

A cluster of recently excavated, steep-sided sand quarries to the south and east of Chelford. Landscaping has produced more gently shelving banks in places, and disused workings soon flood. These waters are managed largely for shooting. Farmwood Pool, however, is left undisturbed as a refuge for wildfowl. This reserve is largely surrounded by gorse and birch scrub with some planted trees. The shoreline, still only sparsely vegetated with clumps of rushes, varies in width from a narrow strip to wider beaches, several metres across, on which waterfowl loaf and preen. A recently constructed island is little vegetated at present.

Catchpenny Sand Quarry is bordered on one side by closely grazed pasture, but with planted willow scrub and coarse grassland around the rest of its banks. There is limited growth of marginal vegetation at the water's edge. The pool is stocked with trout for fishing.

The huge Acre Nook Sand Quarry is still being worked. Different strata of the sand have different qualities, so the quarry is worked 'dry' to allow separate extraction of the different grades, and it will be some time yet before the huge excavation is allowed to flood. Nevertheless a sizeable pool has already developed in the older part of the workings, with marsh vegetation of rushes and reedmace spreading.

149

The surrounding farmland is used for a mixture of arable crops and pasture. It is well wooded with neatly maintained hedgerows, some of which have recently been replanted. The Mosses wood consists primarily of developing birch woodland with some old oaks.

Species

The chief ornithological interest of the area lies in the waterfowl and other birds associated with the quarries, although woodland and farmland species are also well represented. The dry sandy soil of the district appears well suited to the Red-legged Partridge released in recent years as game. Many birds appear to be hybrids between the Red-legged Partridge and the closely related Chukar from the eastern Mediterranean. Large numbers of Pheasant and Mallard are also released on the Withington estate – over 1,000 of the ducks may be seen in late summer. A few Grey Partridge nest in the arable areas.

In autumn stubble fields attract gleaning Canada Goose. In winter large mixed flocks of Tree Sparrow, Greenfinch, Linnet and Chaffinch, with a variable proportion of Brambling, are attracted to the same food source. Yellowhammer are generally also present, but the few Corn Bunting that nest locally seem to move away in the autumn. In some winters thousands of Woodpigeon are attracted by a good acorn crop in the local woods, and careful scanning will reveal up to several dozen of the bluer, more compact Stock Dove, which spend a greater part of their time on stubbles. Parties of Siskin feed silently in alders by marl-pits then twitter noisily as the flock moves on to another tree. A flock of Skylark is usually present in the harvested fields by Longshoot Lane, where the Lapwing flock is occasionally joined by a few brown Golden Plover.

Wildfowl are increasing as the vegetation of the quarries develops. Given the extent of rearing operations, Mallard are likely to remain the dominant species, but up to 400 Teal have roosted in the farthest corner of Farmwood Pool during the winter months, flying out at dusk to feed in the marshy bottom of Acre Nook Sand Quarry, or to sift alder and other seeds from marl-pits throughout the area. Shoveler are few here, preferring better vegetated waters, but up to 25 or so may be present for a time in late autumn. A search of the Mallard flocks in winter may lead to the discovery of a few Pintail, the odd Gadwall, or even a feral Red-crested Pochard (which species seems to feed much more on the surface than do most diving ducks). A resident winter flock of Wigeon, which grazes the banks of Catchpenny Pool, has numbered around 100 birds of late. The practice of tipping seed into the shallows to feed the ducks prior to the start of the shooting season has led to unusual behaviour, with at times dozens of Mallard diving to retrieve this exceptional concentration of food.

Of the true diving ducks, Tufted Duck are the most often present in sizeable numbers, particularly in late summer when gatherings may exceed 200. In winter less than 50 is more normal. Ruddy Duck are present for most if not all of the year. Winter flocks at Farmwood are increasing and regularly exceed 100. Pochard are usually less numerous, although generally present from July to March. Small numbers of Goldeneye feed at Farmwood from October to April, increasing to perhaps 20 or more towards spring, and one or two 'red-headed' Smew are seen annually. Up to 10 Cormorant visit Farmwood Pool on winter days.

Farmwood Pool has already provided records of all three diver species despite its recent origin, and the Black-throated Diver has also occurred

Ruddy Duck – winter

at Catchpenny Pool. Black-necked Grebe have been seen in spring and autumn on both Farmwood and the Dairyhouse Pool. A Slavonian Grebe visited Farmwood in 1985.

The area supports a good variety of nesting waterfowl. Great Crested Grebe nest on two or three pools – well grown young once begged for food as late as 14 November – and several pairs of Little Grebe breed at Acre Nook. Canada Goose nest beside flooded quarries and by pits in fields, and the yellow goslings appear in the first or second week of May. Prospecting Shelduck may visit briefly in April.

Tufted Duck breed by all the quarries, and broods of Ruddy Duck have been seen at Dairyhouse and Withington Hall Pools, where an aberrant white-headed drake, with bubbling display audibly and visually identical to that of a normally plumaged bird, summered in two recent years.

During the mid-winter period when days are shortest, up to 10,000 gulls roost on Farmwood Pool rather than fly back to the estuaries each night. The composition of this roost is broadly similar to that at Rostherne, but now contains larger numbers of Herring (1,000 or more) and Great Black-backed (over 100) Gull. Common Gull are surprisingly scarce. Although this roost is not so thoroughly watched, Iceland Gull are found quite frequently each winter, with the occasional Glaucous Gull or storm-driven Kittiwake. The large gulls feed by day on Danes Moss tip south of Macclesfield.

The narrow sandy beaches of the flooded quarries, and especially the damp bottoms of operational pits, are attractive to waders. Little Ringed Plover and Common Sandpiper nest annually, Redshank and Oystercatcher have bred and Ringed Plover may attempt to do so. Lapwing nest in the bottom of Acre Nook as well as on neighbouring pastures. Snipe occur from autumn to spring, and a few Dunlin may visit at almost any time. Curlew often stop to bathe in the autumn when Ruff may also arrive. Other waders have included Oystercatcher, Greenshank, Little Stint, Knot and Bar-tailed Godwit.

Spring passage brings mixed flocks of pipits, wagtails and Reed Bunting to the banks of Catchpenny Pool, and large swarms of hirundines over all waters. There have been several sightings of Hobby within a few minutes' flying distance of the quarries in the last few years. Terns are recorded annually on either spring or autumn passage, with perhaps a Little Gull, and Osprey have appeared in three years.

Mosses Wood contains both Great and Lesser Spotted Woodpeckers, and the larger Green Woodpecker feeds on heathy ground around Farmwood Pool. The Mosses also holds Long-tailed and occasional Marsh Tits, good numbers of breeding Redpoll and Spotted Flycatcher, and a territorial Wood Warbler or two in some years. Woodcock rode over all local woods and both Tawny and Little Owl are common. This last species favours old, free-standing oaks in Astle and Withington Parks, as well as hedgerow trees. Listen for their yelping calls by day, particularly at the end of a shower in spring, or wait at dusk between February and June for the curlew-like 'hoot' of the males. At times three or four may be calling at once from adjacent territories.

Sand Martin dig their nest-holes out of freshly exposed faces in active quarries, but accurate assessment of their numbers is difficult, for not all holes dug are used and one tunnel may lead to two or perhaps more nests. The number of birds around the colony is no guide either for social visits by birds from other colonies are not infrequent. Kingfisher more often nest in the banks of local brooks although they regularly fish at Farmwood Pool.

Timing

Dusk visits are obviously necessary in spring for owls and Woodcock, or in winter to see the gull roost, but otherwise timing is not critical. Migrants concentrate over and by the pools in spring under similar conditions to those which bring birds to other meres and flashes, namely a southerly airstream with showers. Autumn movements, here as elsewhere, are seldom so marked.

Winter visits at weekend may coincide with shoots. If, on arrival at Farmwood Pool, shots can be heard from the Catchpenny Lane or Acre Nook areas, it is advisable not to visit those pools.

The pools freeze fairly rapidly in severe weather. Farmwood Pool, being fairly deep, stays open longest.

Access

It is not possible to walk around the quarries, but viewing is generally practicable from the network of roads through the area.

Farmwood Pool lies immediately to the west of the A535 Alderley Edge-Holmes Chapel road (SD 810730) and may be viewed from various points, but to best effect in winter from a gateway at the southern end. A telescope will be essential here due to the scale of the lake. To reach Catchpenny Pool, travel south along the main road for a mile (1.3 km) then take the first turning on the left, Catchpenny Lane, by the telephone box (SD 802713). The pool lies on the right after one kilometre.

Continue eastward along Catchpenny Lane for a further half mile (1 km), and turn left into Lapwing Lane. This lane is straddled by the huge, still operational Acre Nook Sand Quarry. Viewing here is difficult and restricted to glimpses over the quarry gates. The Mosses wood lies beyond the quarry to the right of the road and has a bridlepath running through it. Lapwing Lane then rejoins the A535 to the north of Farmwood Pool.

In winter stubble fields off Catchpenny Lane and Congleton Lane can be productive. The best fields in any given season can only be found by touring the lanes.

Calendar

All year: Waterfowl include Great Crested and Little Grebe, Canada Goose, Tufted and Ruddy Ducks. The gamebird presence is assisted by keepers. Farmland species include Kestrel and numerous Little Owl. Hole-nesting species such as Stock Dove and Tree Sparrow favour mature trees. All three woodpeckers and Tawny Owl present in woods, with Marsh Tit, Nuthatch and common woodland species. Redpoll in Birchwoods. Kingfisher along Peover Eye.

December/February: Winter wildfowl include Wigeon, Teal, Pochard and Goldeneye, with flocks of Tufted and especially Ruddy Ducks; occasional Smew, Gadwall, Pintail, perhaps a few Shoveler. Cormorant dine on fish here. Severe weather or storms may bring a diver or other scarce water-bird. Snipe feed in marshy ground. The gull roost on Farmwood Pool may include Iceland or Glaucous Full, possibly Kittiwake after storms. Large flocks of Woodpigeon and Stock Dove after acorns or on stubble, where Skylark may be joined by flocks of Tree Sparrow, finches and buntings. Sparrowhawk harass these flocks.

March/May: Drake Ruddy Duck bubble in display and Sheduck may visit. Wagtails, pipits and Reed Bunting on grassy banks in showery weather in early spring. Lapwing, Little Ringed Plover and Common Sandpiper take up territories, as do Redshank and Ringed Plover in some years. Dunlin or other waders may call in on passage. Hirundines and sometimes terns feed over pools in April and May.

June/July: Waterfowl and waders have young. Numbers of Tufted Duck may reach annual peak in July. Turtle Dove purr in scrub and Wood Warbler trill desperately to attract a mate as the summer advances. Other warblers and Spotted Flycatcher are busy nesting, as are Redpoll in the Mosses and Sand Martin in the quarries. Corn Bunting at the edge of cornfields.

August/November: Newly released Mallard may exceed 1,000 and Shoveler pass through. Black-necked Grebe have occurred. Breeding waders may still be present, joined by migrant Curlew and other species. Terns and hirundines may pause on return passage. Coot gather prior to the shooting season, and eclipse-plumaged Wigeon or Pintail mingle with the Mallard.

52 MACCLESFIELD FOREST, LANGLEY RESERVOIRS AND TEGGS NOSE COUNTRY PARK

SJ

Habitat

Lying on the slopes of the Pennines and covering the catchment of a chain of reservoirs, the conifer plantations of Macclesfield Forest are home to a limited but specialised community of birds. Pine, spruce and larch are the principal trees, with some sycamore, and a few other broad-leaved trees, notably beech, along the roadsides. The plantations should improve for birds as the first generation of trees matures, and felling and replanting become more prevalent. The forest is surrounded by upland pasture and rough, sheep-grazed moorland. Red Deer frequent the plantations, emerging into the open by night.

The reservoirs are steep-sided with rocky shores and, as the water level fluctuates markedly in summer, little marginal vegetation has developed. Submerged plants, exposed during dry weather, include the uncommon Shoreweed (*Littorella uniflora*) and the Lesser Marshwort (*Apium inun-*

154

datum), a tiny umbellifer. The lower reservoirs, Teggs Nose, Bottoms and Ridgegate, are heavily fished. Trentabank, the topmost reservoir, is out of bounds to anglers but seldom holds many waterfowl.

Teggs Nose Country Park includes an area of mixed broad-leaved woodland with oak, ash, beech and other trees, and plentiful dead wood. Cattle graze among the trees but there is nonetheless a considerable scrub layer of brambles and other undergrowth. At the bottom of the steep hillside the woodland changes to alder carr, and at higher altitudes it peters out and is replaced by stands of bracken and some heather.

Species

Despite an overall impression of quietness, the forest does have some specialities, and unusual birds turn up with surprising frequency.

During the winter months flocks of Goldcrest, Coal and Long-tailed Tits roam the plantations, their thin calls breaking the misty silence. With perseverance Crossbill are quite likely to be seen, often in flight across the valley, although they sometimes alight in roadside trees. Goshawk are seen with some regularity, perhaps dashing in at twilight in an attempt to snatch a Carrion Crow from the communal roost in larches at Trentabank. Although not intensively watched at this season, the forest has furnished winter records of a variety of other raptors, notably Hen Harrier and once a Rough-legged Buzzard. Raven are sometimes seen, or their deep croaks heard.

Grey Heron

A few common waterfowl winter on the reservoirs. Up to a dozen Goldeneye are always present, and in late winter there is no better place than Ridgegate for watching their display. The drakes alternately stretch out their necks then throw back the head so that the bill points skyward, giving a strange creaking call at the same time. Often the displaying birds swim within a few yards of the roadside wall. A Smew spent several weeks here in 1990.

Towards spring flocks of small finches arrive to feed on seed from the opening larch cones. Siskin are most numerous – flocks of 150 have been seen – with smaller numbers of Redpoll and Goldfinch. All these species are sufficiently acrobatic to feed without descending to the

155

ground, unlike the Brambling which may appear with Chaffinch under beeches at Teggs Nose and elsewhere in March. Throughout March and April cock Siskin utter their wheezy songs and, as spring progresses, their fluttering display flight becomes more frequent. By the end of April, however, most birds have departed.

The west-east valley forms a corridor for migrant birds crossing the Pennines. In early spring parties of Brambling and Chaffinch, the former detected by their nasal calls, fly at tree-top height up the valley. Herds of Bewick's Swan may pass over on the early stages of their journey from Ireland to Siberia, but only rarely do they alight on the reservoirs. Jackdaw move east at greater altitude. Winter numbers of this small crow in Cheshire greatly exceed summer totals, and this regular passage gives some indication of the origin of the winter flocks. A Red-breasted Merganser or two may put in a brief appearance during April when hirundines gather over the reservoirs and Yellow Wagtails return to the pastures. A migrant Osprey may also call in for a meal of trout. There is a recent April record of Firecrest, again probably an eastward-bound migrant.

The breeding avifauna of the plantations is as remarkable for its absentees as for its variety. Broad-leaved woodland species such as Marsh and Blue Tits, Garden Warbler and Nuthatch are scarce or absent. On the other hand Coal Tit and Goldcrest are plentiful, with Spotted Flycatcher and Treecreeper in mature stands where the odd pair of Siskin very probably breeds. Redpoll and Willow Warbler frequent the younger plantations with Tree Pipit in the clearings.

Crepuscular and nocturnal species include roding Woodcock, best seen from the road by Trentabank. Their curious display flight begins in the last few days of February in mild springs, but is better witnessed in May or June when, with the hours of darkness restricted, the performance begins while the light is still good. At a distance the only call to be heard is a sharp squeak, but as the birds pass overhead with deep, slow wing-beats, listen for a series of three or four deep grunts. Tawny Owl are common and make use of old crow nests, there being a lack of the cavities in trees that provide the usual nest-site. Long-eared Owl have bred and may still do so, hunting the moors above the forest. By day their place is taken by Kestrel which hover above the ridges on the lookout for field voles.

A few waterfowl breed on the reservoirs. Both Great Crested and Little Grebes may nest on Bottoms Reservoir, and Tufted ducklings have been reared on Ridgegate. Canada Goose sit conspicuously on nests beneath trees near the water. Common Sandpiper, which feed along the shoreline, evade the anglers by nesting inside the plantations. As the young hatch the adults perch on roadside walls, bobbing and calling anxiously. Of particular interest is the heronry in larches beside Trentabank. Renovation of old nests may start in February, with new nests still being built in April. The Heron fly out to fish in brooks, pools and rivers in the surrounding hills. Returning birds are greeted with much bill-clattering by their mates. During May and June the growing young birds gabble and squawk noisily.

The woodlands at Teggs Nose come into their own during the summer. Wood Warbler trill beneath the oaks and are more easily located than the pair or two in the forest proper. Redstart flit in and out of tree-holes or warble from the cover of a thorn bush. Pied Flycatcher are seen most years and occasionally stop to breed. All three woodpeckers are seen, although the Lesser Spotted is decidedly scarce. Nuthatch and Tree Pipit also nest, and a few Red-legged Partridge have appeared recently.

Autumn passage brings the occasional rarity to the forest – Honey Buzzard and Wryneck have been noted – but the area is best known for heavy movements of commoner species. On any cloudy or misty day from mid-August to November, migrant pipits and wagtails, and later thrushes and finches pass low over the ridges above the forst, where the skilled observer can separate the various species by their calls. White Wagtail often feed beside the reservoirs in late August and September. Autumn passage of these pearly grey birds down the Pennines is inadequately documented. Migrant Brambling are often recorded here even when they appear to be absent elsewhere in the county. Easterly winds bring the largest movements. On 12 October 1980 over 5,000 Redwing arrived from the east between 8.10 and 9.20 am, along with smaller numbers of Blackbird and grey, continental Song Thrush, and a hundred or so each of Siskin and Redpoll. Similarly, on 29 October 1983 some 5,700 thrushes flew west in just over three hours. Tired migrant thrushes and finches will often settle in the scrub and woodland at Teggs Nose, where they make easy pickings for the resident Sparrowhawks.

Timing

Evening visits are advisable for watching roosting and crepuscular species. Clear mornings are best for raptors. On cloudy days mist may obscure the valley although on cold winter days when fog blankets the lowlands the sun may well be shining on the hills.

Diurnal passage over ridges above the forest is heaviest on autumn days with mist, hazy cloud or total overcast, although very large movements have occurred with a clear sky and light wind from an easterly quarter. Passage stops abruptly in heavy or persistent rain or in high winds. On bright, sunny days migrants fly too high to be seen, although a few calls may be heard.

Teggs Nose and Trentabank may be crowded at weekends particularly in summer, but few people wander far from the roads into the forest.

Access

The forest lies east of Langley village to the south-east of Macclesfield. Immediately through Langley village a left turn, Holehouse Lane, leads to a car park at the foot of Teggs Nose (SD 946717). Follow the path up the hill and explore scrubby areas to the right. A larger car park at the summit of Teggs Nose (SD 949731), signposted off the A537 Macclesfield to Buxton road, provides an easier walk to look out over the valley from the promontory near the quarry exhibition – a good vantage point on passage days.

Otherwise continue up the main road and Bottoms Reservoir appears on the left. Carry on up the road for Ridgegate and Trentabank Reservoirs. A lay-by alongside Trentabank (SD 963713) allows good views of the heronry and is also one of the best viewpoints for the forest as a whole. For watching autumn migration continue up the road past Trentabank to the hill-top, then walk right along the footpath on the ridge and wait. If there is a passage, birds will pass low over this ridge.

The Forest Chapel road is generally most productive for Crossbill, although these may be seen from any of the tracks through the forest.

Calendar

All year: Tufted Duck; Sparrowhawk, Kestrel, Tawny Owl, possibly Long-eared Owl; Goldcrest, Long-tailed and Coal Tits, Crossbill.

December/February: Goldeneye on the reservoirs, with perhaps a few Pochard, Teal or Wigeon; Goshawk and other raptors occasionally; possibly Raven; Carrion Crow roost in large numbers

March/May: Goldeneye displaying by March when Canada Goose take up territory and Heron renovate nests; Woodcock start to rode and Crossbill may be nesting. Passing migrants in March include Jackdaw, Chaffinch and Brambling. Finch flocks in early spring include Siskin, Redpoll and Goldfinch. In April hirundines and Yellow Wagtail pass through and Red-breasted Merganser may visit. Summer visitors arrive including Common Sandpiper and Tree Pipit.

June/July: Young Heron fledge during this period; Great Crested Grebe, Tufted Duck and Common Sandpiper may also have young. Redstart, Wood Warbler and perhaps Pied Flycatcher at Teggs Nose. Possibility of Siskin in the conifers.

August/November: Summer visitors depart. Goldeneye may return from August, more likely in October. Diurnal passage includes Meadow and Tree Pipits and White Wagtail in August and September, Meadows continuing to pass through in October. Pied Wagtail more numerous in October and a few Grey Wagtail likely; Siskin from mid-September; Chaffinch and Brambling in October. Large-scale thrush movements in October/November including Redwing, Fieldfare, Blackbird and Song Thrush.

53 RIVER DANE VALLEY

Habitat

The River Dane is a clean trout stream forming the boundary between Cheshire and Staffordshire. Its waters are rich in invertebrates (look for Banded Agrion damselflies in the lower reaches) which provide food for a good number of riparian birds. Danebower is a gritstone hill topped with peat moorland. Rocky slopes and mixed woodlands, including those at Shell Brook, support a diverse range of breeding species. There are Red Deer in the woods.

Species

Golden Plover still breed on the Danebower moors in small numbers, but have been increasingly disturbed by ramblers. Red Grouse are easily seen however, and there is a chance of Twite or a passing Merlin. Curlew

159

nest on moorland and rough pastures, and Ring Ousel often feed in the pastures around the quarry chimney. Wheatear nest commonly along rocky slopes, where Cuckoo seek pipit nests, and there are several pairs of Little Owl in the area. Birds soaring above the Allgreave-Gradbach ridge have included Raven and Peregrine. There are recent summer records of Hobby and Fieldfare. Dippers, Grey Wagtail and Kingfisher are commonly seen along the river, especially below Danebridge, and Common Sandpiper are frequent passage migrants.

Spotted Flycatcher are plentiful in summer in trees overhanging the river, and Pied Flycatcher sometimes breed. Redstart, Wood Warbler and Tree Pipit also occur. The Shell Brook woods hold a wide range of woodland species. Buzzard are occasionally seen, and the trout pool at Danebridge has been known to attract passage Osprey.

In winter, when many birds have left the moors, there is a remote chance of encountering a wandering predator such as a harrier or Short-eared Owl.

Timing
The valley is visually attractive at all seasons, but is far richer in birds during the summer months, especially April to June. Many birdwatchers visit the Danebower chimney in March to look for early Wheatear and Ring Ousel. The moors are quiet in winter, but persistent visits should eventually be rewarded.

Access
For the upper Dane valley, the public footpath northwards from Danebower to the Cat and Fiddle offers a good chance of moorland species in early spring, before the rambling season intensifies. The lane below Cutthorn Hill and its continuation as a footpath up the brook is a good place for moorland edge species, as is the rocky slope alongside the minor road running eastward from the Rose and Crown at Allgreave.

Access to the valley further west is easy from Danebridge: a footpath follows the river downstream for a mile (1.3 km) before crossing into Staffordshire (SJ 966643). The Shell Brook woods are cut through by footpaths in places.

Calendar
All year: Red Grouse, Little Owl, Dipper, Grey Wagtail, Kingfisher, Sparrowhawk, woodland birds.

March/May: Golden Plover, Curlew, Meadow Pipit and Skylark return to the moors in March; Ring Ousel and Wheatear appear on scree slopes, where Cuckoo often perch in May; Wood Warbler, Redstart, Pied and Spotted Flycatcher sing in woods from late April.

54 SANDBACH FLASHES

**OS Map 118
SJ**

Habitat

A series of shallow pools formed in recent decades as a result of salt-mining, the flashes lie in a triangle between Sandbach, Middlewich and Crewe. The larger flashes at Elton Hall and Watch Lane have extensive muddy margins attractive to wading birds. The Elton Hall flashes are a diurnal roost for wildfowl, and an adjacent disused sludgebed is popular with wildfowl and waders. Watch Lane and several of the smaller flashes have marginal stands of reedmace (*Typha*) or reed-grass and an introduced stand of the true reed (*Phragmites*) is spreading at Watch Lane. The most important *Typha* bed is at Fodens Flash, a small pool backed by carr of alder and willow – the only woodland of consequence in the area. This carr is notable for its lichens, containing many species scarce in Cheshire. Across the road from Fodens Flash a partly derelict market garden is producing a useful cover of willow and hawthorn scrub. This site, and industrial wasteland in the area, furnish a good supply of weed seed for winter finches and other birds. Sunken rushy areas in pastures and tall thorn hedges form further valuable habitats.

A pool between Watch Lane Flash and the Trent and Mersey Canal is

161

fed in part by a saline spring. The inland saltmarshes which develop in such sites are a botanical speciality of Cheshire. This particular site holds Lesser Sea Spurrey, Reflexed Saltmarsh Grass, Sea Aster and other species typical of coastal marshes. Their seeds may originally have been carried inland by birds, or perhaps on barges plying up and down the Weaver valley. However, Wild Celery, a recent arrival at Watch Lane, is more likely to have travelled on the muddy boots of some birdwatcher from the Weaver Bend at Frodsham where the plant thrives.

Species

With over two hundred species recorded to date, the Flashes were one of the best known birdwatching sites in Cheshire, but rapid siltation of the Elton Hall flashes has reduced the attractiveness of the site in recent years. Of particular interest is the passage of waders, although the Witton Flashes have now largely replaced an impoverished Sandbach as the prime wader site in the area. Winter wildfowl are also varied, and movements of passerines can be heavy.

Spring passage begins in March with Little Ringed Plover one of the first immigrants. Wheatear passage traditionally starts around 21 March, and birds linger so long around rabbit burrows as to give rise to suspicions of breeding. In April parties of passing Linnet pause to feed on waste ground, cock birds detach themselves from the flock to sing, and the whole party keeps up an excited twittering. South-westerly winds and showers at this time may bring large movements of Meadow Pipit. Feeding flocks spread out across the short turf bordering Watch Lane and other flashes in company with Pied, White and Yellow Wagtails, Reed Bunting and the occasional pink-breasted Water Pipit. Common Sandpiper, en route to their Pennine nesting streams, also mingle with these flocks, snapping at yellow dung-flies on cow-pats. Rarities at this season have included Little Bunting and Grey-headed Wagtail accompanying the pipit flocks and, if the wind blows from the east in mid-April, there is just a chance of a migrant Osprey deflected westward from the usual line of passage.

Wader passage picks up gradually during April, with larger numbers in May. Most of the typical autumn species occur in small numbers. Arctic Ringed Plover in May and early June are often accompanied by Sanderling. Dunlin, almost constantly present in small numbers, may utter their purring song.

Fodens Flash comes into its own during the summer months with Reed Bunting and Sedge and Reed Warblers nesting in the marsh; Ruddy Duck, Great Crested and Little Grebes on the flash; and Willow Tit, Treecreeper, Spotted Flycatcher, sometimes Lesser Spotted Woodpecker and possibly Water Rail in the carr. The adjacent market gardens are alive with Whitethroat in the nettle-beds and Willow Warbler in the scrub. Bullfinch are common here, their presence betrayed by a thin whistle or a white rump glimpsed as a bird flies into a thorn bush. Grasshopper Warbler nest in good years, but have been harassed by birdwatchers in the past. Although retiring by nature, Grasshopper Warbler do have regular song perches, and once these have been identified prolonged viewing is possible without disturbing the bird.

The area of the flashes as a whole supports important breeding populations of several wetland species. Little Grebe are present on many of the smaller pools, totalling perhaps a dozen or more pairs. Throughout the spring Great Crested Grebe can be seen displaying, at times very close to the car park, from the end of Watch Lane. A pair of grebes will face each other so that they are almost touching, and shake their heads vigorously from side to side. In more advanced versions of this display the birds may rear up out of the water and shake limp water-weeds or algae in their bill.

One other aquatic species nesting on all pools is the Coot. Throughout the breeding season territorial Coot may be seen rearing up out of the water and thrashing away with legs and beak at any intruding rival, while non-breeders of the same species swim meekly in a sociable flock. Shelduck nest annually. Birds return from the moult from December onwards and by spring they too are displaying aggressively. By the time the ducks are sitting on eggs, the drakes will be busy driving ducks of all species, and even Heron, off their adopted flash.

Few waders now breed, although Little Ringed Plover still nest by Watch Lane and Elton Hall Flashes and on waste ground in the area. A pair once bred on the lorry park in Fodens Motor Works. Ringed Plover have also attempted to nest. Redshank may be seen displaying from December onwards, but rarely settle at Sandbach.

Lesser Whitethroat are relatively common in overgrown hedges at Watch Lane, Elton Hall and elsewhere, but are more often heard than seen. Little Owl breed in hedgerow trees throughout the area. Their yelping calls are often heard by day, especially in showery weather. A few Corn Bunting nest around cereal fields, and Yellow Wagtail are wide-spread. The local population of this species is of particular interest since aberrant birds resembling Sykes' or Blue-headed Wagtails occur from time to time, and have even been seen feeding young on several occasions.

'Autumn' wader passage may begin by the end of June with the odd Greenshank or 'black' Spotted Redshank, presumably failed or non-breeders. Common Sandpiper passage peaks in July when the odd Turnstone or Sanderling may also occur, and Green Sandpiper increase, their liquid calls carrying on the twilight air. As Elton Hall Flash has become more overgrown, these birds have become a major feature of autumn passage. Ruff, Greenshank and Spotted Redshank are regular in August, with just a possibility of a Wood Sandpiper. Little Stint or Curlew Sandpiper may latch on to parties of Dunlin, and one or two godwits of both species turn up annually, as does the occasional Grey Plover, even quite late in the autumn.

The flashes have provided records of rare waders almost annually. These have included Wilson's Phalarope (twice), Pectoral (eight), White-rumped, Spotted, Western, Stilt and Upland Sandpipers and Lesser Yellowlegs – all from North America, and Avocet, Marsh Sandpiper and Temminck's Stint from continental Europe. Altogether more than 25 birds of this last-named species have been logged at the flashes, nearly half of them in spring, including a party of six at Watch Lane in May 1973.

Other autumn migrants tend to be neglected by birdwatchers, but are not without interest. Whinchat are regularly present, perching on fence-posts around Watch Lane, although numbers are decreasing, and Red-start flicker along the hedgerows. The line of Crack Willows at Elton Hall provides rich pickings for passing warblers. A small but regular passage of Water and Rock Pipits is most obvious during the first few days of October when birds comb the edge of Watch Lane Flash, picking fresh-water shrimps from amongst the debris. In some years Garganey are present among the Teal, but they often escape detection through their habit of sleeping for much of the day. When seen with their heads up however, the stripy face pattern, with broad supercilium, and the heavier bill are diagnostic.

In winter the Elton Hall flashes are an excellent locality to see all the common dabbling duck species. Of particular interest is the flock of Pintail which has visited the site annually since the 1960s. Numbers vary between 25 and 60 from year to year. The Teal is the most numerous duck – over 950 have been counted, the constant 'prip . . . prip' of the drakes merging with the deeper calls of Pintail and the loud 'whee-oo' of Wigeon. A flock of 100 or more of this latter species join with Coots to graze the pastures around the flash. In severe weather less usual fowl appear, perhaps a family party of Bewick's or Whooper Swans or a small flock of White-fronted Goose.

So long as the weather remains mild large numbers of Lapwing (up to 3,000 or more) feed on surrounding pastures and roost on the sludgebed at Elton Hall. Up to 200 or more Snipe conceal themselves in the marshes where they are hunted by hovering Kestrel, or by Sparrowhawk which adopt a peculiar slow flight to enable them to spot the stripe-backed waders crouching in the rushes. A dozen or so Dunlin may be present right through the winter, and a few Redshank, Ruff and Golden Plover wander down from their haunts around Northwich and Middlewich. The sloping field to the north of Pumphouse Flash regularly supports several dozen Moorhen.

A flock of Skylark winters on the stubble fields between Elton Hall and Railway Flash – this species is remarkably local hereabouts at this season. Fieldfare and Redwing strip berries from the hedges and may fall prey to a Peregrine, sallying out from a perch on a nearby electricity pylon. A Great Grey Shrike is as likely to turn up here as anywhere in Cheshire, although the chances of encountering one are still very slim.

At Elton Hall as elsewhere, the behaviour of the large flocks of birds gives warning of the presence of predators. A hovering Kestrel may cause only local consternation amongst the smaller waders and Starling. A passing Merlin or soaring Sparrowhawk will cause the Lapwing flocks to scramble, and the impending arrival of a Peregrine or migrant harrier (rare here) causes panic among the ducks as well.

Watch Lane holds a few diving ducks in winter, but it freezes over rapidly and ducks and Great Crested Grebes are then displaced to the coast. A few Jack Snipe winter in the *Typha* beds along with the odd Water Rail, and a Green Sandpiper may feed in the north-eastern corner of the flash. The pool below the canal is a regular haunt of Kingfisher. A holly hedge to the north of this pool is popular with roosting Greenfinch and Linnet, and in some winters a sprinkling of Twite have joined the commoner finches. Muck-spreading on nearby fields attracts Corn Bunting and Yellowhammer. Stonechat are regular winter residents in the area when their population is at a high level, and can be seen perching on thistle stems and fence-posts.

In winter Fodens Flash is a good place to see Water Rail. These shy birds perform particularly well in frosty weather when they feed by open puddles or ditches in the willow carr. Willow Tit are resident – as good a place as any to get to know this species for Marsh Tit are almost unknown here. A long-established roost of Magpie in scrub behind the flash has held over 470 birds, possibly the largest gathering recorded in Britain. Long-eared Owl have been recorded in at least three winters, roosting in scrub. Their status in the county is shrouded in mystery.

Timing

Showery weather from a southerly quarter in spring and wet or stormy weather in the autumn are more likely to bring down migrants. In winter duck numbers tend to increase during the day as feeding birds are flushed off field ponds and minor flashes back to the roosts. Prolonged frosts concentrate waterfowl at Elton Hall where the river Wheelock provides some open water.

Access

Turn south off the A533 Middlewich-Sandbach road by The Fox public house just north of Sandbach station. Continue round the perimeter of the lorry works until a narrow humpback bridge over the canal is reached (SJ 733612). For Fodens Flash turn right immediately at this bridge and park at the roadside by the flash shortly after the first corner. A bridlepath runs westward through the carr just beyond the flash.

For Watch Lane Flash return to the canal bridge and take the other fork. Turn left by the telephone box into Red Lane (SJ 729611) and continue round until Watch Lane appears as a minor road joining from the right. Car parking at the end of Watch Lane allows good views of the flash. A second car park is reached by driving round the flash, stopping at intervals to view over the hedges.

To reach Elton Hall turn right out of this second car park, right at the main road past the chemical works, then left after one kilometre at the first crossroads. This road runs between Elton Hall Flash (to the east) and Pumphouse Flash.

Visitors should not wander off the roads at Elton Hall or Watch Lane.

Calendar

All year: Great Crested and Little Grebes, Mute Swan, Shelduck (most of year); Lapwing, Dunlin (not breeding); Little Owl along hedgerows; Willow Tit and Bullfinch common at Fodens Flash.

December/February: Wigeon, Teal, Pintail at Elton Hall; Water Rail at Fodens; Lapwing and Snipe widespread, with a few Ruff, and both Jack Snipe and Green Sandpiper at Watch Lane; Sparrowhawk and perhaps Peregrine hunt the area; Corn Bunting join Yellowhammer flocks; a few Stonechat in mild winters. Magpies form huge roost at Fodens Flash.

March/May: Breeding waders appear in March and April, followed by passage birds in April and May: Little Ringed Plover, Ringed Plover, Oystercatcher, Common Sandpiper, Sanderling and other species. Water Pipit, White and Yellow Wagtail may join flocks of Meadow Pipit and Reed Bunting; Wheatear generally present from late March. Wildfowl depart and summer visitors arrive.

June/July: Breeding species include Little and Great Crested Grebes and Ruddy Duck; Little Ringed Plover by flashes and on waste ground; Reed, Sedge and perhaps Grasshopper Warblers, Whitethroat and Spotted Flycatcher all at Fodens Flash; Lesser Whitethroat and Reed Bunting widespread. Wader passage resumes in July.

Sandbach Flashes

August/November: Autumn duck flocks include Shoveler and one or two Garganey sleeping amongst the Teal. Sprinkling of passage waders; Whinchat and Redstart pass through in small numbers. Small passage of Rock and Water Pipits in October, as winter visitors, including Water Rail, arrive. Duck flocks build up in late autumn.

55 NORTHWICH AREA

Habitat

Several sites lying in and around Northwich offer a considerable diversity of habitats encompassing woodland, freshwater, reedbeds and industrial sludgetanks. Most of these are prone to disturbance and some of them difficult of access. It is therefore sensible to combine visits to several sites.

Northwich lies at the heart of the Cheshire salt and chemical industry. Consequently a great deal of land has been left in a semi-derelict state, with plentiful scrub and rough grassland. Flashes, subsidence pools formed as a consequence of underground brine-pumping, formerly constituted some of the county's richest bird habitats, but the best, at Witton, are gradually being 'reclaimed'. Cheshire County Council has an unfortunate habit of designating prime wildlife sites for tipping. Marbury Mere and Pickmere may also have formed as a consequence of the dissolution of rock salt, but by natural means and over a much longer period of time.

55A Billinge Green Flashes
OS ref: SJ 682712
Habitat

A series of four shallow flashes straddling the Trent and Mersey Canal to the south of the town. The northernmost pool has a well developed fringe of aquatic plants, including the scarce Cowbane, but is heavily fished and supports few wildfowl. An area of damp scrub to the south hold warblers in summer and roosts of various species in winter. A pool to the west of the railway is grazed on all sides and has trampled muddy margins which attracts waders. A few wildfowl are often present. The two canalside flashes are littered with sunken boats and other debris. They too have grazed margins and attract waders. The larger, southern pool also has a sizeable strand of phragmites which provides shelter for wildfowl. There is much scrub around the flashes.

Species

Little and Great Crested Grebes breed along with the occasional pair of Tufted Duck. Ruddy Duck frequent the canal-side reedbed and may breed. A pair of Mute Swans nested until recently and Canada Goose are colonising the area. Shoveler occur on autumn passage when Pochard and Tufted Duck may be more numerous. Small flocks of Wigeon and Teal visit in winter when over a hundred Mallard may be present. Coot flocks graze the waterside pastures, and the related Water Rail skulks in the reeds and damp scrubby areas.

Curlew

From August until March flocks of Curlew feed in pastures between Northwich and Middlewich, roosting on an inaccessible chemical sludge-bed. Up to two or three hundred visit the flashes to drink and bathe. In the autumn they may be joined by the occasional Whimbrel. Several hundred Golden Plover feed with Lapwing in fields along 'King Street' (the A530) to the east. Often a few Redshank or Ruff accompany them through the winter, and these two species will visit the flashes, along with Snipe. Passage waders in spring or autumn regularly include one or two Dunlin, Green and Common Sandpipers, and Little Ringed Plover.

Nesting birds in the scrubby areas include Turtle Dove and Sedge Warbler, with both Common and Lesser Whitethroats. Little Owl yelp from hedgerow oaks, and Reed Warbler chatter in the reedbeds. Both

Great and Lesser Spotted Woodpeckers visit the area, favouring dead elms. In winter the scrub supports roosts of Redwing, and regularly over a hundred Magpies.

Timing
Waders may be flushed off adjacent fields as the day progresses, so morning visits are recommended. As dusk approaches Curlew may return to bathe before going to roost.

Access
Take the A530 'King Street' south from the A556 (T) Broken Cross roundabout south of Northwich (SJ 685727). Turn right after half a mile (1 km) onto the first minor road reached and park beside the main fishing flash. Other flashes are visible from the railway bridge or by walking south along the canal towpath.

Calendar
All year: Little and Great Crested Grebes, Mute Swan, Tufted Duck and Coot, Little Owl, Greater and Lesser Spotted Woodpeckers present nearby.

December-February: Wildfowl regularly include Wigeon, Teal, Pochard and Tufted Duck, Water Rail seldom visible in scrubby areas where Redwing and Magpie roost. Golden Plover and Lapwing feed along 'King Street' with few Redshank, Ruff and Snipe, Curlew also winter.

March-May: A few waders pass through, notably Dunlin, Common Sandpiper, Little Ringed Plover, Reed and Sedge Warblers arrive with Whitethroat and Lesser Whitethroat.

June-July: Warblers continue to sing. Waterfowl may have young. Waders return from July, with Green and Common Sandpipers regular at this time.

August-November: Curlew and other waders return during August, with Green Sandpiper present daily. Warblers mostly depart by September when wildfowl start to return.

55B WITTON FLASHES AND BUTTERFINCH BRIDGE
OS ref: SJ 665750 and 662754

Habitat
The huge Witton Flashes have been filled with alkali waste and now resemble sludgebeds. Shallow rainwater pools form in wet weather and attract passing waders, and hordes of gulls from the adjacent rubbish tip. A tall embankment separates the grassy Ashton's Flash from the relatively bare Neumann's Flash to the north. The flashes support a range of lime-loving flowers which are otherwise hardly known in Cheshire: Fragrant Orchid, Hoary Mustard, Ploughman's Spikenard and Yellow-wort are all abundant. The area in general is well endowed with hawthorn and other scrub.

Immediately to the north-west of the Witton Flashes a narrow tributary flows underneath the road to join the Wincham Brook. To the west of the road it widens out onto mudflats, bordered on one side by phragmites reeds, and on the other by a stand of Sea Club-rush, Sea Aster, Lesser Sea Spurrey, and several other species present make this one of the best inland saltmarshes in the county. Above this marsh is the embankment of Marbury No. 1 sludgebed (commonly referred to as 'Butterfinch Bridge'). This tank is used to accommodate dredgings from the Weaver Navigation and formed an important site for passage waters, but is now near the end of its life. The flowery banks of the tank support a wide range of butterflies.

To the east of the Witton Flashes lie the two small flashes at Marston. In many respects these are similar to the Billinge Green pools, with dead hedges and other relics emerging from the water. They have less marginal cover however, and are more heavily fished.

Species

Witton Flashes are best known for their large winter gathering of gulls, in particular for the larger species which scavenge on the neighbouring tip. Herring Gull predominate from October to March, with often well over 1,000 present. Seven thousand were estimated at Christmas 1986. They are accompanied by several hundred Great Black-backed Gulls at times, generally a few dozen Lesser Black-backed Gull (although hundreds occur in the autumn), and a sprinkling of 'white-winged' gulls. Often two or three of these northern birds are present, with Iceland as likely to occur as Glaucous. 'Yellow-legged' gulls may occur in late summer and a Franklin's Gull appeared in May 1987.

Up to a dozen Heron roost on the flats by day, but their presence is eclipsed by the huge number of Lapwing. Up to 11,000 have been counted, with 5–8,000 in most years. They are accompanied by Golden Plover, varying in numbers from a few dozen to several hundred. These are the birds which feed along 'King Street', and may be joined by a few Ruff or Redshank, although Curlew seldom visit in any numbers. So long as the weather remains mild, up to 300 Snipe may feed on Neumann's Flash, but with the onset of frosts they disperse, and the plovers move out to the west.

Depending on rainfall, Neumann's Flash may remain wet throughout summer and into the autumn. Conditions have proved attractive to waders, especially in autumn, and to some extent the site has taken over from Sandbach in both the diversity and numbers of birds attracted. Over 100 Dunlin and more than 50 Ringed Plover have been present on occasion, with a dozen or more Ruff and Redshank and a good variety of other species. Over the years, the list of rarities has included Dotterel, Stilt and Broad-billed Sandpiper, Avocet, Temminck's Stint and Wiison's Phalarope. Both Ringed and Little Ringed Plovers breed.

Shelduck have bred in the vicinity and both Tufted and Ruddy Ducks summer at Marston. In winter a few Pochard and Goldeneye also occur there, and small parties of ducks of various species may dabble by flood pools at Witton. Water Rail lurk in the Butterfinch Bridge reedbed.

Scrubland species nesting locally include Turtle Dove, Whitethroat, Lesser Whitethroat and Garden Warbler, with a few pairs of Grasshopper Warbler in bramble thickets and Reed Warbler beside Wincham Brook. Long-tailed and Willow Tits are also common. A curiosity is the pair or two of Meadow Pipit which nest among rough grass at the sides of the sludgetanks – the species is absent in summer from much of the Cheshire plain. Wheatear occur along the embankments on passage.

In winter the occasional Blackcap or Chiffchaff is found in the scrub, and towards dusk several hundred Pied Wagtail gather on the mud at Witton before flying off west at sunset towards Winnington. Two scarcer visitors have been Great Grey Shrike, seen in several winters, and Long-eared Owl roosting in thorn scrub.

Timing

Gull flocks reach their peak between mid-December and the end of January, but Glaucous or Iceland Gull may turn up at any time from late summer to spring. Plover flocks are at their largest around full moon in autumn and early winter. Severe weather soon drives them westwards. Wader passage is best in wet weather in May-June and August-October. Visits at any time of day may be rewarding, but gulls start to leave for the estuaries in mid-afternoon. Dusk visits are advisable to hear Grasshopper Warbler in summer and to see the wagtail flocks in winter.

Access

The Marston Flashes straddle the B5075 half a mile (1 km) to the south of its junction with the A559 Lostock to Warrington road (SJ 666742). Continue south along the B5075 from Marston and Neumann's Flash appears on the right. Limited viewing is possible from this point, but most birdwatchers follow minor roads round to the western side of the flashes where gaps in the fence allow access to view. The bank-tops have been much used by dog-walkers and other members of the public, but it appears that usage of the site for waste disposal is about to be resumed and access may be curtailed. Butterfinch Bridge lies half a mile (1 km) to the north of the tip entrance along the same road.

Calendar

All year: Heron roost at Witton for much of the year. Scrubland species include Long-tailed and Willow Tits.

December-February: Herring, Great and Lesser Black-backed Gulls, Glaucous and Iceland Gulls feed on tip and loaf on flashes. Flocks of Lapwing, Golden Plover and Snipe roost by day. A few Redshank or Ruff may winter. Pied Wagtail gather in large numbers at dusk prior to roosting. Water Rail at Butterfinch Bridge. Possibility of Long-eared Owl, Great Grey Shrike, Blackcap or Chiffchaff. Few wildfowl at Marston: Wigeon, Teal, Pochard, Tufted Duck.

March-May: Gull and plover flocks disperse. Light wader passage; Redshank, Ringed and Little Ringed Plovers display. Scrubland comes to life as warblers arrive and take up territory.

June-July: Breeding waders and Shelduck may have young. Warblers continue to sing well into June: Grasshopper, Reed and Garden Warblers, Whitethroat and Lesser Whitethroat among others. Turtle Doves, now scarce, purr from the edge of thickets. Lapwing flocks start to reform by the end of June and the first passage waders appear in July.

August-November: Wader passage at its most varied; plover flocks increase in size. Juvenile warblers roam the scrub, sometimes with mixed flocks of tits. In September they take berries from elder and other bushes, and perhaps utter subdued practice songs before departing. Lesser Black-backed Gull may predominate in the diurnal roost.

55C MARBURY (BUDWORTH) MERE AND PICK MERE

OS ref: SJ 655768 and 683772
(See map on p. 170)

Habitat

The Country Park lies within the grounds of the now demolished Marbury Hall. It consists for the most part of dog-walking grassland, the scrub which provided much ornithological interest having been largely cleared away. However mature planted woodland or mixed broad-leaved trees with some conifers encircles the park.

The mere, often referred to as Budworth Mere to distinguish it from Marbury Mere near Whitchurch, is fringed by a narrow belt of phragmites reeds for much of its perimeter. In places these reeds thicken out to form substantial beds, notably at the western end where a small woodland reserve has been set aside as a memorial to T.A. Coward, the great Cheshire naturalist. Other parts of the shoreline are subject to grazing and trampling by cattle. A sandy spit by the mouth of the Kid Brook on the north bank attracts bathing gulls and sometimes waders. The mere is subject to heavy disturbance by a sailing club based at the eastern end, and by members of the public visiting the park.

Species

The mere seldom supports large numbers of wildfowl, but most of the common species occur regularly in winter. A few Goldeneye are usually present, and Cormorant fly in from Rostherne. The mere attracts more than its fair share of divers and the rarer grebes, with one or two in most winters. Canada Goose are becoming more frequent and skeins of Pink-footed Goose pass over occasionally in mid-winter. A Bittern is sometimes seen in winter or spring.

In spring the reedbeds attract a good variety of waterfowl. Gadwall and Shoveler have displayed in recent years, the latter species having bred successfully, and Tufted and Ruddy Ducks nest annually, as do Little and Great Crested Grebes. Reed Warbler are present from late April, by which time the wintering Water Rail have departed.

Budworth Mere is probably the best place in Cheshire to see Kingfisher, for several pairs nest in the vicinity, and birds often dash low over the water within a few metres of the mereside footpath, their approach being heralded by a ringing 'chee' call. Grey Wagtail also nest. A heronry has been founded in recent years and held over 60 nests in 1990.

Spring passage over and by the mere involves essentially the same species as at Tatton Mere (site 49), but Sand Martin tend to arrive here even earlier in March and Common Sandpiper are generally better represented with six or more around the shoreline in late April. Oystercatcher may occur at this time. Other passage waders are more likely to be seen in autumn, when Dunlin, a Green Sandpiper or a Redshank may feed at the mouth of Kid Brook.

Terns occur at Marbury more regularly and in better numbers than at any other inland site in the county. Black Tern are more likely to appear in the autumn, but Common and Arctic Tern usually appear on both migrations. The occasional Little Gull is also seen.

All three species of woodpeckers nest locally. The woodlands fringing the park hold a good variety of birds including Marsh Tit, plentiful Long-tailed Tit and Nuthatch, with Blackcap, Spotted Flycatcher and Chiffchaff in summer. The first Chiffchaff often sings at the mereside well before the end of March.

Pick Mere, some two kilometres to the east of Marbury Mere, attracts a similar range of species in winter and on passage, but lacks the woodland species. Its margins support Sedge and Reed Warblers and Reed Bunting, and damp fields alongside the mere are popular with migrant pipits and wagtails.

Timing

The sailing club is active on most days with even remotely favourable weather, but the presence of the boats generally only concentrates waterfowl in the western end. Here they may be disturbed by visitors to the Country Park, so in fine weather early morning visits are advisable. Tern passage is most likely in wet, windy weather from mid-April to June and again from July to September. Black Tern arrive especially on easterly winds.

Pick Mere is often worth a visit at passage times, especially during showery weather in spring. Winter visits may turn up unusual waterfowl.

Access

The Marbury Country Park is signposted off the minor road between Anderton and Comberbach (SJ 648763). Otherwise it may be reached by continuing northward up the private road from Butterfinch Bridge. There is free access to the south-western shores of the mere through the park. To reach Pick Mere either follow minor roads from the park, turning right in Comberbach and continuing through Great Budworth to Pickmere village, or take the B5391 eastwards from the A559 Lostock-Warrington road. From Pickmere village follow signs for 'Pickmere Lake'. Park at the fairground end and walk the very muddy footpath along the south bank of the mere, examining fields for migrants.

Calendar

All year: Woodland birds include Nuthatch, Treecreeper, Long-tailed and Marsh Tits, and all three woodpeckers. Great Crested and Little Grebes frequent the meres all year unless driven off by frosts. Heron and Kingfisher seen daily.

December-February: Wildfowl include Pochard and Goldeneye, Wigeon and Teal. Pink-footed Goose overhead occasionally and rare grebes or divers seen most winters. Cormorant fish in the meres. Water Rails and Snipes along boggy parts of shoreline.

March-May: Sand Martin and Chiffchaff arrive by the end of March with other hirundines and Swift following in April. Common Sandpiper and occasionally other waders pass through in April and May. Ruddy Duck and perhaps other waterfowl take up residence by reedbeds. Terns and sometimes a Little Gull may feed over meres.

June-July: Residents and summer visitors busy feeding young, including Reed Warbler, Blackcap and Spotted Flycatcher. Common Tern, or perhaps other tern species, visit occasionally.

August-November: Terns pass through in appropriate conditions until September, a few waders, such as Dunlin, Redshank or Green Sandpiper until October. Winter wildfowl then returning.

Habitat

The four huge sludgetanks at the Woolston Deposit Grounds SSSI are managed in part as a nature reserve by the Eyes Conservation Group in agreement with the Manchester Ship Canal Company. Part of the site is still in use to accommodate dredgings from the Ship Canal. Beds No. 1 and No. 2 lie between the canal and the Mersey. No. 1, east of the motorway viaduct, consists primarily of rough grassland, but sand extraction has created a number of pools which attract waders and wildfowl. No. 2 is currently being used for pumping and has mudflats which are an important feeding and roosting areas for waders and gulls. No. 3 lies to the north of a meander of the river. This bed is shallowly flooded and contains extensive beds of *Typha* and some phragmites. The western half of the bed is covered in nettles, willow scrub and other rank vegetation. The westernmost No. 4 bed again lies between the river and the canal. It has reached the end of its life as a sludgetank and is developing a dense cover of willow scrub and rank herbage. All the tanks have steep embankments with rough grassland and scrub. In places taller poplars and willows grow alongside the river whose banks are covered in parts by hawthorn, elder, bramble and increasingly Himalayan Balsam and Japanese Knotweed. The river and canal are severely polluted, but both may hold wildfowl in severe weather and grebes have recently been observed catching fish on the river as the water quality slowly improves. A rubbish tip to the east of the reserve attracts large numbers of scavenging gulls and crows.

Species

In all, over 200 species have been recorded at the Eyes, including all five grebes, the three woodpeckers, and four species of owl.

Lying next to the Mersey, the flooded tanks inevitably attract large numbers of dabbling ducks moving inland from the estuary. The Mersey valley Pochard flock also spends time here, making this an excellent place to see winter wildfowl. Typically a thousand or more Teal are present, sometimes several times this figure, with several hundred Mallard and Pochard, a hundred or so Shoveler and Tufted Duck, and from a few dozen to several hundred Pintail. Ruddy Duck are increasing in numbers. Typically 20–30 will be present in mid-winter, but in mild seasons over 100 may remain into December and in 1986 128 were on the Ship Canal in February. Other standard duck species occur less frequently or in smaller numbers, and scarce or rare species such as Ferruginous and Long-tailed Duck, Green-winged Teal, Common Scoter and Smew have been noted. In late autumn and winter Pink-footed Goose occasionally fly over and have been known to alight briefly.

The extensive shallow marsh of No. 3 Bed forms excellent nesting habitat for wildfowl. Teal, Shoveler, Mallard, Pochard and Tufted Duck are all present in good numbers in the summer,and this is probably the most important site in Britain for breeding Ruddy Duck. Gadwall breed annually, and Pintail, Wigeon and Garganey are suspected of doing so in some years. A drake Ring-necked Duck moulted at the Eyes between May and August in three summers in the mid-1980s. Pochard broods are conspicuous between mid-June and the end of July – in 1981 17 were recorded. Broods of Tufted and Ruddy Ducks are more likely to appear in July and August respectively. Broods of the various dabbling ducks remain hidden in the marsh and are less easily seen.

Other breeding waterfowl have included Shelduck, with a pair or two of Mute Swan in most years, and Canada Goose in 1990. Up to 20 pairs of Little Grebe arrive in spring and stay to nest. In July and August they gather in groups of thirty or more on the open water before dispersing. A pair or two of Great Crested Grebes have appeared since the introduction of fish.

The Eyes support important nesting populations of several other marshland birds. More than 150 singing Sedge Warbler and over 100 Reed Bunting are present in summer, with up to thirty pairs of Reed Warbler. Water Rail may be heard squealing at any time of the year and there can be little doubt that several pairs nest. Bearded Tit and Marsh Harrier have both appeared on passage, with the latter now annual. Emergent tussocks are favoured as nest sites by up to 450 pairs of Black-headed Gull, whose presence attracts migrant Little Gull in spring. Common, Arctic and Black Terns may visit in spring or autumn, and hundreds of Swift often feed overhead.

The scrubby embankments are favoured by Grasshopper Warbler, with fifteen or more pairs present in good seasons, and up to eight pairs of Whitethroats and fifty of Willow Warbler. A pair of Stonechat or Whinchat nests in some years. Blackcap and Willow Tit nest along the better wooded stretches of riverbank, where Kingfisher are often seen, with Sand Martin in the banks of the Ship Canal.

The scrub and *Typha* on No. 3 Bed hold large roosts of Starling from spring to autumn, comprising some tens of thousands of birds at times. In autumn Pied Wagtail roost, with perhaps a few thousand Starling in early September. In most years there is a sizeable Swallow roost, regularly up to 3,000 birds but 10,000 in September 1985. Inevitably, a Hobby is often in attendance and has provided some spectacular performances. From October to early winter thousands of Redwing and other thrushes may shelter by night. Mist-netting by day has revealed significant passage of various passerines through the Eyes, with perhaps 300 Reed Bunting being ringed in a typical autumn. Warblers and Goldcrest pass through in moderate numbers.

In winter roosts dwindle as food supplies diminish, although Magpies seldom seem to go hungry and over 200 continue to roost in the scrub. Finches, notably Linnet, flock to feed on weed seed on the drier parts of muddy tanks. A sprinkling of Chiffchaff remains in willow scrub during most winters, and two Firecrest wintered in 1989/90. Merlin are seen annually in very small numbers and one or two Short-eared Owl hunt field voles in grassy areas. A Peregrine may visit from time to time.

Wader passage is much smaller than formerly, due to changes in the pumping regime into the tanks. Spring passage is typically light, although Common Sandpiper are seen regularly in late April and early May, and recently bred for the first time. Little Ringed Plover appear annually and usually attempt to breed. The inland spread of Ringed Plover has resulted in this species also breeding. Autumn passage is much more reliable, and although not as common as formerly, 10–15 Ruff can be expected in August and September. Most wader species which are likely to occur inland appear sooner or later, with Knot, Grey Plover, Sanderling and

Turnstone annual. Recent rarities have included Buff-breasted, Pectoral and White-rumped Sandpipers, Red-necked Phalarope and Temminck's Stint. Dunlin occur at almost any time of the year and can exceed 100 in autumn and winter. Several dozen Snipe are also present at these seasons, but number are notoriously difficult to estimate. A flock of up to 2,000 Lapwing often attracts 500–1,000 Golden Plover.

Timing
Whatever the timing of a visit there is always something to be seen. Even nocturnal visits might produce an array of surprising noises. Spotted Crake have been heard in the last two springs in the early hours. Morning visits are generally most productive for birdsong. As gulls pass through on their way to roost in the late afternoon these should be checked for rarities. Easterly winds in spring or autumn are likely to produce Black Tern, and in October and November large movement of Thrushes may take place. Grounded waders are most likely in wet weather.

Access
Access is strictly limited to permit holders. Permits are available, at a cost of £3 per year (£6 for a family), from Brian Ankers, 9 Lynton Gardens, Appleton, Warrington, Cheshire W4 4ED. A stamped addressed envelope should be enclosed and cheques made payable to the Eyes Conservation Group. A permit entitles the holder to visit the Eyes on any number of occasions during the year and to make use of the several hides either planned or already in existence.

The Eyes is not an easy reserve to find but is best approached by visitors from outside the area by leaving the M6 at Junction 21 and taking the A57 signposted to Warrington. After some 200 yards (200 m) turn left down Weir Lane and park by Woolston Weir (SJ 654888). All permit holders receive a map of the reserve giving details of the best viewing points and those areas which are out of bounds.

Calendar
All year: Mute Swan, Teal, Shoveler, Pochard, Tufted Duck; Water Rail, Moorhen, Coot; Snipe, Black-headed Gull; Kingfisher, Willow Tit.

December-February: Large flocks of wildfowl including Pintail and several hundred diving ducks. Pink-footed Goose occasional overhead. Short-eared Owls and occasional Merlin hunt grassland. Peregrine and Hen Harrier possible. Lapwing and Snipe present in flocks with smaller numbers of Golden Plover, Ruff and occasional influxes of Dunlin. Magpie roost in scrub where few Chiffchaff often winter. Linnet and other finches flock to weedy tanks.

March-May: Little and Great Crested Grebes return; prospecting Shelduck and occasional Garganey visit as Ruddy and other ducks take up territory. Wigeon and Pintail may show signs of nesting. Common Sandpiper and few other waders pass through, and little Ringed Plover arrive. Reed Bunting appear from March onwards, with warblers arriving in April and May. Little Gull and terns may pass through in late April and May. Starling roost likely to form as first broods fledge in mid-May.

June-July: Wildfowl broods appearing include Pochard, Tufted Duck,

Teal, Gadwall and perhaps Shoveler. Many hundreds of moulting Pochard, Shoveler and Mallard gather on No. 2 Bed. Gull colony gives impression of great activity, and hundreds of Swift may wheel overhead. Warbler song tails off in July. Starling continue to roost in thousands. Common Sandpiper passage resumes in early July, and Little Grebe gather on open water later in the month. Flocks of migrant Shelduck heading for the moult are often seen on late July evenings.

August-November: Little Grebe depart in early autumn. Ruddy Duck broods still appearing in August. Small flocks of Shelduck sometimes appear in mid-autumn. Shoveler flocks reach huge proportions, perhaps 500 or more, in September and October when Ruddy Duck usually exceed 100. 50–100 Canada Goose have become a feature of recent autumns. Wader passage includes Ruff, Dunlin, Ringed Plover and other species. Snipe and Lapwing flocks reform. Terns occasional until September. Warblers depart during August and September, when birds from outside the area pass through. Swallow roosts in early autumn replaced by Pied Wagtail and incoming thrushes in October. Goldcrest and Reed Bunting pass through in October. By November large numbers of Teal have usually returned.

Reference
The Eyes Conservation Group produce a comprehensive annual report obtainable (from the address given above for permits) at a cost of £2.50.

57 LOWER WEAVER VALLEY: ACTON BRIDGE TO KINGSLEY

Habitat

The river Weaver was canalised to facilitate the export of salt from the Cheshire wiches. It is still used on a small scale in association with the chemical industry, and increasingly by pleasure craft. Continuous dredging is necessary to keep the canal open, the silt being pumped into large riverside lagoons to drain. Such sludgetanks at Acton Bridge and Kingsley are both excellent bird habitats, showing quite different stages of vegetational succession. At Acton Bridge recent pumping has left areas of open mud and small pools with low, marshy vegetation, while at Kingsley, where the lagoon has been unused for some years, a phragmites reedbed has developed with scrubby margins and a sizeable, shallow pool.

The Weaver itself is fringed by reeds in places, notably by the side channel to Dutton locks, and there are further reedy cut-off pools between here and Kingsley. The valley bottom is intensively farmed, both for arable and dairying, but there are a number of ancient woods on the steeper valley sides. Warburton's Wood, at Kingsley, is a particularly good example, being a reserve 'of the Cheshire Conservation Trust. In May the blossom on the Wild Cherry trees can be spectacular. Small-leaved Lime and Wild Service tree are present, both being rare in the county, and many unusual fungi appear in autumn.

Species

In winter small numbers of dabbling ducks feed at the sludgebeds, but that at Kingsley is shot over on occasions. Reed Bunting pick seeds from flattened grasses at both sites, and Water Rail lurk in the Kingsley reeds. Tree Sparrow and Yellowhammer flock to stubble fields, and may be joined by local Corn Bunting. A wintering Green Sandpiper may feed at Acton Bridge, or rise unexpectedly from the side of the Weaver. Snipe are regular in damp ground, along with a Jack Snipe or two. From mid-afternoon parties of gulls call in at Acton Bridge to bathe on their way to roost around the Mersey estuary.

April brings passage migrants to the valley. At Acton Bridge White and Yellow Wagtail dart around the pools where Little Ringed Plover stoop to feed. Whitethroats dance over the banks and Lesser Whitethroat rattle from cover. Depending on the state of the tanks, Sedge Warbler may settle, and Reed Warbler sing from the Dutton reeds. Common Sandpiper flicker along the river, and may hop over the bank onto the sludgebed perhaps to join a Green Sandpiper or two. In May wader passage increases. Dunlin are more likely and parties of arctic Ringed Plover drop in. Other species, such as Greenshank, may call in. Shelduck have bred. Cuckoo occur in small migrant parties, calling noisily from the telephone wires above the riverbank, and gliding down to snap up caterpillars.

Meanwhile at Kingsley, Reed and Sedge Warblers have taken up territories in the reedbed, and a Grasshopper Warbler or two may sing from bramble patches. Cuckoo often enter the reeds and may lay in Reed Warbler nests – unusual behaviour in the region. Towards dusk a Water Rail may start its eerie calling. A variety of scrubland birds breeds around the lagoon and across the water. Turtle Dove nested until recently and may still do so. On the open water look for broods of Mallard, Coot and Little Grebe. Less common species may also nest, for example Ruddy Duck.

Great and Lesser Spotted Woodpecker are resident in the woodlands, along with a good variety of typical woodland species. Marsh Tits are more numerous along the Weaver valley than elsewhere in Cheshire.

Autumn brings drab Shoveler, more Teal and perhaps a Garganey to the sludgebeds. Acton Bridge is especially favoured for feeding, the summer's crop of buttercups and Redleg providing abundant seed. Green Sandpiper may reach double figures, and a sprinkling of other waders also appears. A variety of small passerines feeds in the wet bottom of the tank; pipits, wagtails and Reed Bunting especially. In drizzly weather, parties of terns sometimes fly along the Weaver, but are intent on their travels and take no notice of the pools alongside. Turtle Doves join Stock Dove and buntings in stubble fields.

Timing

Early morning visits are likely to be most productive at Acton Bridge, but any time of day will do. The crucial factor is the activity of dog-walkers, some of whom unfortunately allow their animals to run over the sludge-tank, scaring off the birds which take time to return. Unless shooting is taking place Kingsley is less prone to disturbance.

Access

For Kingsley lagoon, head east from Kingsley (south east of Frodsham) along the B5153, turning left onto Ball Lane after a quarter of a mile (0.5 km). There is space to park at the right-angle bend where the track to Hall o'th' Hey farm branches off to the north (SJ 557758). Walk up to the farm and a cart-track continues down to the river. At the river bank turn right for the lagoon, which may be viewed by climbing the bank, or turn left to follow the bottom of Warburton's wood. Members of the Cheshire Conservation Trust can obtain further access to the wood.

From Kingsley it is possible to walk through to Acton Bridge, following the riverbank for much of the way. Alternatively park on the side road off the A49 beside the Weaver swing bridge (SJ 601761). A private road and public path follows the Weaver westwards past the lagoon, which again may be viewed by climbing the bank. Be careful when first topping the bank, or all the birds may be flushed by your sudden appearance. Continue along the riverside to Dutton locks. Here a path skirts the reedbed. Cross the river at the locks and continue downstream for further reedy pools.

Calendar

All year: Marsh Tit, woodpeckers, Stock Dove, Corn Bunting and Tree Sparrow.

December-February: A few waterfowl, Green Sandpiper, Water Rail, Reed Bunting.

March-May: Green Sandpiper, Ringed Plover, Little Ringed Plover, Dunlin, Common Sandpiper, other waders and Shelduck at Acton Bridge. Warblers here and at Kingsley include Reed, Sedge and perhaps Grasshopper. Cuckoo often conspicuous.

June-July: Rather a quiet time, but waterbirds have young, and families of Marsh Tit are sometimes conspicuous around Kingsley and Dutton. Wader passage resumes in July.

August-November: Wader passage continues, Green Sandpiper especially. Dabbling ducks gather in eclipse plumage. Turtle Dove in early autumn with other seed-eaters in stubble fields.

58 FRODSHAM MARSH AND THE WEAVER BEND

Habitat

The Mersey estuary supports wildfowl and wader populations of inter-national importance but, unfortunately, is for the most part inaccessible to the casual birdwatcher. However the Frodsham Marshes, a stretch of flat grazing marsh between the M56 motorway and Manchester Ship Canal, together with the 'estuary' of the river Weaver which flows into the canal, provide opportunities to see most if not all the estuarine species, and others too.

Frodsham Score lies to the north of the Ship Canal and consists of an area of closely-cropped turf bordering the tidal mud-flats of the Mersey. The estuary is severely polluted by the various chemical works in the vicinity. Nevertheless considerable numbers of Shelduck and waders feed out on the mud.

Much of the marsh is taken up by huge sludgetanks into which dredgings from the Ship Canal are pumped to drain. Ultimately the tanks revert to pasture, but while still wet they may form habitats of outstand-ing value for wildfowl and waders. It appears that sludge deposited of late has been too polluted to support much life, and birds are only usually present when high tides force them off the estuary. Bulldozing during construction work on the retaining banks of the tanks often result in a good crop of weed-seed on the disturbed ground. Established banks develop a cover of scrub and rough grassland.

The low-lying fields on the remainder of the marsh are bordered by tall thorn hedges and drained by deep ditches which contains stands of phragmites. Some fields are devoted to cereal crops, the resultant stubble providing winter feeding for many birds.

The Weaver Bend consists of a meander of the river Weaver extending to some 2 miles (3 km) between the motorway bridge and the Ship

182

Canal, where it overflows into the estuary through the Weaver Sluice. The Bend contains extensive mud-banks which are exposed at low tide, depending on the operation of locks and sluices on the canal. These banks, and the riversides which are lined with marsh vegetation in places, attract wildfowl and waders. A sludge tank immediately above the Bend attracts considerable numbers of waders at times. The Bend is subject to increasing disturbance from water-skiers.

Species

In winter a wide range of wildfowl visit the Bend. Tufted Duck and Pochard feed near the junction with the Ship Canal and may be joined by a few Scaup, often brown immature birds. Goldeneye are often present in small numbers and one or two 'redhead' Smew are fairly regular. Ruddy Duck arrive in severe weather when the flow of the river keeps the Bend open after meres have frozen. Cormorants and Great Crested Grebe are also more likely to appear under such conditions. Scarcer diving ducks, such as Long-tailed and the American Ring-necked, have been recorded.

Numbers of surface-feeding ducks fluctuate wildly, not least due to the early morning visits of wildfowlers. The vast flocks on the Mersey form an enormous reservoir from which birds move into the Weaver. To give some idea of the potential involved, the following figures are the highest species totals on the Mersey Marshes from monthly counts in 1988: Shelduck – 2,060; Wigeon – 6,000; Teal· – 7,000; Mallard – 1,095; and Pintail – 3,960. Much higher numbers are noted in more severe winters. Some of these birds are occasionally seen on the Score, and up to several hundred Teal and a smaller number of Wigeon often visit the Bend. Pintail are more likely to be seen flying over heading for stubble fields inland.

A flock of Canada Goose has taken up residence, replacing the herd of Mute Swan which occurred prior to the catastrophic decline of the 1970s. Swans seen now are almost as likely to be Bewick's or Whoopers. Small flocks of grey geese, either Pink-footed or White-fronted, spend a few days on the Marsh in most winters. In February 1984 a party of eight Bean Goose was seen.

Many other birds inhabit the fields. Up to 5,000 Golden Plover roost on the sludge tanks and feed on the fields or Score along with 2–3,000 Lapwing. Several times a day the alarm calls of Lapwing and the excited whistling of Golden Plover signal the approach of a predator. The whole flock rises with a rush of wings which must prove bewildering for the incoming Peregrine, often an inexperienced immature bird, or smaller Merlin, for which these heavy plovers are outside the normal range of prey species.

Other waders attach themselves to the plover flocks: Snipe, Redshank and Dunlin, perhaps a Ruff or two, or even a Black-tailed Godwit. All these species, and in some winters a few Little Stint, are more likely to be seen on the Bend. Two hundred or more Snipe and even larger numbers of Dunlin may feed here. The highest tides may flush several thousand Dunlin and other waders off the Mersey to roost on the sludge tanks.

Short-eared Owl quarter the embankments on the lookout for small mammals and birds. Four or five of these pale, long-winged owls hunt here each winter. In good vole years there may be a dozen or more, they roost close together on the ground and may be flushed, one after the other, by a farmer or shooter walking across the tanks until several are in the air at once. Hen Harrier are occasional visitors.

Stubble fields attract flocks of Woodpigeon, Stock Dove and finches including dozens or hundreds of Chaffinch, Brambling and Greenfinch, with smaller numbers of Linnet and possibly a few Twite. In snowy weather hundreds of Skylark from further inland gather on the stubbles and winter thrushes strip any remaining berries off the hedges before being forced to feed on the ground. A Great Grey Shrike is seen between Frodsham and Helsby in some winters. Coveys of Grey Partridge inhabit most fields. They are as common here as anywhere in the region south of the Mersey and partridge shoots are held in most winters. A few Red-legged Partridge are seen.

Many of the winter flocks remain intact during March before dispersing as spring approaches. Two to three thousand Golden Plovers may still be present in late April, by now showing the extensive black on the under-parts which characterises the northern race. Spring arrives late in high latitudes, so these birds time their departure accordingly. Many Woodpigeon nest late, so there may still be a thousand or more on the Marsh in early May.

Garganey are recorded in most springs, occasionally in March but more likely in April or May. A series of small pools above the Ship Canal is particularly favoured. Oystercatcher, Ringed and Little Ringed Plovers all breed locally in small numbers, and by April they are back in territory. Common Sandpiper pipe as they fly beneath the river banks, and other passage waders such as Ruff and Greenshank may occur amongst the Dunlin on the Bend. Sanderling and northern Ringed Plover move through in May and early June, when there is more chance of a Curlew Sandpiper or perhaps a Temminck's Stint. Other rarities at this season have included Dotterel, Collared Pratincole, Red-necked Phalarope, Broad-billed and Stilt Sandpiper. Common, Arctic and Black Tern may pass through, sometimes flying straight on upstream without stopping.

Passerine migrants include Wheatear and Reed Bunting in late March, joined by Yellow Wagtail and a sprinkling of Rock or Water Pipit in April. Goldfinch and Linnet move through in parties, and may fall victim to a lingering Merlin. Short-eared Owl usually remain into April. Reed Warbler appear in stands of phragmites and Sedge Warbler chatter along the ditches. The thin reeling song of the Grasshopper Warbler emanates from bramble clumps on the sides of the tanks, where Whinchats nest in ever dwindling numbers – victims of drought in their African winter quarters. A small nesting population of Meadow Pipit shares the same embankments.

By July return passage is already underway. Often a single adult Little Stint or brick-red Curlew Sandpiper portends the main passage which is due to follow a month later. These are birds which may have lost their eggs or perhaps not bred at all, hence their early arrival. 'Dusky' Spotted Redshank may even appear in late June, with Greenshank and Ruff almost certain to be seen at some time in July. Redshank and Dunlin increase, and Curlew start to build up on the fields where they probe with their long bills for earthworms. Swift gather in hundreds over the Bend and up to forty Heron roost on fields nearby.

Wader passage picks up during August and September. Several hundred Dunlin are often present and high tides may force other species to roost on the tanks. A thousand or more Ringed Plover may appear there with Knot more likely in September, and a few Sanderling or Turnstone in either month. On the Bend a dozen or so Curlew Sandpiper in August may increase to 30 or so in September, although in some years almost none are seen. Redshanks similarly increase to 200–300. Ruffs find the river to their liking and up to 50 may be present. Black-tailed Godwit are also frequent if erratic in their occurrences. Little Stint are usually late in passing through. Small numbers in August may increase to fifty or more in September and October,with a few remaining later.

Most wader species appear at some stage on the ICI tank above the Bend where they may allow very close views. Green Sandpiper tend to stay further upriver towards the motorway bridge, where Snipe become more numerous in late autumn, by which time the plover flocks have returned to the fields and several hundred Curlew may be present.

In addition to species mentioned above, most waders that occur regularly in Britain are noted from time to time. Frodsham offers a better chance of seeing truly rare waders than anywhere else in the region. These have included three Black-winged Stilt, two Buff-breasted Sandpiper, four White-rumped, seven Pectoral and two Baird's Sandpipers, one Sharp-tailed and one Stilt Sandpiper, four Wilson's and a Red-necked Phalarope amongst others, all since 1980! In August 1990 a Long-billed Dowitcher arrived in breeding plumage.

By August increasing numbers of ducks feed on the river; Teal, Wigeon and Shoveler in drab, eclipse plumages. One or two Garganey often consort with the much more numerous Teal. Little Grebe feed on small fish which they pursue beneath the algal blanket on the water. Terns pass through in autumn as well as spring. Black Tern and Little Gull are now more likely to linger for a few days, hawking up and down the river and picking flies off the surface. White-winged Black Tern have occurred several times.

Swarms of House Martin gather over the river before leaving for the south, and hundreds or even thousands of Swallow roost with Sand Martin by night in reedbeds by the Ship Canal and elsewhere. A Hobby or two now appear annually, scything in at dusk and perhaps at dawn also to cut down hirundines. Another rarity that turns up with some regularity is the Spotted Crake, a short-billed relative of the rather more numerous Water Rail.

During August and early September parties of Yellow Wagtail feed in damp fields, and loose groups of Sedge Warblers, up to 20 strong, move through the reedy ditches. Goldfinch and Linnet form noisy flocks, including many young birds, to feed on the ripening seed of thistles and ragworts. Many of these birds have moved on by October when Rock or Water Pipit appear briefly at the riverside and a few Twite may drop in. On overcast days with an easterly breeze southward passage of pipits and Skylark may be heavy, and small parties alight to feed beside the tanks. Reed Bunting may also be prevalent at such times.

Timing

Afternoon visits at weekends are perhaps the most likely to clash with water skiers, although there is a risk of this at almost any time. Dawn or dusk visits may coincide with wildfowlers' activities. Otherwise there are good birds to be seen at almost any time, and plenty of habitat to cover apart from the Bend itself.

The highest tides are likely to flush waders off the Mersey, and at such times the sludge-beds should be checked carefully. Consult tide tables for the predicted height of tides.

In severe weather wildfowl may concentrate on the river which remains unfrozen. Thrushes and larks also gather, having been driven west by snow.

Access

Leave the M56 at Junction 12 and follow signs into Frodsham. After passing beneath a footbridge the road descends towards a set of traffic lights. Turn right shortly before the lights into Ship Street and follow this lane round until a bridge over the motorway is seen on the left (SJ 520785). Turn left, pass over the bridge, and continue along the unmade road until a gate bars the way. A footpath continues from here up to the Bend. Once the motorway is crossed, the roads on the marsh are private, and while many visitors drive as close to the Bend as practicable, this is a potential cause of friction with landowners and tenants, so is left to the conscience of the individual.

Alternatively, continue through the lights in Frodsham and pass along the main shopping street before turning right down Marsh Lane. This lane passes over the motorway where, now a private road, it forks (SJ 512779). Take the right-hand fork to reach the Bend. This track runs alongside then climbs the bank of No. 5 tank. From here the path to the Bend is obvious. The left-hand fork leads alongside the sludge-tanks and up to the pumping station by the Ship Canal. Walk left from here to view the 'canal pools'. On the highest tides walk left for several hundred yards to a position opposite the old magazine out on the Score to view wildfowl and waders with a good chance of Peregrine.

Calendar

All year: Lapwing, Redshank and Dunlin at almost any time. Grey and a few Red-legged Partridges. Little Grebe, Canada Goose and Shelduck usually present.

December-February: Wigeon, Teal and perhaps Pintail; Pochard, Tufted Duck and Goldeneye, perhaps Smew and Scaup; Ruddy Duck and scarcer waterfowl in frosty weather; wild geese and swans may visit. Peregrine, Merlin and Short-eared Owl hunt the marshes, with perhaps a Hen Harrier or Long-eared Owl. Large flocks of Lapwing and Golden Plover often joined by Ruff, Black-tailed Godwit or other waders. Snipe and Curlew on damper ground. Stubble fields hold large numbers of pigeons, finches and, after snow, Skylark, Fieldfare and Redwing in fields and hedgerows. Water Rails in reedbeds. Possibility of Great Grey Shrike.

March-May: Winter flocks disperse and raptors move back north in March and April, when Wheatear, pipits, wagtails and Reed Bunting appear by the Bend, along with incoming Goldfinch and Linnet. Northern Golden Plover remain into May in breeding plumage. Breeding Ringed and Little Ringed Plovers arrive. Passage waders include more Ringed Plover, Sanderling, Common Sandpiper, Ruff, perhaps Greenshank and others. Terns move through quickly. Garganey likely from March onward.

June-July: Whinchat, Meadow Pipit and Grasshopper Warbler around tanks; Sedge and Reed Warblers in reeds. Large feeding concentrations of Swift over river. Return wader passage begins in July: odd Curlew Sandpiper, Spotted Redshank, Greenshank, Ruff. Dunlin, Redshank and Curlew increase. Diurnal roost of Heron.

August-November: Wader passage most marked August to early October, with Dunlin, Ruff, Redshank, Black-tailed Godwit, Curlew Sandpiper, Little Stint, occasional Turnstone, Sanderling or rarer species. Estuarine waders such as Ringed Plover, Knot on tanks at high tides. Garganey regular on river with Teal and other ducks during August and September. Black and other terns pass through, perhaps Little Gull. Hobby likely at Swallow roosts in August-September. Warblers and Yellow Wagtail move out followed by Linnet and Goldfinch flocks. Spotted Crake may lurk in reeds in September; Water Rail increase in October. Also in October, small passage of Water and Rock Pipit and Twite; passage of larks and Meadow Pipit may be heavy. Winter thrushes and finches arrive October-November, followed by owls and raptors. Plover flocks reassemble.

ADDITIONAL SITE:
HALE HEAD

OS ref: SJ 473809 (Sheet 108)

Hale Head, a low sandstone bluff, juts out into the Mersey estuary from the north bank opposite Frodsham Marsh, and offers an alternative viewing point for estuarine species. It is approached by a minor road south from Hale Village, with limited parking at the southern end. From here a track leads down to the disused lighthouse.

As the tide rises flocks of Dunlin and other waders may concentrate offshore, with attendant raptors and a range of wildfowl, including the Mersey specialities, Teal, Wigeon and Pintail. Corn Bunting and Yellow Wagtail breed in the arable fields.

Footpaths follow the shoreline to east and west. Pickerings Pasture, 1 ½ miles (2.5 km) to the east, is a reclaimed rubbish tip, landscaped to attract wildlife, and boasting a wader scrape. To the west of Hale Head, Oglet Shore provides further viewing of estuary birds. More direct access is available down Dungeon Lane which skirts Speke airfield.

59 DELAMERE FOREST
OS Map 117/118
SJ

Habitat

Delamere Forest derives its name from the medieval hunting forest of Mara, this definition being legal rather than physical. Indeed until recently the character of the forest was one of dry heathland on sandy soils with boggy, sphagnum-filled hollows and odd stands of pine trees. Now much of the area has been ploughed for arable farming, and almost all the heathland has been lost under conifers.

Abbots Moss is a floating bog – a mat of sphagnum moss floating over several metres of liquid peat and water. It is noted for its bog plants, such as Cranberry and bog Rosemary, and for dragonflies, notably the White-faced Dragonfly, Green Hairstreak butterflies and Orange Underwing moths flutter around the birch trees, Grass Snakes and lizards are sometimes seen. The bog is gradually drying out as a consequence of sand-quarrying operations nearby which have lowered the water-table.

The various sand-quarries are of some ornithological importance, and not only for aquatic and waterside species. Bulldozing of topsoil and 'overburden' allows the germination of arable weeds whose seeds attract finches and doves. Unlike the Chelford quarries, these pits are worked 'wet', that is they are allowed to flood while still operational and sand is pumped out through hoses. Silt draining back in from the stock-piles forms shallow beaches which attract gulls and waders and which eventually develop a covering of reedmace.

Species

The mature plantations support rather few species of birds. Crossbill are seen annually in flocks of up to fifty or more and breed in some years, Siskin too may breed annually in very small numbers but proof is seldom forthcoming. They are far more numerous in winter and especially in spring. The high-pitched squeaks of Goldcrests and Coal Tits, feeding in the tops of conifers, can be heard at all seasons. Wrens nest amongst the ferns beneath the pines, where Chaffinch and Treecreeper sing, in summer they are joined by Blackcap, Chiffchaff and Spotted Flycatcher. A few pairs of Sparrowhawk are also present, and Kestrel hunt the cleared areas. Tawny Owl are common, but the smaller Long-eared Owl has become rare and elusive, it should be sought in winter, roosting in willow scrub. Nightjar formerly bred in some numbers but there are no recent records although much habitat remains suitable, in some springs Brambling extract seeds from ripening cones in the flat crowns of pines.

Green Woodpecker seek out ants in open, sandy areas, and bound away when disturbed on whirring wings, their yellow rumps flashing. In June the noisy young of this species or the Great Spotted Woodpecker may be heard shouting for food from a nest in a shattered conifer or bogside alder. Willow Tits frequent these same alders and birches, and wander into the plantations to feed, as do numerous Nuthatch which nest in roadside oaks and chestnuts. Other birds which favour broad-leaved trees around the edges of the conifers are Wood Warbler, Pied Flycatcher and Redstart – all present in very small numbers.

Recent plantations, with trees between six and twelve feet (2–4 m) tall, are quiet in winter but alive with nesting passerines in summer. Tree Pipits sing from the tops of isolated birches or in parachuting display-flight, and Whitethroats warble a few, scratchy phrases during their briefer, low-level display, the fluty cadences of Willow Warbler mingle with the ringing songs of Yellowhammer and the stammer of Reed Bunting, here nesting in unusually dry habitat. Redpoll and Linnet fly out into surrounding fields in small groups to feed, while Dunnock and Long-tailed Tit are much less conspicuous. Toward dusk a Grasshopper Warbler may sing. Garden Warbler and Bullfinch favour taller, denser stands until such time as the foresters remove the lower branches from the trees.

Seed-eating species attracted to weedy, disturbed ground beside operational sand-quarries include Turtle Dove and more numerous Stock Doves. Corn Bunting nest in cornfields in the area and also visit the quarries which now offer a richer supply of seed than do sprayed croplands. The largest colonies of Sand Martins in Cheshire are established in recently exposed faces.

The most conspicuous feature of the quarries is the diurnal gathering of gulls from late summer until spring. Lesser Black-backed Gull often exceed a thousand in the autumn, and Common Gull are even more numerous in winter. Late on winter afternoons large flocks of gulls of all common species gather to drink and bathe before moving out to their roosts by the estuaries. At this time an Iceland or Glaucous Gull may appear.

In spring pairs of Black-headed Gull take up territory and may display, and would probably nest if rafts or islets were provided. The Common Tern which appear from time to time in summer might also be encouraged to breed.

A few waders occur on passage. Common Sandpiper and Dunlin are the most frequent species in both spring and autumn, with perhaps a Greenshank or Green Sandpiper at the latter season. Whimbrel pass through the area each May and sometimes alight in fields. With luck a small flock may be seen flying low to northward uttering their tittering, multiple whistle, or even pausing to deliver the full, bubbling song. Little Ringed Plover have bred on the sandy beaches and in winter a few Snipe and Jack Snipe crouch amongst stands of reedmace.

Little and Great Crested Grebe nest on the flooded quarries, and Black-necked Grebes have been seen. Shelduck display in April, but only Mallard, Tufted and Ruddy Ducks nest with any regularity. Up to twenty or thirty each of Pochard and Tufted Duck occur in winter, when up to a dozen Goldeneye and a few Teal are usually present.

Timing

That part of the forest closest to Delamere station attracts large numbers of day-trippers, especially on sunny days, but there are always more remote areas relatively free from disturbance. Morning or evening visits in spring are best for birdsong. Dusk visits in summer might reveal some of those nocturnal species of which little is now known in Delamere. Evening visits to the sand-quarries in winter may result in a sighting of an unusual gull attending the pre-roost gathering.

Access

The forest area straddles the A54 Chester to Winsford and A49 Warrington to Whitchurch roads. Access to the plantation is generally unrestricted along Forestry Commission rides. Some of the better sites are listed below.

59A Delamere Switchback

Take the B5152 Frodsham road northward from the A556. Pass over the railway bridge and continue for almost a mile (1.5 km) before turning left onto a minor road just before Hatchmere (SJ 552713). Tracks lead north and south from this road into the plantations. Explore this area for woodland birds; Nuthatch, Treecreeper, Green Woodpecker; Siskin in winter and spring, possibly summer; perhaps Crossbill; Redstart, Wood Warbler and perhaps Pied Flycatcher.

59B Fourways Sand Quarry

OS ref: SJ 574688

Visible from western end of Hogshead Wood or from A556 half a mile (1 km) to east of B5152 Delamere junction (parking difficult). Tufted Duck and few other wildfowl; Little Ringed Plover and occasional passage waders; large numbers of Common and Lesser Black-backed Gulls, possibly Iceland or Glaucous Gull; Turtle Dove in summer and Stock Dove all year. Sand Martin nest in banks.

59C Hogshead Wood

OS ref: SJ 583690

An area of young plantations lying to the west of the A49 opposite Nunsmere. This area tends to be less disturbed than other parts of the forest, and supports good numbers of scrubland species. Bulldozed areas are particularly attractive to butterflies. Part of the wood has been taken for a new quarry, which remains dry at the time of writing.

59D NUNSMERE
OS ref: SJ 590690
A disused quarry adjacent to the A49 half a mile (1 km) to the south of the A556 crossroads,with banks overgrown with birch scrub. Turtle Dove, Garden Warbler, Willow Tit, Bullfinch and Redpoll nest; Green Woodpecker feed in more open areas. Breeding waterfowl include grebes and Tufted Duck despite occasional water-skiing. Winter wildfowl are few in number but have included Long-tailed Duck. An increase in water sports seems imminent and may ruin the site for waterfowl.

59E ABBOTS MOSS
OS ref: SJ 587685
A forestry track runs eastward from the A49 immediately to the south of Nunsmere. Walk down this, turning left at the end then bear right where a striped pole bars the road. This ride leads between two floating bogs ringed with alder and birch trees, and through conifer plantations. Green Woodpecker, Willow Tit and Tree Pipit nest, with Redstart in some years. Crossbill, Siskin and Sparrowhawk possible at any time of year.

59F PETTY POOL AND PETTYPOOL WOOD
OS ref: SJ 618701
Travel east along the A556 from A49 crossroads and turn right very shortly at another set of lights. After 1 ¼ miles (2 km), at the end of a line of large houses, a footpath leads into the plantations. Parking is not possible immediately by this entrance, so it will be necessary to park elsewhere and walk back. Rides lead through the plantation to the pool. Breeding waterfowl include Ruddy Duck. Siskin are plentiful in spring; plantation species and few Wood Warbler appear in summer. Rhododendrons by pool hold roosting finches, often including Brambling, in winter.

59G NEWCHURCH COMMON
OS ref: SJ 600688
Continue south along the minor road past Pettypool Wood and take the first right, signposted to Nova Scotia. Turn right at the end and park at the quarry entrance. A bridle-path runs between the two quarries, the smaller of which is used for water-skiing. These pools are favoured by Goldeneye, Tufted Duck and Pochard with a few Teal in winter, when

Jack Snipe can generally be found in the reedmace. A sprinkling of waders occurs on passage, and large numbers of gulls may be present in winter. Scaup and Common Scoter have occurred. Stubble fields in the vicinity often hold finch flocks.

The *Whitegate Way*, which passes the southern end of the smaller pool, should be followed westward from Newchurch Common to view the Gull Pool, now devoid of nesting gulls, but supporting breeding Little Grebe, Tufted and Ruddy Ducks. From here it is possible to follow paths through to Abbots Moss and Nunsmere.

Calendar

All year: Sparrowhawk and Kestrel by day, Tawny and possibly Long-eared Owls by night. Woodland species include Green and Great Spotted Woodpeckers, Nuthatch, Treecreeper, Long-tailed and Willow Tits. Coal Tit and Goldcrest plentiful. Redpoll and often Bullfinch in birches, Crossbill and perhaps Siskin in pines. Stock Dove and Corn Bunting in arable areas. Little Grebe and Tufted Duck on quarries and pools.

December-February: Teal, Pochard and Goldeneye; Snipe and Jack Snipe by quarries. Common Gull abundant, Glaucous and Iceland Gulls occasional. Brambling may feed under beeches.

March-May: Shelduck visit; Ruddy Duck move onto breeding pools. Passage waders may include Dunlin, Common Sandpiper, Whimbrel, Brambling and plentiful Siskin in mature conifers. Crossbill may have young. Breeding species, including warblers, move into young plantations.

June-July: Grebes, Tufted and Ruddy Ducks may have young. Little Ringed Plover and Sand Martin in quarries. Black-headed Gull may summer and Common Tern appear at times. Turtle Dove feed along weedy banks. Young plantations hold Tree Pipit, Whitethroat, possibly Grasshopper Warbler, Linnet, Redpoll, Reed Bunting and Yellowhammer. Nightjar formerly bred and might still occur. Crossbill may be augmented by irrupting flocks from further north. Redstart, Pied Flycatcher and Wood Warbler locally.

August-November: Summer visitors depart and plantations become quiet. Waders such as Dunlin, Greenshank and Green Sandpiper may drop in by quarries where Lesser Black-backed Gull gather in their hundreds.

Habitat

The Peckforton Hills form a ridge of sandstone standing isolated in the middle of the Cheshire Plain, with Beeston Castle surmounting a solitary hill to the north, the tops of the hills are heathy by nature, but most of the summit of Peckforton Hill has been planted with conifers. There are however considerable tracts of oak woodland on the steeper slopes, and birch and bracken are spreading extensively across remaining open areas. Bulkeley Hill has numbers of old chestnut and oak trees, but is largely covered by birch woodland. Climbing Corydalis is a characteristic plant of the woodlands, with Cow-wheat locally plentiful. In summer Purple Hairstreak butterflies dart around the sunlit crowns of oak trees.

Bickerton Hill, now named Larkton Hill by the National Trust, lies at the south end of the ridge. It is capped by probably the best remaining heathland area in Cheshire. In late summer Oak Eggar months fly over the heath, where bilberries fruit in profusion. The deep purple flowers of Bell Heather, pinker bells of Cross-leaved Heath, growing in the damper areas, and later flowers of Heather attract bees and butterflies to this rich source of nectar. At the highest point of the hill are the Iron Age ramparts of Maiden Castle, now largely overrun by bracken.

Species

The tracts of older oak woodland are particularly rich in woodland species, with a notable concentration of Pied Flycatchers, especially in the Burwardsley woods. Wood Warbler, Marsh Tit and a few Redstart are also present, and all three species of woodpecker breed. Pied Flycatcher and Wood Warbler may also be seen within the grounds of Beeston Castle, along with other more common woodland species. The castle is infiltrated by early Chiffchaff each March, and the hills in general would repay much closer attention than they have received to date as a focus for migrants. Conifer plantations may be expected to hold specialist birds.

Bickerton Hill in particular supports a few pairs of Tree Pipit, Nightjar formerly bred, and much habitat remains suitable. The dialect name of 'Leitchfowl', restricted to the Peckforton Hills, is Saxon in origin and suggests the birds were here before Beeston Castle was built by the

Pied Flycatcher

194

Normans. Even now nocturnal visits in late spring or summer might reveal a churring bird.

The isolated nature of the hills attract migrant raptors,and although the area remains little known ornithologically, there have been many records of Buzzard, Peregrine and Raven, and a Honey Buzzard was once watched overhead. Buzzard are perhaps most likely to appear in August and September when young birds are dispersing from Welsh strongholds.

Timing

Most accessible sites in Cheshire are invaded by trippers at weekends, Beeston Castle especially so, but it is usually possible to find relatively quiet footpaths on the Peckforton Hills. Spring visits are optimal for woodland species, but there is exploratory work to be done here, with autumn and winter populations poorly known.

Access

The hump of Beeston Castle (SJ 537593) can be seen from afar, lying just to the west of the A49 south of Tarporley. Minor roads are well sign-posted, and there are car parks at the foot of the outer wall. The castle is managed by English Heritage, and there is an admission charge. The keep, unfortunately very popular with day-trippers, is an excellent view-point from which various raptors have been seen. Minor roads skirt the Peckforton Hills on either side, with a network of public footpaths well marked. The Burwardsley woods are best approached from the west, following the signs for the Candle Workshops into the village, but turning left past the Pheasant Inn opposite a telephone box (SJ 523565). This is a no-through road and parking may be difficult. The lane deteriorates into a track which soon passes an area of old oakwood on the right. Explore along footpaths through the woods.

Bickerton (Larkton) Hill is best approached from Bickerton village, just south of the A534. Take Goldford Lane which runs beside the church-yard. There are signposted access points at various points along the lane. Foot- and bridle-paths cross the heath and woods. An area of oak woodland at the south-west corner of the hill may be rewarding.

Calendar

All year: woodpeckers, Marsh Tit, Goldcrest, woodland birds. Redpoll and Bullfinch among other scrubland birds on the heaths.

December-February: Resident woodland birds in wandering flocks jointed by territorial Marsh Tit. Possibility of Raven or Peregrine.

March-May: Spring migrants arrive, including Pied Flycatcher, Wood Warbler, Tree Pipit, Redstart. Greater likelihood of Raven.

June-July: Breeding species less conspicuous by July, being busy feeding young. Many birds, including Stock Doves, feed on bilberries at Bickerton.

August-November: Woodland quiet. Buzzard may visit on dispersal from Wales.

61 ECCLESTON AND THE DEE AT EATON

Habitat

The village of Eccleston lies on the west bank of the river Dee and is the most reliable place in Cheshire to see Hawfinch. The village itself is characterised by lichen-rich sandstone walls and a mixture of mature evergreen and broad-leaved trees. The Dee skirts Eaton Park to the south, with its old, hollow trees and its park lake. Lime and other trees beside the lake support what may be the region's only wild population of mistletoe, curiously so since the park is a noted haunt of Mandarin Duck, the oriental symbol of fidelity.

Species

The mature timber of Eaton Park houses many hole-nesting birds; Stock Dove, Jackdaw and Little Owl at the larger end of the scale, Nuthatch, Marsh Tit and Tree Sparrow at the smaller end. Of special interest are the few pairs of Mandarin which also nest in hollow trees. Whether these released birds can sustain themselves in the long term remains to be seen, but they are welcomed by most birdwatchers. The increasing local rabbit population regularly attracts Buzzard.

The Eaton Estate also played a big part in the establishment of feral Greylag Goose in Cheshire, with numbers of birds increasing steadily from the 1960s until the present day, when there may be 200–300 birds in the county at times. Good numbers of Greylag Goose often consort with the Canada Goose beside the park lake. In recent years a small population of Snow Goose has begun to breed, producing blue-phased young as well as hybridising with the Canadas and Greylags. Similar feral populations are growing in other parts of England. It is an unfortunate fact that birdwatchers constantly neglect feral populations during the early stages of establishment. Here there is a chance for the Cheshire Snow Goose to be consistently monitored.

From autumn until early spring, the lakeside trees hold one of the county's two main inland Cormorant roosts, with several dozen birds regularly present. Numbers increase towards evening, but even at mid-

196

day the odd bird may perch hopefully near to a bunch of mistletoe. Towards spring some birds show characteristics of the continental race – the origin of inland Cormorant continues to arouse speculation.

As the days lengthen, warblers and other migrants appear in riverside trees, and itinerant Common Sandpiper skim low across the river. In the early morning Nuthatch pipe from the tree-tops and woodpeckers drum on hollow branches, the rattle of Lesser Spotteds being in longer bursts than those of the Great. As morning wears on, their display becomes less frequent as do the laughing calls of Green Woodpecker.

It is in March and April that Hawfinch become conspicuous. Listen for their explosive, vaguely Robin-like 'tick' from the tops of trees near the river, or in the village where birds may be seen in song flight.

By May the first feral goose broods are hatching. In addition to pure-bred Canada, Greylag and Snow Geese, there may be odd hybrids between species. The incidence of 'mongrels' in winter flocks throughout the region is increasing. Mandarin Duck may also be seen with ducklings along quieter reaches of the river. Kingfisher too breed locally and may be seen at any season.

Mandarin

From about the middle of June, Hawfinch again become conspicuous, often around the church, as they bring their offspring to feed in cherry trees. By mid-August, when the cherries are finished and the Hawfinch fade away again, breeding warblers have also become elusive and autumn passage is under way. Careful observation along the banks of the Dee, a large river with north-south orientation, might produce surprises with regular coverage. Common and Green Sandpipers do appear, following the river banks, and with the onset of autumn parties of Siskins appear in the alders.

Timing

Hawfinch are most reliably present in March-April and June-August, but with luck may be encountered at other seasons. The Deeside footpath attracts its share of visitors, so Mandarin are most likely to be seen in the early morning, before disturbance drives them away. This is however a pleasant walk at all seasons.

Access

Take the A483(T) southwards from the A55(T) roundabout (at SJ 390625) turning left after half a mile (1 km) onto a minor road signposted to Eccleston. Park in the village or on Ferry Lane, from which footpaths follow the riverbank in either direction.

Eaton Park is strictly private, but interrupted views of the park lake can be obtained by following the path southwards for a little over a mile (2 km), although when the trees are in full leaf watching is more difficult. The goose flock may be visible at times from the Aldford/Huntington road (B5130) near the Crook of Dee (SJ 425615).

Hawfinch are most likely to be seen in the area around the church.

Calendar

All year: feral Canada, Greylag and Snow Geese, Mandarin Duck, woodpeckers, Kingfisher, Nuthatch, Marsh Tit; possibly Buzzard.

December-February: Cormorant roost at its peak; feral goose flock includes Greylag and Snow Geese, with possibility of wild birds. Kingfisher and Mandarin on river with few other waterfowl.

March-May: Hawfinches displaying in early spring, when woodpeckers drumming near river in early morning. By mid-May goslings hatching.

June-July: Hawfinch reappear with young birds; Mandarin may have young; geese now moulting.

August-November: Cormorant roost reassembles and geese become more mobile.

62 GAYTON SANDS AND THE INNER DEE MARSHES

Habitat

The saltmarshes of the Dee estuary have spread rapidly this century following the construction of embankments to reclaim the Sealand area, and the diversion of the main river channel to the Welsh side. Their spread has been accelerated by the arrival of Common Cord-grass which has stabilised mudbanks throughout the inner estuary and is now threatening to cover the beaches at West Kirby and Hoylake in the Dee mouth, despite attempts to curb its spread. Within the saltings tidal creeks and gutters persist, and in places shallow, brackish pools have formed. Upper parts of the marshes are heavily grazed by sheep but elsewhere such saltmarsh plants as Sea Aster, Scurvy-grass and Sea Purslane flourish. The marshes now extend from beyond the Cheshire border at Burton Point seaward as far as Heswall. Off Denhall Lane at Burton a part of the grazing marsh is managed as a refuge by the Dee Wildfowlers Club. Pools here and below the Decca station towards Neston attract waders. At Neston the character of the marsh changes since it is not grazed, and from here past Parkgate to Gayton it is owned by the RSPB. The reserve extends to 5,000 acres (2,040 hectares) and includes a small reedbed near to the sewage works at Neston.

The Wirral Way, a disused railway track, runs parallel to the coastline from Neston north-westward. It is lined with scrub and passes through farmland, which includes stubble fields in winter.

To the south of the Burton Marshes and separated from the estuary by the Wallasey-Wrexham railway embankment lies an area of flat fields. Formerly saltmarsh, these Shotwick fields now attract plovers and occasionally geese. A reserve has been purchased here by the RSPB, and excavation of scrapes and pools is underway, but it will be some time yet before visiting will be possible to what seems destined to be an outstanding birdwatching site.

199

Species

The Dee was once famous for its wild geese, but excessive disturbance early this century drove away the already dwindling remnants of the former flocks. Since the establishment of Gayton Sands RSPB reserve however numbers of wildfowl wintering in the estuary have risen markedly. The Pintail is well adapted to the open, estuarine environment, its long neck enabling it to detect approaching predators from considerable distances. Several thousand are present on the edge of the saltmarsh from September until March. Up to 5,000 Shelduck feed in the channel off Gayton; and between 2,000 and 4,000 Mallard, from 1–3,000 Teal, and up to 3,000 Wigeon frequent the outer edge of the marsh in the same area. Teal and Wigeon also feed in the wildfowl refuge off Denhall Lane. In severe winter skeins of Pink-footed Goose move into the area and may alight on grazing land at Burton or Shotwick. Less often a smaller flock of White-fronted Goose may arrive. Family groups of Bewick's Swan may also take up residence for short periods. An American Wigeon was seen in March 1988.

Farmland, marshland and estuarine waders meet in the inner Dee in winter. Several hundred Golden Plover and Lapwing may feed on the Shotwick fields or Burton Marsh. Spotted Redshank, Greenshank and Green Sandpiper are occasionally present at the Decca Pools and elsewhere, and at high tide estuarine species gather to roost on the marshes. (A roost on the pasture at Burton will hold several thousand birds: Oystercatcher, Knot and Dunlin, Curlew and Redshank. The last two species also roost well out on the marsh at Parkgate.)

The saltmarsh plants produce vast quantities of seeds which are floated up the various creeks by the tide and deposited in masses along the tideline. This abundance of seed draws vast flocks of finches to the edge of the marsh. Between Parkgate and Gayton the top outer edge of the sandstone sea-wall is yellow with lichens encouraged to grow by the droppings of the winter finches. These may include over 1,000 Chaffinch and even more Greenfinch. Brambling are erratic in their appearances but may number 1,000 or even 5,000 when other food is scarce. Linnet are most numerous in autumn, but several hundred winter. A few dozen Twite winter further out on the marsh, but at times move to the landward edge where their distinctive twanging calls help to separate them from Linnet. Where there are thistles, as in the rougher pastures bordering the marsh, Goldfinch may gather.

Bramblings

House and Tree Sparrows bulk up the finch flocks even more, and Corn Bunting occur in small numbers. Skylark feed out on the marsh, as do hundreds of Reed Bunting, although these birds are less prone to flocking than finches. A sprinkling of Lapland Bunting is reported annually. Usually these dumpy, short-tailed bunting are seen only in flight when their call, 'ticatic', followed by a whistled 'teu', gives them away to those familiar with the species.

Rock Pipit move into the Dee in October, remaining until April. They feed along the gutters and forage amongst the debris at the high water mark. While counts of 1–200 Rock Pipit are possible a few Water Pipit may also be seen below the car park at Parkgate and around the Neston reedbed. Water Pipit in winter have warmer brown upperparts and whiter underparts than Rock Pipit, with a clear white supercilium (eyebrow stripe). Towards spring they become greyer above and develop a pink flush on the breast which loses its streaking. In late March and April up to 30 such birds, though usually ten or less, may be seen either at Neston or Burton, frequenting the grazing marsh.

The profusion of birds feeding on the marsh and the mudflats beyond attracts predators, and this is one of the best sites in the region to see raptors. Kestrel hover in search of small mammals, and Sparrowhawk steal in low from the landward side hoping to snatch an unwary finch. Hen Harrier quarter the marsh systematically, gliding along just above the ground with their wings held in a shallow V. When prey is spotted the wings are folded back abruptly and the hawk drops from sight. Not infrequently Merlin can be seen in the air simultaneously, apparently taking advantage of the harrier's flushing of larks or small waders which the falcon then pursues. Towards dusk the Hen Harrier fly in to roost amongst the cord-grass off Parkgate. Between three and seven birds, including up to three grey males, have roosted here from October to April since 1980 or earlier. The Merlin, between three and five in a typical winter, may roost nearby. Peregrine also hunt the area, and can generally be seen during a morning's watch.

The other characteristic predator of the marshes from autumn to spring is the Short-eared Owl. Numbers fluctuate in response to vole populations, and in some winters almost none are seen. In a good year however ten or more may be present, with several in the air at once. Although not strictly predators, marauding Raven, which have infiltrated the area in recent winters from their Welsh mountain strongholds, deserve a mention. Up to six have been seen at Denhall.

One final feature of winter birdwatching, but one that happens very infrequently now as the marsh continues to grow and the open water becomes more distant, is the flooding of the marshes by the highest tides. As normally dry parts of the marsh are inundated, small mammals must break cover and swim for higher ground. Shrews, voles, mice and rats all fall victim to the owls and harriers, or to the more numerous gulls, or to the Heron which line the advancing tide. Water Rail too are driven out of the cord-grass, and if the marsh floods completely they fly up onto the sea-wall and take cover under parked cars, in fields, or in gardens. Not all the rails make it to safety, for some are eaten by Heron. Finches, larks and buntings are also displaced from the marsh and move to coastal fields, as do Snipe and a few short-billed Jack Snipe.

Towards spring Red-breasted Merganser often arrive and display on the pools off Denhall Lane. Wheatear appear along the sea-wall from March when Meadow Pipit pass over in large numbers, and in April both

Yellow and White Wagtails may be numerous. April and May bring a light passage of marshland waders, some of which have attained smart plumage by the latter month. If a high pressure system becomes established over the continent at this time, south-easterly winds may bring Marsh Harrier in place of the departing Hen Harrier. In 1980 a Montagu's Harrier arrived under similar conditions. These migrant birds seldom stay for more than a day or two. A Garganey or two may appear at this season.

A few pairs of Mallard and Shelduck nest on the marshes, and Teal, Shoveler or other duck species may occasionally do so. Redshank and Oystercatcher nest in small numbers along with a sprinkling of Black-headed Gull. Common Tern nest just over the border in Clwyd and often fish in the Dee or the pools on the marsh.

The reedbed at Neston holds breeding Reed and Sedge Warblers, with further pairs of the latter species and a few Grasshopper Warbler in scrub elsewhere along the edges of the marsh. Stonechats increase in numbers given mild winters and may then nest along the landward edge of the marsh. Reed Bunting and Skylark nest commonly. Twites have nested more than once and are seen in most summers – an interesting extension of their normally upland breeding range. Quail have been heard in most recent summers uttering their trisyllabic call from the marsh or nearby cornfields, and there is a history of evening sightings of Hobby in the area.

Marshland waders are rather more conspicuous on spring passage than in winter, but much larger numbers may occur in autumn. Maximum counts of Greenshank roosting off Parkgate at this season have varied between 30 and 70 and up to 16 Spotted Redshank have been seen off Burton – in the 1970s counts in excess of 100 were not exceptional. Black-tailed Godwit are frequent, Curlew Sandpiper and Little Stint are noted annually in small numbers, and Ruff occur more reliably with up to 40 in good years. Scarce or rare species are found from time to time, with Wood and Pectoral Sandpipers, Grey and Wilson's Phalaropes, Temminck's Stint and Long-billed Dowitcher in recent years. Spoonbill and Spotted Crake have occurred on a number of occasions, and Purple Heron and Crane more rarely. Single Little Egret were seen in spring and autumn 1989. As at Red Rocks and Hilbre, diurnal movements of thrushes and finches may be heavy given east winds in late autumn.

Timing

The marshes may appear quiet between tides, but activity increases as the river channel floods and waders are forced onto the marsh to roost. Raptors and owls then become more active. Only the very highest tides (33 feet (10–11 m) or more) are now likely to flood the marsh as well. A following wind on the day of the highest tides might still have the same effect.

On high tide days the car park at Parkgate fills up with birdwatchers very quickly, so it is advisable to take up a good position an hour or two before the tide. Evening visits give views of harriers entering the roost as the light fades.

Prolonged east or south-east winds in May are a sign that passage harriers may occur, or perhaps even some overshooting southern heron. Similar winds in September or October may bring eurasian waders to the pools.

Access

Access is essentially restricted to a series of lanes and footpaths which run the length of the landward side of the marshes from Burton north-westward to Gayton. The whole area lies to the west of the A540 Chester to Hoylake road.

To view Burton Marshes, take Denhall Lane westward from Burton village until the marshes, here sheep-grazing, appear in front (SJ 302736). Pools here may hold waders at any time, Wigeon and Teal in winter and mergansers in spring. An unmade road runs north from here to Neston, with birdwatching all the way. The Decca pools, beyond Denhall House Farm, are particularly productive and can be viewed by climbing the bank opposite.

The other main vantage point is the site of the old baths at Parkgate, now a car park. From Parkgate village take the road along the front north-westward until it swings away from the marsh. Here fork left along a side road with speed ramps which leads to the car park (SJ 273791). Watch from here for raptors and possibly rails. Walk northwards along the sea-wall for further views of finches and perhaps Water Pipit. A path which leads inland from the car park connects to the Wirral Way.

Walk southwards from Parkgate along the edge of the marsh to reach Neston reed-bed. Raptors may also be seen here in winter, Water Pipit in spring and warblers in summer.

The Shotwick fields are viewed by taking the industrial estate road westward off the A550(T) south of Shotwick village (SJ 338708).

Calendar

All year: Shelduck, Oystercatcher, Redshank and Lapwing breed; Black-headed Gull always present and a few pairs nest. Reed Bunting and Skylark nest commonly, with perhaps Stonechat or even Twite. Heron stalk along the shoreline.

December-February: Huge flocks of finches gather along edge of marsh; Chaffinch, Brambling, Greenfinch, Linnet, fewer Twite and Goldfinch, joined by House and Tree Sparrow, perhaps Corn Bunting. Hundreds of Skylark and Reed Bunting out on marsh, with Rock and a few Water Pipits in creeks. Lapland Bunting annual. Snipe, Jack Snipe and Water Rail may be flushed into view by high tide. Lapwing and Golden Plover at Burton or Shotwick, where perhaps joined in severe weather by grey geese or wild swans. Pintail, Teal and Wigeon in thousands out on marsh, and Shelduck on flats. Spotted Redshank and Greenshank occasional. Peregrine, Merlin, Hen Harrier and Short-eared Owl hunt marshes daily, with commoner Kestrel and Sparrowhawk. Raven may appear.

March-May: Wildfowl mostly depart in March, but Merganser appear at Burton. Wader flocks disperse a little later; a sprinkling of stints or 'shanks' may pass through in April or May. Raptors still regular to early April, then progressively scarcer. Marsh Harrier possible in May. Pink-breasted Water Pipit in March and April.

June-July: A few Pintail, Teal, Shoveler may linger along with small numbers of non-breeding waders such as Bar-tailed Godwit. Common Tern fly out from Shotton (Clwyd) to fish in marsh pools or the Dee. Grasshopper, Reed and Sedge Warblers in Neston reed-bed. Quail in some years.

August-November: Wader passage in August may bring Spotted Redshank and Greenshank in large numbers which continue into September when Little Stint and Curlew Sandpiper may also appear. Rarer waders more likely in September or October, when raptors also return.

63 HILBRE ISLAND AND THE DEE MOUTH

OS Map 208
SJ

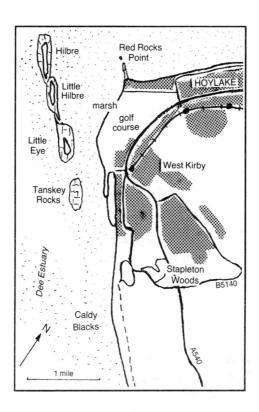

Habitat

Hilbre, at just under 12 acres (5 hectares) and with cliffs rising to 55 ft (17 m) on the exposed western side, is the largest of a group of three islands lying about a mile (1.5 km) to the west of the north-west tip of Wirral in the mouth of the Dee estuary. At low tide the islands are accessible, with caution, across the sands from West Kirby, but at high tide they are cut off from the mainland. All three islands are composed of red sandstone and topped with rough grassland. Apart from a few bushes on Hilbre and some bracken on Middle Eye, there is little cover for birds and, other than an old, roofless lifeboat house and a small, often full seawatching hide, even less shelter for birdwatchers. Since 1957 detailed notes have been kept of the island's birds by members of the Hilbre Bird Observatory.

The West Hoyle Bank, a large sandbank to the west of the islands, is regularly used by Grey Seals which haul themselves out of the water there. At high tide the seals are often seen bobbing below the cliffs of the island.

205

At low tide sands are exposed stretching from Hoylake and West Kirby to Hilbre, but there are a number of deep runnels to trap the unwary. These extensive flats are the feeding grounds for thousands of shorebirds – waders and gulls. A deep water channel, which approaches the shore off Caldy some 2 miles (5 km) up the estuary, often holds sea-ducks.

Species

In excess of 225 species have been recorded at Hilbre. Few breed because of the restricted habitat. Shelduck are perhaps the most appealing to the casual visitor. Cormorant rest on sandbanks offshore at low tide.

Vast flocks of waders winter in the estuary. In late July the first Dunlin, perhaps a thousand or more, return from the tundra. They are joined by flocks of white-bellied Sanderling, on the way to winter quarters on African beaches, which continue to pass through during August and September. Up to 20,000 Oystercatcher, sometimes more, arrive in August and remain in similar or even larger numbers right through the winter. August also sees the peak of Ringed Plover passage; Dunlin, Curlew and Redshanks continue to increase; and early Knot, some of them 'red' summer-plumaged birds, black-bellied Grey Plover and godwits of either species may arrive. Turnstone reach 200–300 on Hilbre in August and September, flicking over seaweed and pebbles in their search for food. Grey Plover may exceed 1,000 in September as Knot increase, reaching several thousands by October. A speciality of the island is the flock of Purple Sandpiper which builds up from mid-October into November, reaching perhaps 40–50 birds in total.

Knot flock

By the end of the year the Knot flocks are usually 10,000 or even 40,000 strong. There may be 10,000–20.000 Dunlins, several hundred Bar-tailed and over 1,000 Black-tailed Godwit, with a similar number of Curlew and of Redshanks. Hundreds of Grey Plover and a smaller number of Ringed Plover will also be present, with Oystercatcher still abundant and highly conspicuous.

By no means all of these birds will use the outer estuary at any one time, and many commute between the Dee and the Alt or Ribble estuaries. High tide roosts may gather on the two lesser Hilbre islands, which should be left undisturbed at high tide for this purpose. At times the crowding there may be so severe that Dunlin have been known to settle on the backs of Knot.

Quite often the roosts are disturbed by a Peregrine, several of which hunt the estuary daily in winter. Rather less often a Merlin appears.

Lacking the burst of speed with which Peregrine take their prey, Merlin rely on persistence instead and may be watched towering and swooping for minutes on end as some unfortunate wader seeks to throw the falcon off its tail.

Numbers of waders in the estuary are falling by March. North-bound Sanderling pass through in April and May as the Purple Sandpiper flock also returns north, perhaps to Greenland. By June only a few Oystercatcher, Curlew and Redshank remain, with occasional birds of other species.

Shelduck also haunt the outer estuary in moderate numbers. In most winters they are joined by at least one small party of Brent Goose, usually dark-breasted birds. This is a scarce species in the region as a whole. A favourite haunt is around the Tanskey Rocks south of Little Eye, where Wigeons may be seen resting over the high tide. Large numbers of dabbling ducks winter on the marshes of the inner Dee, but few wander this far out. Occasionally parties of Pink-footed Goose fly over from the Southport mosslands and continue up the Dee or into Wales, and Pintails may fly over from Gayton Sands. In March herds of Icelandic Whooper or Siberian Bewick's Swans pass over.

The deep-water channel off Caldy often holds a flock of Scaup. Up to 400 have been counted although they can be elusive. At high tide look for the grey-backed drakes bobbing offshore with the chocolate-coloured ducks. Often a few Goldeneye are present also, and perhaps a Merganser or even a Long-tailed Duck. In rough weather the occasional sea-duck shelters on West Kirby Marine Lake.

Visitors to Hilbre often go there specifically for the sea-watching. Given two or three days of strong north-westerlies in the autumn Leach's Petrels will appear. Ideal conditions are infrequent, and in some years non-existent, but most autumns produce at least a handful of birds. Outstanding among recent years were 1978 when 959 passed by on 27 September, 1980 with 337 on 14 September, 1983 with 265 on 19 October and 243 on 13 September 1987. Most birds beat westward into the wind close by the north end of the island. Exhausted birds may settle for a while on the sea. Storm Petrels occur only rarely among the larger Leach's.

The same autumnal storms blow in other exciting seabirds. Arctic Skua, which occur occasionally in spring and at any time from July to October, are more numerous at such times, with a few bulky Great Skua and an increased chance of the delicate Long-tailed or heavy Pomarine. One or two Long-tailed Skua are reported during most prolonged windy spells in autumn. Grey Phalarope are not seen every year but odd birds may appear under such conditions. As Kittiwake stream past look out for the tricoloured wing pattern of rare Sabine's Gull. Hilbre now accounts for one or two records of this high arctic bird every year. Sometimes more, with others seen from the north shore of Wirral. A flock of Little Gull, which varies greatly in size from year to year, winters in Liverpool Bay and these birds too may be blown inshore.

Seawatching is not limited to autumn storms however. Divers occur at any time from September to April, and just occasionally in summer too. Daily totals seldom rise above ten, with Red-throated Diver by far the most numerous species. Great Northern Diver are seen on only a handful of days each year, and Black-throated even less often. Up to twenty or more Great Crested Grebe may be counted offshore in late autumn, with smaller numbers during the winter and into spring. The smaller grebes are seldom noted – only three or four a year – with Red-necked more likely than Black-necked or Slavonian.

Fulmars fly within sight of land between March and October when the wind blows from the west or north-west. On windy days more than fifty may be logged. Manx Shearwater appear under similar conditions between June and September, with seldom more than a dozen even on good days. Gannet are seen from March to November.

Few ducks frequent the open sea off the Dee mouth. Common Scoter may be seen in any month, perhaps least often in late winter and early summer. Occasionally rafts of up to a hundred bob offshore, but more usually small parties fly past in lines, the black drakes and browner, pale-cheeked ducks easily recognisable by their stocky outline and rapid wing-beats. The heavier Velvet Scoter is rarely seen.

Terns occur offshore from April to October. Common Tern are generally the most numerous, and occur throughout the summer. Dozens may be counted on spring days, but from July to September much larger numbers may be seen. Recent reports suggest that the majority of these birds are Common Tern, although Arctic Tern also pass through in quantity. The status of these two species is in need of study.

The scarcer Little Tern passes the Dee mouth from mid-April to late May with perhaps 15–20 birds on a good day, and again on the return passage. Up to 150 a day may occur in August and September. Noisy Sandwich Tern show a similar pattern of occurrence with a predominance of autumn records. Fifty to a hundred pass by on better days in late April or May, and several hundreds may be counted in August. A few late birds are seen in October. The Roseate Tern is a very scarce migrant, not reliably seen even once a year. Black Terns are a little more frequent.

Both Guillemot and Razorbill occur offshore with a small moulting flock in Liverpool Bay in summer. These birds may be accompanied by chicks, too young to fly, which have nonetheless swum considerable distances from their breeding colonies, perhaps in North Wales or on the Isle of Man. The browner-backed, shorter-tailed Guillemot is the more frequent of the two species. Only single figures of either are likely on any day from November to June, but larger numbers may come within range given onshore winds in autumn – perhaps 100 Guillemot and 10–20 Razorbill. Other auks occur only rarely. Over the five years from 1980–1984 there were just eleven sightings of Puffin, three Little Auk, and one Black Guillemot, all seen from Hilbre and emphasising the island's pre-eminence as the Cheshire seawatching site.

Movements of passerine migrants have been studied intensively at Hilbre. Spring passage begins in March with the first Chiffchaff, Wheatear and Ring Ousel, and the start of a movement of Meadow Pipit which reaches its peak in the first few days of April, when over a thousand may pass in a day.

Migration is at its height in late April or early May when, given suitable conditions, the bushes may be full of migrants shortly after dawn. The Willow Warbler is the principal species involved. Spring passage at Hilbre is in fact more varied than autumn. Sedge and Grasshopper Warblers, Common and Lesser Whitethroats, Redstart and Whinchat are typical spring migrants. Tree Pipit are also prevalent – 61 were logged one May morning in 1983. Most summer visitors occur in at least small numbers. The shortage of cover on Hilbre means that migrants are unlikely to stay for more than a few hours. Considerable numbers of Goldfinch and Redpoll pass in April and May, with perhaps thirty or so of either species at Hilbre on some days. Tree Sparrow also pass through.

Emigration of summer visitors picks up in August, when the largest autumn totals of Willow Warblers occur. On occasion over a hundred of these dainty birds will descend on Hilbre. Variety on the island on autumn passage is somewhat restricted, but Garden Warbler occur more often at this season than in spring, with perhaps the odd Pied Flycatcher. A few Black Redstart are noted each year, in either spring or late autumn. Yellow-browed Warbler have appeared several times in late autumn. Relatively few diurnal migrants pass over, these preferring to follow the mainland coastline.

Immigrant winter thrushes and Starlings fly over the island in large numbers from the end of September onwards, when finch movements may also be heavy. Renewed movement of plovers, larks and thrushes may follow winter frosts. Snow Bunting are seen occasionally.

Timing

For seawatching, strong winds from a north-westerly quarter are ideal, and a persistent blow for two or more days in September or October will bring in petrels, Little Gull and skuas. Tide tables should be consulted and visits timed around the high tide. Particular attention should be paid to the state of the tide when visiting Hilbre (see under Access).

In April and May the largest arrivals of warblers and other passerines take place with south-westerly winds curving up from Spain, or on south-easterlies. Birds arrive shortly after dawn, rest and feed briefly then move on. Few remain by mid-morning. In autumn east or north-east winds bring in the birds.

Severe winter weather may bring large westward movements of birds seeking milder conditions. A thaw following prolonged cold induces return movements.

Access

To visit Hilbre a permit is necessary, available from the Department of Leisure Services and Tourism, Wirral Borough Council, Concourse, West Kirby, Wirral, Merseyside. Individuals may apply for a yearly permit for up to five people.

The walk across the sands to Hilbre can be tricky and should not be attempted in foggy conditions. It is usual to set out from the end of Dee Lane, West Kirby, at least 3½ hours before high tide and head for the southernmost (i.e. left-hand) island, Little Eye, thereby avoiding treacherous gutters. Visitors are then forced to remain on the island until at least two hours after high tide when it is again possible to return to the mainland. The state of the tide clearly places constraints on those wishing to visit the island at dawn to see migrants. Regular visitors to the island will inevitably make contact with members of the observatory who may offer further advice on early morning visits. Most early risers will however be satisfied with the possibilities offered by the Red Rocks area.

At Caldy a loop of minor roads leads westward off the B5140 to a clifftop car park (SJ 223851) from which the Scaup flock and other ducks may be seen. The marine lake at West Kirby is obvious from the end of Dee Lane, and should be checked for waterfowl.

Calendar

All year: Few nesting species, but Cormorants and Kestrels present for much of year.

December-February: Vast flocks of estuarine waders including Black-tailed Godwit, Turnstone and Purple Sandpiper on Hilbre. Perhaps a few Brent Goose. Scaup and other sea-ducks off Caldy. Peregrine and Merlin hunt the waders. Red-throated Diver and Great Crested Grebe on sea; possibly rarer divers or Red-necked Grebe. Severe weather brings westward movement of Lapwing, Golden Plover, Skylark and thrushes, with wandering Pink-footed Goose. Snow Bunting a possibility.

March-May: Winter duck and wader flocks disperse. Spring passage brings Sanderling, perhaps Whimbrel, and other wader species. Purple Sandpiper depart by mid-May. Seawatching improves, with possibility of Fulmar, Gannet and Kittiwake from March onwards, and perhaps a skua. Terns appear during April. Passerine migration starts in March; heavy movement of Meadow Pipit in early April. Passage peaks late April-early May with falls of Willow Warbler, with other warblers and chats. White and Yellow Wagtails also regular, with steady passage of hirundines.

June-July: Common Tern offshore, with Fulmar, Gannet and Manx Shearwater in windy weather, Razorbill and Guillemot from July onwards. Small numbers of non-breeding waders summer in the estuary, and by late July Sanderling and other species start to return.

August-November: Wader flocks increase. Early birds may be in breeding plumage. Purple Sandpiper return in October and November. North-westerly gales in September and October, or even early November, bring Leach's Petrel; Arctic, Great, perhaps Pomarine and possibly Long-tailed Skuas; Kittiwake and Little Gull with the occasional Sabine's Gull. Manx Shearwater until end of September, Fulmar and auks into October, and Gannet until November; Common Scoter throughout the period. Large gathering of terns in early autumn. Falls of warblers in August or September consist mostly of Willow Warbler or Chiffchaff, with the occasional rarity. Diurnal passage in October and November of winter thrushes, Starling, Chaffinch, Linnet and Greenfinch, and buntings (which may include Snow Bunting).

ADDITIONAL SITE;
STAPLETON WOODS

A small but varied woodland in which most typical woodland birds may be seen. All three woodpeckers, Wood Warbler, Pied and Spotted Flycatchers are present in season, and what may be Wirral's only Marsh Tit. The woods are well situated to receive migrants at passage seasons.

Access

From West Kirby southwards on the A540. A small car park is situated on the right a short distance after the grammar school (SJ 236861). The wood is divided into two by the public footpath, with mature beech and oak trees below the path and more open birch woodland above. Numerous paths run through the woods, but the most productive skirts the southern edge, at the boundary with open fields.

64 RED ROCKS, HOYLAKE

Habitat

Red Rocks Point at Hoylake, the north-west tip of Wirral, consists, like Hilbre Island (site 63) of a sandstone outcrop. The farthest point, Bird Rock, is cut off by the tide and is then popular with roosting waders, provided it is not occupied by anglers. Gardens at the point contain a number of bushes attractive to migrants. Around the corner into the estuary a line of mature sand-dunes runs south to West Kirby, separating the golf course from the shore. Between the dunes and the beach lies Red Rocks marsh, a haunt of Natterjack Toads (and reserve of the Cheshire Conservation Trust), with its reedbed and alder thickets.

Species

In excess of 235 species have been recorded at Red Rocks, making this one of the richest areas for birdwatching in the region. Sedge Warbler and possibly Reed and Grasshopper Warblers and Stonechat are the only breeding birds of note, although Kestrel may hunt the dunes.

Many of the Dee's estuarine waders can be seen feeding off the marsh and, as the tide rises, in flight out of the estuary past the point. These birds used to roost on the beach here, but were frequently disturbed by horse-riders and dog-walkers, so now usually roost elsewhere. Peregrine are frequently seen hunting waders over the estuary.

As at Hilbre, movements of passerine migrants have been studied intensively, and there is a great deal of similarity between movements at the two sites. March brings the first spring visitors, and emigrant Goldcrest visit the gardens. Meadow Pipit passage is also heavy in early spring. Westward passage of Collared Dove is a feature of April, with up to 300 or more on the best days. One or two Barbary Dove are occasionally reported with these birds, but beware a pale colour form of Collared Dove which also occurs.

Conditions suitable for a fall are infrequent. Prolonged southerly winds and poor visibility may ground Willow Warbler and small numbers of other migrants at the point soon after dawn. Such days are rare however, and the vast majority of migrants pass straight through. White Wagtail are seen more regularly on the west coast of Wirral than anywhere else in Cheshire. It seems probable that these pale, slender wagtails are moving up the west coast of Britain towards Icelandic rather than continental breeding grounds. Up to 45 or so may frequent the beach at Red Rocks between mid-April and mid-May, with 350 the record count. The native Pied Wagtail will often be present alongside for comparison. Spring rarities have included a Great Reed Warbler which remained in the reed-bed for three days in May 1975, and a Red-backed Shrike present in gardens at the point on 20 May 1979. Hoopoe have occurred on several occasions. Given the nature of movement through the site, many of the rarities reported are seen by only one or two observers.

Diurnal autumn migrants, following the coastline southwards, start with Swifts in July. Sizeable movements of hirundines may follow as autumn progresses. Tree Pipit may be picked up overhead by their rough

211

'teez' calls. Notice that their flight undulates more evenly, and lacks the jerky irregularities typical of Meadow Pipit.

Easterly winds in autumn, as in spring, may also bring in rarities. An Aquatic Warbler remained in the reedbed for a week in autumn 1976. Other rarities have included Tawny Pipit, Wryneck, both Icterine and Melodious Warblers, and one September dawn a Great Spotted Cuckoo. On 30 October 1982 an American Black-billed Cuckoo was photographed.

From mid-September to mid-October parties of Blue Tit fly westward along the north coast of Wirral and either drop into the reeds at Red Rocks or continue westward across the sands past Hilbre into Wales. They are accompanied by smaller numbers of other tits and the occasional Treecreeper or woodpecker. Ringing has shown these to be local birds dispersing after the breeding season.

From late September into November immigrant winter visitors fly over the Dee mouth in large numbers. Movement is most concentrated at the point in the second half of October. Hundreds, even thousands of Starling, Redwing, Fieldfare and Chaffinch may be counted in a day, with smaller numbers of Linnet, Greenfinch and other species. Snow Bunting may also join in these movements, and from this season onwards small parties visit the area intermittently until April.

Winter frosts may initiate weather movements. With the onset of severe weather Golden Plover, Lapwing, Skylark, thrushes and other birds fly west into Wales, perhaps on the way to Ireland.

Timing

The height of the tide is critical to concentrate waders at the roost on West Kirby shore. A tide of 25 ft (8 m) or less will leave large areas of flats exposed,and the waders will not be forced to gather. Conversely tides of 30 ft (10 m) force the birds off the foreshore altogether to roost on fields inland or else fly out the tide in distant flocks high above the Dee. A tide of around 26.2 ft (9 m) is ideal. The observer should preferably be in position two hours before the tide, but should be prepared to move as waders may roost and feed either along the north shore or further into the Dee.

Spring arrivals of migrant passerines are assisted by winds from a southerly quarter. Dawn visits are advisable at Red Rocks, although a search of the bushes here and along the coast may reveal lingering migrants later in the day. In autumn east or north-east winds bring in the birds. Rarities do not turn up with the same regularity as at some east coast stations, and the casual visitor is unlikely to see anything very special, but persistence will eventually be rewarded.

Dispersal movements may be witnessed at Red Rocks on any fine morning in the autumn, but for diurnal movements of long distance migrants conditions are more critical. Low cloud with a fresh or strong breeze from a southerly quarter will result in heavy, visible passage for the first two hours after dawn especially, although movement may continue throughout the day. There is little passage with strong wind, mist or fog, but with clear skies and light wind the birds will fly too high to be seen.

Access

From the Hoylake roundabout on the A553 turn north onto a minor road then first left into Stanley Road (SJ 214889). Park at the far end and walk right to the point (SJ 203886) for seawatching or to scan the flats, or turn left, when the marsh is soon obvious between the beach and the golf-course. Migrants may frequent the reedbed or bushes in the dunes. The best cover is a small poplar plantation at the north end of the marsh. Waders gather to roost on the beach just to the south of the marsh, and observers should wait above the high tide mark. The flocks are some-times flushed by inconsiderate dog-walkers and horse-riders, but bird-watchers should appreciate that the birds need their rest, and set a better example.

Calendar

All year: Stonechat resident along dunes in some years. Certain wader species may be present all year due to non-breeding birds summering in the estuary.

December-February: Dee wader flocks and Shelducks offshore, with hunting Peregrine. Severe weather brings westward movement of Lapwing, Golden Plover, Skylark and thrushes, with wandering Pink-footed Goose. Snow Bunting a possibility.

March-May: Passerine migration starts in March, peaking late April-early May. Similar species involved as at Hilbre, but White and Yellow Wagtails along Red Rocks shore, and westerly movement of Collared Dove. Rarities may appear. Terns offshore from April.

June-July: Common Terns offshore. Small numbers of non-breeding waders. Grasshopper Warbler and Stonechat breed along the coast. Mediterranean Gull seen with some regularity.

August-November: Falls of common warblers in early autumn, with perhaps the odd rarity. Locally bred tits and other species on dispersal. Diurnal passage in October and November of winter thrushes. Starling, Chaffinch, Linnet and Greenfinch, and buntings which may include Snow Bunting. Seawatching may be excellent at this season, with skuas and petrels after strong westerlies. Unlike at nearly Hilbre Island, a four hour minimum stay is not essential.

65 NORTH WIRRAL SHORE

The north shore of Wirral, running east from Hoylake to New Brighton, is largely given over to market gardens, defended from the sea by a fixed dune system. The whole area may prove attractive to migrants, given the right weather conditions. Rarities have included Great Grey Shrike, Richard's and Red-throated Pipits, Pallas' Warbler, Yellow-browed Warbler and Britain's fourth Desert Warbler.

During onshore gales, the entire coastline offers good seawatching, especially at high tide in autumn. Vehicular access to the top of the sea wall is no longer guaranteed, but the car park at Dovepoint is a useful vantage point.

65A DOVE POINT, MEOLS

OS ref: SJ 234907

Reached by driving to the easternmost point of Hoylake promenade. After north-westerly gales in September, petrels, skuas and shearwaters may be seen. Leach's Petrel often come closer to shore here than at any other vantage point along the coast. Dove Point, like New Brighton (site 66), allows the luxury of seawatching from a car, an important factor in a gale. However, the state of the tide is critical. Unless the East Hoyle sandbank is completely flooded, passing birds will be too distant for adequate views. On less windy days this sandbank is worth checking, particularly in August, when numerous gulls and terns roost on its easternmost end. In recent years, Mediterranean Gull have been seen regularly between here and Hoylake.

65B MEOLS–LEASOWE COMMON

OS ref: SJ 250910

In migration periods, the Common, immediately behind the sea-wall, is particularly good for Wheatear, Whinchat, Ring Ousel and pipits, whilst

Leach's Petrel

Snow Bunting, Twite, Stonechat and Black Redstart are often present in winter. The hedges and ditches are attractive to warblers, and Grasshopper Warblers regularly breed. Access to the market gardens is limited, but they can be viewed from the public footpath and private road (a public right of way).

Moreton Brick Pit holds Great Crested Grebe, and is a favourite bathing place for gulls. Mediterranean and Glaucous are regular, and Ring-billed has been seen on a number of occasions.

Access

The area lies between Dovepoint and the Leasowe lighthouse (SJ 262918). Lingham Lane runs south from the lighthouse. The hedges on either side of this lane are probably the easiest to cover, and in any case, a walk down to Moreton Brick Pit (SJ 252907) is worthwhile. The junction between Lingham Lane and the Birkett is probably the best spot for migrants, and Kingfisher are sometimes present in winter.

Separated slightly from other sites on the north shore, Ditton Lane provides a patch of willow and alder cover. Though this area may be full of migrants, covering it often proves frustrating for a single observer. Ditton Lane runs east-west between the A551 coast road and the Birkett (SJ 258913).

66 NEW BRIGHTON OS Map 108
(See map on p. 113 (site 42))

Habitat
The one-time holiday resort of New Brighton stands on the corner of the Mersey estuary at the east end of the north Wirral shore. Unusually for the area, the beach here is rocky. A sewage outfall is a further attraction for touring gulls. New Brighton itself has little to offer to birdwatchers, who stand with their backs to the town looking out. The Mersey ferries at Seacombe jetty, to the south, are followed by a mixture of gulls and terns.

Species
New Brighton is best known for the shelters on its promenade, which provide cover for seawatching during autumn storms. The Irish Sea is largely landlocked, so contains fewer seabird species than more exposed Atlantic or North Sea coasts. North-westerly gales can produce birds in any month, but the chief attraction is in autumn when hundreds of Leach's Petrel may appear offshore. The Mersey mouth lies in the angle between the Lancashire and North Wales/Wirral coast, so persistent gales, lasting over two or more days, funnel birds into the river. Under such conditions petrels may be seen upriver as far as Seacombe Ferry, and odd birds appear over inland meres and flashes. Many beat out of the river mouth past Fort Perch Rock, some of them being blown back to make further passes. The range of other seabirds involved is similar to those at Hilbre or Seaforth. Pomarine and Long-tailed Skuas and Sabine's Gull are virtually annual in appearance.

From late summer to spring Turnstones frequent the rocky beach, and may be joined in winter by a few Purple Sandpipers. Eider are occasionally seen off Fort Perch Rock. Gulls around the sewage outfall may include uncommon species.

Gulls following the Mersey ferries at Seacombe have included Little and Mediterranean as well as Kittiwake. Little Gull are almost always present in the river, although usually on the Liverpool side. The river mouth is at its narrowest here, so watches at passage times allow reasonable views of terns, including Black Tern following easterly winds. Rarer gulls and terns have been recorded.

Timing
For seawatching, strong winds from a north-westerly quarter are ideal, and a persistent blow for two or more days in September or October will bring in petrels, Little Gull and skuas. At low tide the sea retreats a considerable distance from the shore, although watching is still practicable from New Brighton, and during the strongest blows petrels may be seen flying over the beach at Leasowe. Tide tables should be consulted and visits timed around the high tide.

Access
During storms and in winter months, there is seldom any difficulty in parking along the seafront at New Brighton. View from the shelters near to the fort, or from a parked car.

216

The sewage outfall lies towards the southern end of the promenade along the Mersey shore. Traffic is prohibited here, but a walk along the front to check the gulls will also give a chance to scan for waders, possibly including Purple Sandpiper, feeding on the rocky shore.

The Seacombe ferries ply across the river from a pierhead some 2 miles (3 km) upriver from New Brighton. Watch the boats from vantage points south of the terminal.

Calendar

December-February: Purple Sandpiper with Turnstone on beach. Gulls at sewage outfall and following ferries. Occasional sea-ducks or auks in river.

March-July: Tern passage in spring and birds feed offshore in summer. Otherwise quiet except during onshore gales.

August-November: Turnstones return from August, few Purple Sandpiper later. Tern passage along river may bring rarer species. Greater likelihood of uncommon gulls. Petrels and skuas after storms.

SELECT BIBLIOGRAPHY

The authors wish to thank the authors and organisations for a source of information from the following publications.

Books

Cooper, J.H. & Wood, J.C. (1986) *A Checklist of the Birds of Bolton*, Bolton RSPB Group

Craggs, J.D. (1982) *Hilbre, The Cheshire Island*, Liverpool University Press

Green, G. & Cade, M. (1989) *Where to Watch Birds in Dorset, Hampshire, and the Isle of Wight*, Christopher Helm

Hardy, E. (1979) *Birdwatching in Lancashire*, Dalesman

Hollom, P.A.D. (1952) *The Popular Handbook of British Birds*, Witherby

Hutcheson, M. (1985) *Cumbrian Birds*, Frank Peters, Kendal

Madders, M. (1985) *Birdwatching in the Lake District*, Bartholomew guides

Madders, M. & Welstead, J. (1989) *Where to Watch Birds in Scotland*, Christopher Helm

Mitchell, W.R. & Robson, R.W. (1973) *Pennine Birds*, Dalesman

—— (1974) *Lakeland Birds*, Dalesman

Prater, A.J. (1981) *Estuary Birds of Britain and Ireland*, Poyser

Sharrock, J.T.R. & E.M. (1976) *Rare Birds in Britain and Ireland*, Poyser

Spencer, K.G. (1973) *The status and distribution of Birds in Lancashire*, Turner & Earnshaw, Burnley

Wilson, J. (1974) *The Birds of Morecambe Bay*, Dalesman

Wilson, J.D. (1985) *Birds and Birdwatching at Pennington Flash*, Pennington Flash Joint Committee

Annual Reports

Birds in Cumbria (1984/9), Cumbria Naturalist Union

Cheshire Bird Reports (1978/84), Cheshire Ornithological Association

Fylde Bird Club Reports (1986/8)

Lancashire Bird Reports (1987/9), Lancashire and Cheshire Fauna Society

Lancaster and District Birdwatching Society Annual Reports (1980/9)

Seaforth Bird Reports (1985/7), Lancashire Trust for Nature Conservation

Walney Bird Observatory Annual Reports (1985/8)

CODE OF CONDUCT
FOR BIRDWATCHERS

Today's birdwatchers are a powerful force for nature conservation. The number of those of us interested in birds rises continually and it is vital that we take seriously our responsibility to avoid any harm to birds.

We must also present a responsible image to non-birdwatchers who may be affected by our activities and particularly those on whose sympathy and support the future of birds may rest.

There are 10 points to bear in mind:
1. The welfare of birds must come first.
2. Habitat must be protected.
3. Keep disturbance to birds and their habitat to a minimum.
4. When you find a rare bird think carefully about whom you should tell.
5. Do not harass rare migrants.
6. Abide by the bird protection laws at all times.
7. Respect the rights of landowners.
8. Respect the rights of other people in the countryside.
9. Make your records available to the local bird recorder.
10. Behave abroad as you would when birdwatching at home.

Welfare of birds must come first

Whether your particular interest is photography, ringing, sound recording, scientific study or just birdwatching, remember that the welfare of the bird must always come first.

Habitat protection

Its habitat is vital to a bird and therefore we must ensure that our activities do not cause damage.

Keep disturbance to a minimum

Birds' tolerance of disturbance varies between species and season. Therefore, it is safer to keep all disturbance to a minimum. No birds should be disturbed from the nest in case opportunities for predators to take eggs or young are increased. In very cold weather disturbance to birds may cause them to use vital energy at a time when food is difficult to find. Wildfowlers already impose bans during cold weather, birdwatchers should exercise similar discretion.

Rare breeding birds

If you discover a rare bird breeding and feel that protection is necessary, inform the appropriate RSPB Regional Office, or the Species Protection Department at the Lodge. Otherwise it is best in almost all circumstances to keep the record strictly secret in order to avoid disturbance by other birdwatchers and attacks by egg-collectors. Never visit known sites of rare breeding birds unless they are adequately protected. Even your presence may give away the site to others and cause so many other visitors that the birds may fail to breed successfully.

Disturbance at or near the nest of species listed on the First Schedule of the Wildlife and Countryside Act 1981 is a criminal offence.

Copies of *Wild Birds and the Law* are obtainable from the RSPB, The Lodge, Sandy, Beds. SG19 2DL (send two 2nd class stamps).

Rare migrants

Rare migrants or vagrants must not be harassed. If you discover one, consider the circumstances carefully before telling anyone. Will an influx of birdwatchers disturb the bird or others in the area? Will the habitat be damaged? Will problems be caused with the landowner?

The Law

The bird protection laws (now embodied in the Wildlife and Countryside Act 1981) are the result of hard campaigning by previous generations of birdwatchers. As birdwatchers we must abide by them at all times and not allow them to fall into disrepute.

Respect the rights of landowners

The wishes of landowners and occupiers of land must be respected. Do not enter land without permission. Comply with permit schemes. If you are leading a group, do give advance notice of the visit, even if a formal permit scheme is not in operation. Always obey the Country Code.

Respect the rights of other people

Have proper consideration for other birdwatchers. Try not to disrupt their activities or scare the birds they are watching. There are many other people who also use the countryside. Do not interfere with their activities and, if it seems that what they are doing is causing unnecessary disturbance to birds, do try to take a balanced view. Flushing gulls when walking a dog on a beach may do little harm, while the same dog might be a serious disturbance at a tern colony. When pointing this out to a non-birdwatcher be courteous, but firm. The non-birdwatchers' goodwill towards birds must not be destroyed by the attitude of birdwatchers.

Keeping records

Much of today's knowledge about birds is the result of meticulous record keeping by our predecessors. Make sure you help to add to tomorrow's knowledge by sending records to your county bird recorder.

Birdwatching abroad

Behave abroad as you would at home. This code should be firmly adhered to when abroad (whatever the local laws). Well behaved birdwatchers can be important ambassadors for bird protection.

This code has been drafted after consultation between the British Ornithologists' Union, British Trust for Ornithology, the Royal Society for the Protection of Birds, the Scottish Ornithologists' Club, the Wildfowl Trust and the Editors of British Birds.

Further copies may be obtained from The Royal Society for the Protection of Birds, The Lodge, Sandy, Beds. SG19 2DL.

INDEX TO SPECIES BY SITE

Species are listed by the reference numbers of the sites. Species mentioned in the General Introduction to certain Sub-regions are identified by the following letters:

A Solway and the Border Country   C The Lake District
B Vale of Eden   D Morecambe Bay

221